# KEYS to SUCCESS

# HOW TO ACHIEVE YOUR GOALS

# KEYS to SUCCESS
## BRIEF EDITION

## Carol Carter
## Joyce Bishop
## Sarah Lyman Kravits

**Editorial Consultant:**

Richard D. Bucher
Professor of Sociology
Baltimore City Community College

**Prentice Hall**

Upper Saddle River, New Jersey 07458

Library of Congress Cataloging-in-Publication Data
Carter, Carol.
   Keys to success: how to achieve your goals / Carol
Carter, Joyce Bishop, Sarah Lyman Kravits; editorial
consultant, Richard D. Bucher.—Brief ed.
      p. cm.
   Includes bibliographical references and index.
   ISBN 0-13-010798-0
      1. College student orientation—United States—
Handbooks, manuals, etc.   2. Study skills—Handbooks,
manuals, etc.   3. College students—United States—Life
skills guides.   I. Bishop, Joyce (Joyce L.), 1950–   .
II. Kravits, Sarah Lyman.   III. Bucher, Richard D.,
1949–   .   IV. Title.
LB2343.32.C37   1999
378.1'98—dc21                         98-33850
                                          CIP

Acquisitions Editor: *Sue Bierman*
Director of Manufacturing
   and Production: *Bruce Johnson*
Managing Editor: *Mary Carnis*
Manufacturing Buyer: *Marc Bove*
Production Liaison: *Denise Brown*
Full Service Production: *Jill Lynch/*
   *North Market Street Graphics*
Formatting: *Christine Crocamo/*
   *North Market Street Graphics*
Creative Director: *Marianne Frasco*
Interior Design: *HRS*
Cover Design: *Wendy Helft*
Marketing Manager: *Jeff McIlroy*
Editorial Assistant: *Michelle Williams*
Printer/Binder: *Banta Menasha*

Reprinted with corrections May, 1999

Printed in the United States of America

10  9  8  7  6  5  4  3  2  1

ISBN   0-13-010798-0

Prentice-Hall International (UK) Limited, *London*
Prentice-Hall of Australia Pty. Limited, *Sydney*
Prentice-Hall Canada Inc., *Toronto*
Prentice-Hall Hispanoamericana, S.A., *Mexico*
Prentice-Hall of India Private Limited, *New Delhi*
Prentice-Hall of Japan, Inc., *Tokyo*
Prentice-Hall Asia Pte. Ltd., *Singapore*

## PHOTO CREDITS:

### Chapter Opening Photos

| Chapter | Source |
|---|---|
| 1 | PhotoDisc, Inc. |
| 2 | Peter Menzel Photography |
| 3 | Larry H. Mangino/The Image Works |
| 4 | Rick Singer |
| 5 | Phyllis Picardi/Stock Boston |
| 6 | John Zillioux/Gamma-Liaison, Inc. |
| 7 | David M. Grossman/Photo Researchers, Inc. |
| 8 | Paul W. Liebhardt |
| 9 | PhotoDisc, Inc. |
| 10 | PhotoDisc, Inc. |

### Interior Photos

| Page | Source |
|---|---|
| 10 | Bob Daemmrich/Stock Boston |
| 16 | Kopstein/Monkmeyer Press |
| 31 | Frank Stewart |
| 48 | Rick Singer/Pearson Education/PH College |
| 60 | Stephen Frisch/Stock Boston |
| 71 | Arnold Zann/Black Star |
| 82 | Rick Singer/Pearson Education/PH College |
| 94 | Beryl Goldberg |
| 100 | Peter Menzel Photography |
| 123 | Frank Siteman/Picture Cube, Inc. |
| 137 | John Zillioux/ Liaison Agency, Inc. |
| 141 | Peter Menzel Photography |
| 155 | Peter Menzel Photography |
| 170 | Will & Deni McIntyre/Photo Researchers, Inc. |
| 183 | Stephen Collins/Photo Researchers, Inc. |
| 204 | Jeff Greenberg/Picture Cube, Inc. |
| 215 | Shackman/Monkmeyer Press |
| 234 | Collins/Monkmeyer Press |
| 241 | Bob Daemmrich/The Image Works |
| 262 | Alan Klehr/Churchill & Klehr Photography |
| 267 | Bob Daemmrich/Stock Boston |
| 270 | Michael P. Gadomski/Photo Researchers, Inc. |

## Our Mission Statement

 Our mission is to help students know and believe in themselves, take advantage of resources and opportunities, set and achieve their goals, learn throughout their lives, discover careers that fulfill and support them, build fruitful and satisfying relationships with others, and experience the challenges and rewards that make life meaningful.

# CONTENTS

# PREFACE

## Keys to Success Owner's Manual

As your authors, we have talked to students across the country. We've learned that you are concerned about your future, you want your education to serve a purpose, you are adjusting to constant life changes, and you want honest and direct guidance on how to achieve your goals. We designed the features of *Keys to Success* based on what you have told us about your needs.

### The Contents of the Package: What's Included

We chose the topics in this book based on what you need to make the most of your educational experience. You need a strong sense of *self*, *learning style*, and *goals* in order to discover and pursue the best course of study. You need good *study skills* to take in and retain what you learn both in and out of class. You need to *manage your time*, *money*, and *relationships* so you can handle the changes life hands you. *Keys to Success* can guide you in all of these areas and more.

The distinguishing characteristics and sections of this book are designed to make your life easier by helping you take in and understand the material you read.

Lifelong learning. The ideas and strategies you learn that will help you succeed in school are the same ones that will bring you success in your career and in your personal life. Therefore, this book focuses on success strategies as they apply to *school, work,* and *life*, not just to the classroom.

Thinking skills. Being able to remember facts and figures won't do you much good at school or beyond unless you can put that information to work through clear and competent thinking. This book has a chapter on *critical and creative thinking* that will help you explore your mind's actions and thinking processes.

Skill-building exercises. Today's graduates need to be effective thinkers, team players, writers, and strategic planners. The exercises at the end of the chapters will encourage you to develop these valuable career skills and to apply thinking processes to any topic or situation.

Diversity of Voice. The world is becoming increasingly diverse in ethnicity, perspective, culture, lifestyle, race, choices, abilities, needs, and more. Every student, instructor, course, and school is unique. One point of view can't possibly apply to everyone. Therefore, many voices will speak to you from these pages. What you read will speak to your needs, offer ideas, and treat you with respect.

User-friendly features. The following features will make your life easier in small but significant ways.

➤ **Perforations.** Each page of this book is perforated so you can tear out exercises to hand in, take with you somewhere, or keep in your date book as a reference.

➤ **Exercises.** The exercises are together at the ends of the chapters, so if you want to hand them all in you can do so without also removing any of the text.

➤ **Internet Research Appendix.** This addition at the end of the book is a terrific resource for information about how to use the Internet for research purposes.

➤ **Definitions.** Selected words are defined in the margins of the text.

➤ **Layout and style.** Full-color photos, graphics, and cartoons will illustrate key points as well as spice up your reading.

➤ **Long-term usefulness.** Yes, most people sell back some of the textbooks they use. If you take a good look at the material in *Keys to Success*, however, you may want to keep this book around. *Keys to Success* is a reference that you can return to over and over again as you work toward your goals in school, work, and life.

## Take Action: Read

You are responsible for your education, your growth, your knowledge, and your future. The best we can do is offer some great suggestions, strategies, ideas, and systems that can help. Ultimately, it's up to you to use whatever fits your particular self with all of its particular situations, needs, and wants, and make it your own. You've made a terrific start by choosing to pursue an education— take advantage of all it has to give you.

# ACKNOWLEDGMENTS

This brief edition has come about through a heroic group effort. We would like to take this opportunity to acknowledge the people who have made it happen. Many thanks to:

➤ Our student editors Michael Jackson and Aziza Davis.

➤ Student reviewers Sandi Armitage, Marisa Connell, Jennifer Moe, and Alex Toth.

➤ Our reviewers: Glenda Belote—Florida International University, John Bennett, Jr.—University of Connecticut, Ann Bingham-Newman—California State University–LA, Mary Bixby—University of Missouri-Columbia, Barbara Blandford—Education Enhancement Center at Lawrenceville, NJ, Jerry Bouchie—St. Cloud State University, Mona Casady—SW Missouri State University, Janet Cutshall—Sussex County Community College, Valerie DeAngelis—Miami-Dade Community College, Rita Delude—NH Community Technical College, Judy Elsley—Weber State University (Ogden, UT), Sue Halter—Delgado Community College, Suzy Hampton—University of Montana, Maureen Hurley—University of Missouri-Kansas City, Karen Iversen—Heald Colleges, Kathryn Kelly—St. Cloud State University, Nancy Kosmicke—Mesa State College in Colorado, Frank T. Lyman, Jr.—University of Maryland, Barnette Miller Moore—Indian River Community College in Florida, Rebecca Munro—Gonzaga University in Washington, Virginia Phares—DeVry of Atlanta, Brenda Prinzavalli—Beloit College in Wisconsin, Jacqueline Simon—Education Enhancement Center at Lawrenceville, NJ, Carolyn Smith—University of Southern Indiana, Joan Stottlemyer—Carroll College in Montana, Thomas Tyson—SUNY Stony Brook, Rose Wassman—DeAnza College, Michelle G. Wolf—Florida Southern College

➤ The PRE 100 instructors at Baltimore City Community College, Liberty Campus, especially college President Dr. Jim Tschechtelin, Coordinator Jim Coleman, Rita Lenkin Hawkins, Sonia Lynch, Jack Taylor, and Peggy Winfield. Thanks also to Prentice Hall representative Alice Barr.

➤ The instructors at DeVry, especially Susan Chin and Carol Ozee.

➤ The instructors at Suffolk Community College, and Prentice Hall representative Carol Abolafia.

➤ Our editorial consultant Rich Bucher, professor of sociology at Baltimore City Community College.

➤ Dr. Frank T. Lyman, inventor of the Thinktrix system.

- Professor Barbara Soloman, developer of the Learning Styles Inventory.

- The people who contributed their stores for *Real World Perspectives:* Anonymous, Clacy Albert, Laura Brinckerhoff, Brett Cross, Erica Epstein, Norma Espina, Jeff Felardeau, Edith Hall, Jacque Hall, Mike Jackson, Miriam Kapner, Karin Lounsbury, Matt Millard, Todd Montalbo, Carrie Nelson, Tan Pham, Chelsea Phillips, Patti Reed-Zweiger, Raymond Reyes, Tim Short, Tom Smith, and Shirley Williamson.

- Kathleen Cole, assistant and student reviewer extraordinaire, and Giuseppe Morella.

- Cynthia Leshin, author of the appendix on Internet research.

- Our editor Sue Bierman and our former editor Todd Rossell.

- Our production team, especially Barbara Cappuccio, Mary Carnis, Marianne Frasco, Steve Hartner, and Nancy Velthaus.

- Our image resource consultant, Florence Silverman.

- The folks in our marketing department, especially Jeff McIlroy, Frank Mortimer, Jr., Karen Austin, Robin Baliszewski, and Christopher Eastman.

- Jackie Fitzgerald, Beth Bollinger, Jennifer Collins, Amy Diehl, Byron Smith, Julie Wheeler, and Robin Diamond.

- The Prentice Hall representatives and the management team led by Gary June.

- Our families and friends.

- Judy Block, who contributed both editing suggestions and study skills text.

Finally, for their ideas, opinions, and stories, we would like to thank all of the students and professors with whom we work. Joyce in particular would like to thank the thousands of students who have allowed her, as their professor, the privilege of sharing part of their journey through college. We appreciate that, through reading this book, you give us the opportunity to learn and discover with you.

# ABOUT THE AUTHORS

**Carol Carter** is Vice President and Director of Student Programs and Faculty Development at Prentice Hall. She has written *Majoring in the Rest of Your Life: Career Secrets for College Students* and *Majoring in High School.* She has also co-authored *Graduating Into the Nineties, The Career Tool Kit, Keys to Career Success, Keys to Effective Learning,* and the first edition of *Keys to Success.* In 1992 Carol and other business people co-founded a nonprofit organization called LifeSkills, Inc., to help high school students explore their goals, their career options, and the real world through part-time employment and internships. LifeSkills is now part of the Tucson Unified School District and is featured in seventeen high schools in Tucson, Arizona.

**Joyce Bishop** holds a Ph.D. in psychology and has taught for more than twenty years, receiving a number of honors, including Teacher of the Year. For the past four years she has been voted "favorite teacher" by the student body and Honor Society at Golden West College, Huntington Beach, CA, where she has taught since 1986 and is a tenured professor. She is currently working with a federal grant to establish Learning Communities and Workplace Learning in her district, and has developed workshops and trained faculty in cooperative learning, active learning, multiple intelligences, workplace relevancy, learning styles, authentic assessment, team building, and the development of learning communities. She also co-authored *Keys to Effective Learning.*

**Sarah Lyman Kravits** comes from a family of educators and has long cultivated an interest in educational development. She co-authored *The Career Tool Kit, Keys to Effective Learning,* and the first edition of *Keys to Success* and has served as Program Director for LifeSkills, Inc., a nonprofit organization that aims to further the career and personal development of high school students. In that capacity she helped to formulate both curricular and organizational elements of the program, working closely with instructors as well as members of the business community. Sarah holds a B.A. in English and drama from the University of Virginia, where she was a Jefferson Scholar, and an M.F.A. from Catholic University.

# OTHER BOOKS
# BY CAROL CARTER

# BECOMING A LIFELONG LEARNER:
## Opening Doors

**W**elcome—or welcome back—to your education. Whether you are right out of high school, returning to student life after working for some years, or continuing on a current educational path, you are facing new challenges and changes. Every person has a right to seek the self-improvement, knowledge, and opportunity that an education can provide. By choosing to pursue an education you have given yourself a strong vote of confidence and the chance to improve your future.

This book will help you fulfill your potential as a learner by giving you keys—ideas, strategies, and skills in a variety of areas—that can lead to success in school, on the job, and in life. Chapter 1 will give you an overview of the educational world. It will start by looking at today's students—who they are and how they've changed—and at the connection between education and success. You will also discover in this chapter how various resources can help you deal with issues and problems and how teamwork plays a role in your success.

In this chapter, you will explore answers to the following questions:

➤ Who is pursuing an education today?

➤ How does education promote success?

➤ What resources are available at your school?

➤ What is your role in a diverse world?

# WHO IS PURSUING AN EDUCATION TODAY?

In various forms, learning took place in the ancient civilizations of Rome, Greece, Byzantium, and Islam. Learning institutions became formalized as universities, similar to those of present day, in medieval Europe as early as the eleventh century. In the early life of the university, students and scholars were men, mostly white, seeking religious and intellectual pursuits. Since their inception at that time, universities have evolved, becoming centers for cultural and social inspiration, intellectual growth, and scientific advancements and research.

Because of federal support and a universal understanding that a formal education should be the right of all people regardless of race, creed, color, age, or gender, universities have become extremely diverse, serving over 14,359,000 people per year in the United States alone. The variety of schools includes community colleges offering certificates and associate degrees, technical schools offering certificates and training in specific technical fields, colleges offering baccalaureate degrees, and universities offering both baccalaureate and advanced degrees. In this new technological age, there are even virtual universities where classes are taken on line.

Today's college students are more diverse than at any time in history. Although many students still enter college directly after high school, the old standard of the student finishing a four-year college education at the age of 22 is a standard no longer. Some students take longer than four years to finish. Some students complete part of their education, pursue other paths for a while, and return to finish later in life. Some go right into the work force after high school and decide to pursue a college degree after many years. The old rules no longer apply.

## The Diverse Student Body

The following facts from the National Center for Education Statistics paint a dramatic picture of how the student population has changed since the 1980s.

➤ Of the undergraduates entering school in the academic year 1992–93, 59 percent were 20 or older, 42 percent attended part-time, 48 percent were financially independent, and 28 percent worked full-time while studying.[1]

➤ From 1980 to 1990, the population of students over the age of 25 grew by 34 percent, while there was only a 3 percent growth for students under 25.[2]

➤ Enrollment from 1984 to 1994 showed strong growth in the female student population (24 percent growth). In the same period of time, male enrollment rose 9 percent.[3]

➤ In 1993, 43.7 percent of all undergraduates were 25 years old or older. Most older students attended part-time, approximately 65 percent.[4]

> Of the entire undergraduate population in the academic year 1992–93, 20 percent were supporting children. Among older students (entering as a freshman at the age of 20 or older), over 40 percent were supporting children.[5]

> More minority citizens are in school, and they comprise an increasingly larger percentage of the student population. From 1976 to 1994, total minority enrollment (including African-Americans, Hispanics, Asians, and Native Americans) went from 15.7 percent of the student body to 24.6 percent.[6]

> In 1994, 38.7 percent of students attended two-year or less-than-two-year schools, compared to 33.3 percent back in 1974.[7]

> In the fall of 1994, 43 percent of undergraduates were enrolled part-time, while 57 percent were enrolled full-time.[8]

> Almost 80 percent of undergraduates were employed at some time during their enrollment in the academic year 1992–93. About 41 percent of undergraduates reported working part-time (from 1 to 34 hours per week), and about 37 percent reported working full-time (35 or more hours per week).[9]

> Students are taking longer to get a degree. Of students graduating in 1993, 64.5 percent took over four years to complete their degrees, and 25.6 percent took more than six years.[10]

These changes have brought with them a new educational experience defined by the varying needs of an increasingly diverse student body. Not so long ago, if you were female, African-American, or handicapped, you had limited opportunity to attend college. Even twenty years ago, you might have given up on an education if you couldn't afford a four-year college, if you were unable to attend classes during the day, or hadn't enrolled immediately after high school and then felt it was too late to return. Now, however, an education is available to a wide range of potential students, regardless of their situations or backgrounds.

Education isn't an automatic guarantee of a higher-level, better-paying job. Statistically, however, a better-educated population means a more efficient work force, more career fulfillment, and better-paid workers. Quality of life can improve when people make the most of their abilities through education.

The decision to take advantage of an education is in your hands. No school can force you to learn. You are responsible for seeking out opportunities and weaving school into the fabric of your life. You may face some of these challenges:

> Handling the responsibilities and stress of parenting children alone, without a spouse

> Returning to school as an older student and feeling out of place

> Learning to adjust to the cultural and communication differences in the diverse student population

*"A journey of a thousand miles must begin with a single step."*

Laotzu

➤ Having a physical disability that presents challenges

➤ Having a learning disability such as dyslexia or ADD

➤ Balancing a school schedule with part-time or even full-time work

➤ Handling the enormous financial commitment college requires

Your school can help you work through these and other problems if you actively seek out solutions and help from available support systems around you. Explore some reasons why the hard work is worthwhile.

## HOW DOES EDUCATION PROMOTE SUCCESS?

Education—the process of developing and training the mind—should be far more than the accumulation of credit hours. If you take advantage of all education has to offer, you will develop the skills and talents you need to succeed in your career—and in life.

How can education help you succeed? Here are some of the ways.

*Education gives you tools for lifelong learning.* You learn facts while you are in school, but more importantly, you learn how to think. While some of the facts and figures you learn today may not apply to the world of tomorrow, your ability to think will be useful always, in everything you do.

 FIGURE 1-1 EDUCATION AND INCOME

MEDIAN ANNUAL EARNINGS OF WORKERS 25 YEARS OLD AND OVER, BY HIGHEST DEGREE ATTAINED AND SEX: 1994

*Source:* U.S. Department of Commerce, Bureau of the Census, *Current Population Reports*, Series P-60, *Monthly Income of Households, Families, and Persons in the United States: 1994.*

FIGURE 1-2 EDUCATION AND EMPLOYMENT

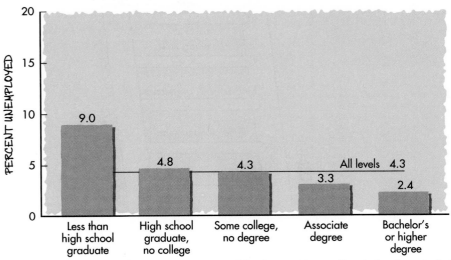

UNEMPLOYMENT RATES OF PERSONS 25 YEARS OLD AND OVER, BY HIGHEST LEVEL OF EDUCATION ATTAINED: 1995

*Source:* U.S. Department of Commerce, Bureau of the Census, *Current Population Reports*, Series P-60, *Monthly Income of Households, Families, and Persons in the United States: 1994.*

**Education improves your quality of life.** Income and employment get a boost from education. *The Digest of Education Statistics 1996* reports that income levels rise as educational levels rise. Figure 1-1 shows average income levels for different levels of educational attainment. Figure 1-2, also from a report in the *Digest*, shows how unemployment rates decrease as educational levels rise.

**Education expands your self-concept.** As you rise to the challenges of education, you will discover that your capacity for knowledge and personal growth is greater than you imagined. As your abilities grow, so do opportunities to learn and do more in class, on the job, and in your community.

**Education enlarges your possibilities.** Education gives you a *base of choices* and *increased power*, as shown in Figure 1-3. First, through different courses of study, it introduces you to *more choices* of career and life goals. Second, through the training you receive, it gives you *more power* to achieve the goals you choose. For example, while taking a writing class, you may learn about careers in journalism. This experience may lead you to take a class in journalistic writing that teaches you about reporting. Down the road, you may decide to work on a newspaper and to make journalism your career. Looking back, you realize that two classes you took in college changed the course of your life.

**Education improves your employability and earning potential.** Learning additional skills raises your competency so you can fulfill the requirements

> "They are able because they think they are able."
>
> Virgil

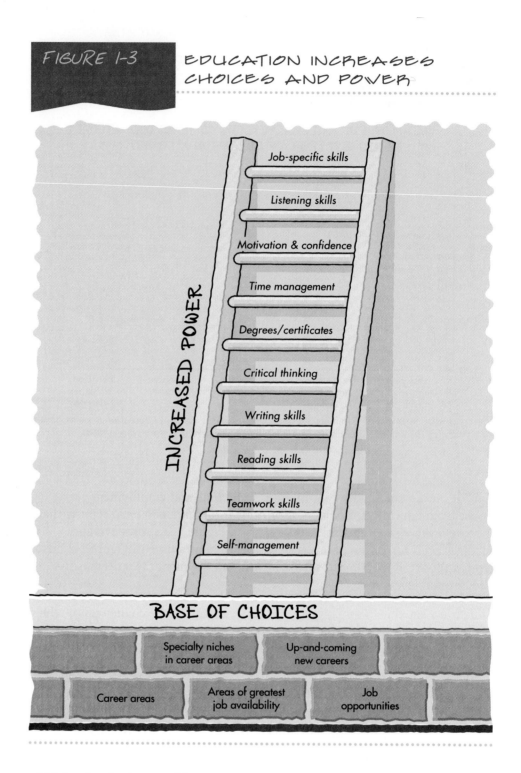

FIGURE 1-3 — EDUCATION INCREASES CHOICES AND POWER

INCREASED POWER

- Job-specific skills
- Listening skills
- Motivation & confidence
- Time management
- Degrees/certificates
- Critical thinking
- Writing skills
- Reading skills
- Teamwork skills
- Self-management

BASE OF CHOICES

Specialty niches in career areas

Up-and-coming new careers

Career areas

Areas of greatest job availability

Job opportunities

of higher-level jobs. In addition, having a college degree makes an impression on potential employers and makes you eligible for higher-salaried positions.

**Education makes you a well-rounded person.** As it widens your understanding about what is possible in the world, education increases your awareness and appreciation of areas that affect and enrich human lives, such as music, art, literature, science, politics, and economics.

Education affects both community involvement and personal health. Education helps to prepare individuals for community activism by helping them understand political, economic, and social conditions. Education also increases knowledge about health behaviors and preventive care. The more education you have, the more likely you are to practice healthy habits in your daily life and to make informed decisions.

Education is more than the process of going to school and earning a degree or certificate. It is a choice to improve your mind and your skills. Any program, no matter the length or the focus, is an opportunity to set and strive for goals. Education is what you make of it. A dedicated, goal-oriented learner will benefit more from school than a student who doesn't focus. If you make the most of your mind, your time, and your educational opportunities, you will realize your potential. Using available resources is part of that process.

# WHAT RESOURCES ARE AVAILABLE AT YOUR SCHOOL?

Resources help you make the most of your education. As a student, you are investing money and time. Whether you complete your studies over the course of six months or sixty years, resources can help you get where you want to go.

Like any company that makes products or provides services, your school is a business. The goal of this particular business is the successful education of all who come through its doors. On pp. 8–9 you will find Table 1-1, a general summary of resources, most or all of which can be found at your school. Most schools offer a student orientation, near the beginning of your first semester, that will explain resources and other important information. Even if your school does not, you can orient yourself. The following sections will describe helpful resources—people, student services, organizations, and course catalogs and student handbooks.

**Resources,** People, organizations, or services that supply help and support for different aspects of college life.

## People

Your school has an array of people who can help you make the most of your educational experience: instructors, administrative personnel, advisors and counselors, and teaching assistants. They're often busy with numerous responsibilities, but their assistance is provided as a standard part of your educational package. Take the opportunity to get to know them, and to let them get to know you. Together you can explore how they can help you achieve your goals.

Instructors are more than just sources of information during scheduled class time. They can also be valuable resources for you to consult. You might ask them to clarify course material or explain homework assignments. They can advise you on course selection in their department, give educational and career advice, and may even be able to introduce you to professionals in your chosen field. Although this book uses the term "instructor" for simplic-

## TABLE 1-1 HOW RESOURCES CAN HELP YOU

| RESOURCE | ACADEMIC ASSISTANCE | FINANCIAL ASSISTANCE | JOB/CAREER ASSISTANCE | PERSONAL ASSISTANCE |
|---|---|---|---|---|
| **INSTRUCTORS** | Choosing classes, clarifying course material, help on assignments, dealing with study issues | | Can tell you about their fields, may be a source of networking contacts | During office hours, are available to talk to you |
| **ADMINISTRATORS** | Academic problems, educational focus, problems with school services | | Can be a source of valuable contacts | Can help you sort through personal problems with instructors or other school employees |
| **ACADEMIC ADVISORS** | Choosing, changing, or dropping courses; getting over academic hurdles; selecting/changing a major | | Can advise you on what job opportunities may go along with your major or academic focus | |
| **PERSONAL COUNSELORS** | Can help when personal problems get in the way of academic success | Services may be free or offered on a "sliding scale" depending on what you can afford | | Help with all kinds of personal problems |
| **FINANCIAL AID OFFICE** | | Information and counseling on loans, grants, scholarships, financial planning, work-study programs | Information on job opportunities within your school environment (work/study and others) | |
| **ACADEMIC CENTERS** | Help with what the center specializes in (reading, writing, math) | | Perhaps an opportunity to work at the center | |
| **ORGANIZATIONS AND CLUBS** | If an academic club, can broaden your knowledge or experience in an area of study; can help you balance school with other enriching activities | | Can help you develop skills, build knowledge, and make new contacts that may serve you in your working life | Depending on the club focus, can be an outlet for stress, a source of personal inspiration, a source of important friendships, an opportunity to help others |
| **FITNESS CENTER(S)** | | Usually free or low cost to enrolled students | | Provides opportunity to build fitness and reduce stress; may have weight room, track, aerobic or dance classes, martial arts, team sports, exercise machines, etc. |

## TABLE 1-1   HOW RESOURCES CAN HELP YOU (CONTINUED)

| RESOURCE | ACADEMIC ASSISTANCE | FINANCIAL ASSISTANCE | JOB/CAREER ASSISTANCE | PERSONAL ASSISTANCE |
|---|---|---|---|---|
| **BULLETIN BOARDS** | List academic events, class information, changes and additions to schedules, office hours, academic club meetings | List financial aid seminars, job opportunities, scholarship opportunities | List career forums, job sign-ups, and employment opportunities; offer a place for you to post a message if you are marketing a service | List support group meetings |
| **HOUSING AND TRANSPORTATION OFFICE** | | Can help find the most financially beneficial travel or housing plan | | Can help commuters with parking, bus or train service, and permits; can help with finding on- or off-campus housing |
| **CAREER PLANNING AND PLACEMENT OFFICE** | | Can help add to your income through job opportunities | Job listings, help with résumés and interviews, possible interview appointments, factual information about the workplace (job trends, salaries, etc.) | |
| **TUTORS** | One-on-one help with academic subjects; assistance with specific assignments | | If you decide to become a tutor, a chance to find out if teaching and working with people is for you | |
| **STUDENT HEALTH OFFICE** | | May provide low-cost or no-cost health care to enrolled students; may offer reduced-cost prescription plan | | Wellness care (regular examinations), illness care, hospital and specialist referrals, and prescriptions |
| **ADULT EDUCATION CENTER** | Academic help tailored to the returning adult student | May have specific financial-aid advice | May have job listings or other help with coordinating work and classes | May offer child-care assistance and opportunities to get to know other returning adults |
| **SUPPORT GROUPS AND HOTLINES** | If school-related, they offer a chance to hear how others have both stumbled and succeeded in school —and a chance to share your story | | | Personal help with whatever the hotline or support group specializes in; a chance to talk to someone whose job is to listen |
| **SCHOOL PUBLICATIONS** | Academic news and course changes | News about financial aid opportunities or work/study programs | Job listings, information about the workplace and the job market | Articles and announcements about topics that may help you |

ity's sake, instructors have official titles that show their rank. From lowest to highest, these include lecturer, instructor, assistant professor, associate professor, and full professor (often just called professor).

Instructors have many time-draining responsibilities outside of teaching. However, you can gain access to your instructors while still respecting the demands on their time. Most instructors keep office hours, and they will tell you the location and times. You are responsible for seeking out your instructor during office hours. If your schedule makes this impossible, let your instructor know. Perhaps you and your instructor can get together at another time. If your school has an electronic mail (e-mail) system that allows you to send messages via computer, you may be able to communicate with your instructor using e-mail.

Teaching assistants are people who help an instructor with a course. You may or may not have teaching assistants in your courses. Often they are studying to be instructors themselves. Sometimes they teach the smaller discussion sections that accompany a large group lecture. They can be a great resource when your instructor is too swamped to talk to you.

Your school's administrative personnel have the responsibility of delivering to you—the student consumer—a first-rate product. That product is the sum total of your education, comprising facilities, instructors, materials, and courses. Schedule a meeting with your dean, the chair of a particular department, or other school administrator if you have an issue to discuss, such as a conflict with an instructor, an inability to get into a class you need, or a school regulation that causes a problem for you. Although administrators don't interact with students as often as instructors do, it is their business to know how the school is serving you.

Advisors and counselors can help with both the educational and personal sides of being a student. They provide information, advice, a listening ear, referrals, and other sources of help. Generally, students are assigned academic advisors with whom they meet at least once a semester. Your academic advisor will help you find out about classes, choose a schedule, explore and select a major or design your own when the time comes, and plan out the big picture of your academic life. Visit your academic advisor more than once a semester if you have questions or want to make changes.

Counselors, although not usually assigned, are available to you at any time, usually through student services. Don't hesitate to seek a counselor's help if you have something on your mind. The ups and downs of your personal life greatly influence the quality of your work in school. If you put some effort into working through personal problems, you will be more able to do your work well and hand it in on time. Occasionally, an illness or family difficulty may interfere with your schoolwork enough to call for special provisions for the completion of your classes. Most colleges are more than happy to assist you during challenging times.

## Student Services

Your school has a variety of services aimed at helping students. Basic services offered by almost every school include the following: academic advising and personal counseling, student health/wellness, career planning and placement, tutoring, fitness/physical education, and financial aid. Depending on your school, you may also find other services: child care, housing and transportation, adult education services (for adults returning to school), disabled student services, academic centers (reading center, writing center, math center, etc.—for help with these specific subjects), various support groups, and school publications that help keep you informed of developments that affect you.

Often a school will have special services for specific populations. For example, at a school where most of the students commute, there may be a transportation office that helps students locate bus schedules and routes, find parking and sign up for permits, or track down car pools. Similarly, at a school where many students are parents, a child-care center may provide day care during class time and also refer students to outside babysitters. You will find additional details about school services in Table 1-1 on pp. 8–9. They can help you earn the maximum benefit from your educational experience.

## Organizations

No matter what your needs or interests are, your school probably has an organization that would interest you or can help you. Some organizations are sponsored by the school (academic clubs), some are independent but have a branch at the school (government ROTC programs), and some are student-run organizations (Latino Student Association). Some organizations focus on courses of study (Nursing Club), some are primarily social (fraternities and sororities), some are artistic (Chamber Orchestra), and some are geared toward a hobby or activity (Runner's Club). Some you join in order to help others (Big Brothers or Big Sisters), and some offer help to you (Overeaters Anonymous).

When you consider adding a new activity to your life, weigh the positive effects against the negative effects. Positive effects could be new friends, fun activities, help, a break from schoolwork, stress relief, improved academic performance, increased teamwork and leadership skills, aid to others, and experience that can broaden your horizons. On the negative side there may be a heavy time commitment, dues, inconvenient location or meeting times, or too much responsibility. Explore any club carefully to see if it makes sense for you. As you make your decision, consider this: Studies have shown that students who join organizations tend to persist in their educational goals more than those who don't branch out.

To find out about organizations at your school, consult your student handbook, ask friends and instructors, or check the activities office or center if your school has one. Some schools, on registration days, have an area where organizations set up tables and make themselves available to talk to interested students. Some organizations seek you out based on your academic achievements. Find out as much as you can. Ask what is expected in terms of time, responsibility, and any necessary financial commitment. Talk to students who are currently involved. Perhaps give an organization a test run to see if you like it.

If you try out an organization, make a commitment that you will stay for the right reasons. Don't be afraid of being labeled a "dropout"; if something becomes more than you can handle, bow out gracefully. In the best of all possible worlds, your involvement in organizations will enrich your life, expand your network of acquaintances, boost your time-management skills, and help you achieve goals.

## College Catalogs and Student Handbooks

Navigating through your school's course offerings, the departments and resource offices, and even the layout of the campus can seem overwhelming. There are two publications that can help you find your way—the college catalog and the student handbook. Most schools provide these materials as a standard part of their enrollment information.

The *college catalog* is your school's academic directory. It lists every department and course available at the school. Each course name will generally have two parts. Take "EN101" or "CHEM205," for example. The first part is one or more letters indicating department and subject matter, and the second part is a number indicating course level (lower numbers for introductory courses and higher numbers for more advanced ones). The catalog groups courses according to subject matter and lists them from the lowest-level courses up to the most advanced, indicating the number of credits earned for each class. See Figure 1-4 for a segment of an actual college catalog from Baltimore City Community College.[11] A course book released prior to each semester will indicate details such as the instructor, the days the course meets, the time of day, the location (building and room), and the maximum number of students who can take the course.

Your college catalog contains a wealth of other information. It may give general school policies such as admissions requirements, the registration process, and withdrawal procedures. It may list the departments to show the range of subjects you may study. It may outline instructional programs, detailing core requirements as well as requirements for various majors, degrees, and certificates. It may also list administrative personnel as well as faculty and staff for each department. The college catalog is an important resource in planning your academic career. When you have a question, consult the catalog first before you spend time and energy looking elsewhere.

---

**COURSE DESCRIPTIONS**

1...

Lab fe...

This cour...
study of th...
techniques o...
imagination an...
oped through im...
ing the first half of ...
the second half is spe...
characters and perform...

**SP 240: ORAL INTERPRETATION OF LITERATURE (3 CREDITS)**

*45 lecture hours.*

This course acquaints students with the general principles of oral reading and the art of oral interpretation of poetry, short stories, and drama. Required student performances in the second half of the course are evaluated.

**SPA—SPANISH**

**SPA 101: SPANISH ELEMENTS (3 CREDITS)**

*45 lecture hours.*

This course teaches students how to function in the language and how the language functions. Emphasis is placed on pronunciation, vocabulary development, and grammatical patterns. The course meets the needs of those who have had no previous instruction in the language. The intent is to develop in the student the ability to speak, read, and write in Spanish.

**SPA 102: SPANISH ELEMENTS (3 CREDITS)**

*45 lecture hours.*

This course continues, for students who have completed SPA 101, the

158

ST 1...
(3 CRL...

*45 lecture ...*

This course in...
responsibilities,...
clerical workers i...
private sector. Topic...
preparation and proce...
office records and busin...
types of office equipment,...
communications, and busine...
relations.

**ST 101: SHORTHAND I (4 CREDITS)**

*60 lecture hours.*

*Prerequisites: ENG 101; SP 101.*

This course introduces the fundamental principles of Gregg Shorthand. Emphasis is on a sound knowledge of shorthand theory as a foundation for reading and writing skills and speed development in shorthand. Individualized instruction is provided.

Pr...
and ...

Corequis...

Lab fee.

This course pro...
for medical secret...
apply previously le...
edge and skills. Stud...
integrated projects that ...

**FIGURE 1-4**

*Source:* 1996-1998 Catalog, Baltimore City Community College.

Your *student handbook* looks beyond specific courses to the big picture, helping you to navigate student life. In it you will find some or all of the following, and maybe more: information on available housing (for on-campus residents) and on parking and driving (for commuters); overviews of the support offices for students, such as academic advising, counseling, career planning and placement, student health, disabled student services, child care, financial aid, and individual centers for academic subject areas such as writing or math; descriptions of special-interest clubs; and details about library and computer services. It may also list hours, locations, phone numbers and addresses for all offices, clubs, and organizations.

Your student handbook will also describe important policies such as how to add or drop a class, what the grading system means, campus rules, drug and alcohol policies, what kinds of records your school keeps, safety tips, and more. Keep your student handbook where you can find it easily, in your study area at home or someplace safe at school. The information it gives you can save you a lot of trouble when you need to find out information about a resource or service. If you call for locations and hours before you visit a particular office, you'll avoid the frustration of dropping by when the office is closed.

Making the most of your resources is one way to adjust to your new environment. Interacting with people around you is another.

# WHAT IS YOUR ROLE IN A DIVERSE WORLD?

Diversity isn't just what happens in an International Students' Club, in a business that tries to hire men and women from different backgrounds, or in an inner-city neighborhood that is home to various cultural groups. Diversity is the mosaic of differences that envelops your life, your communities, your nation, and the world. In addition to races and ethnic groups, diversity also occurs in desires, traditions, religions, family backgrounds, genders, abilities, economic levels, ages, habits, lifestyles, choices, careers, artistic expressions, modes of dress, foods, health conditions, perspectives, opinions, experiences, and more. Diversity touches each of you in a very personal way.

## Diversity Is Real Life

You encounter diversity every day, even if you don't realize it. You are constantly bombarded with images and information in newspapers and magazines, on television, and on the radio that tell you about how different people think and live. People tend to focus on the kind of diversity they can see, such as skin color, hair type, or eye shape, but there are meaningful forms of diversity that aren't visible to the naked eye. People who look similar to you may actually be different in many important ways. Think about the qualities of the people you know. Your fellow student may have a different religion or a hidden disability; your cousin may oppose your political beliefs; your co-worker may have a different sexual orientation. Society is made up of millions of people who transcend labels and have limitless worth.

Diversity has become more important, partly because the world is becoming more interdependent. As people become more aware of other ways of living, they may tune in more to differences between "us" and "them." The knowledge of differences can be a benefit. Unfortunately, it can also be used to spread opinions that others are inferior. The problem is not in the differences but in the way in which people view and treat these differences.

## Ethnocentrism

**Ethnocentrism,**
The condition of thinking that one's particular ethnic group is superior to others.

When groups of people believe that their way of thinking is the only way, or a better way than anyone else's, they are being ethnocentric. Ethnocentrism creates an opinion that one's particular group is better than anyone else's. It's important to be proud of your identity, but it's one thing to think your group is terrific and another thing to think that your group is superior to all other groups.

A group can be organized around any sort of uniqueness—the same skin color, accent, country of origin, ideas, interests, religion, traditions, and much more. The problem arises when celebrating your own uniqueness leads to putting down someone else's. One example is thinking that when someone speaks with an accent, he or she doesn't know as much as you do. Another example is thinking that it is disrespectful for someone not to look you in the eye during a conversation. In certain other cultures, it is considered rude to look people in the eye, especially if that person happens to be an authority.

Ethnocentrism has many negative effects. It can get in the way of effective communication, as you will see in more detail when you read Chapter 8. It can prevent you from getting to know people from different backgrounds. It can result in people being shut out and denied opportunities that all people deserve. It limits you and your potential because it denies you exposure to new ideas that could help you grow and learn. Finally, it can hinder your ability to work with others, which can cause problems for you both at school and on the job.

## Diversity and Teamwork

Much of what people accomplish they owe to teamwork. Think of the path of your accomplishments, and you will find that other people had roles in your success. When you earn a degree, complete a project, or raise a family, you don't do it alone. You are part of many hard-working teams. As the African proverb goes, it takes an entire village to raise a child.

Your success at school and at work depends on your ability to cooperate in a team setting. At school you will work with study groups, complete group projects, interact with instructors and administrators, and perhaps live with a roommate. At work you will regularly team up with co-workers to achieve goals. At home you work with family or housemates to manage the tasks and responsibilities of daily life. Your achievements depend on how you communicate, share tasks, and develop a common vision.

Any team will gain strength from the diversity of its members. In fact, diversity is an asset in a team. Consider a five-person basketball

## How do I make the most of college?

### Matt Millard, University of Wyoming, undeclared major

I decided to attend college so I could have a job doing what I really like instead of just doing it for the money. Even though I haven't decided what I want to do when I graduate, I know that I want to continue learning for a long time. I'd even like to continue on to get a Masters and maybe even a Ph.D. someday. So far, I'm mainly interested in the theater and English, but I'm not quite sure where to go with it.

I try to take steps to better myself. Even though I'd like it to be more often, I work out at racquetball a couple of times a week. I also think it's important to help other people, so I make time to help my friends with their homework and stuff like that. My grades are average so I'd like them to get better. I'd also like to get a little more focused on what I want to declare as a major. Even though I think I'm doing fine handling college, I'd appreciate any suggestions you could give me. What steps do you think I need to take in order to get the most out of my learning?

### Todd Montalvo, University of Alaska, Anchorage, education major—junior year

I think it's very important to do what you love. That will really help your goal of lifelong learning. Even though having money to support yourself and your family is important, it's more important to enjoy what you're doing and feel like you're making a difference. I chose education as my major because I really like being with young people and feel I can influence their lives in a positive way. Plus, my

mother is a teacher. After going to her classes and seeing her teach, I decided it was something I'd enjoy. I've changed my major twice, though, since I started school. I tried the business department but realized after taking an economics class that I just wasn't that interested.

It might be beneficial for you to try different classes in the subjects that really interest you. That way you'll know if you're on the right track. Another suggestion is to join a drama club or try out for a local theater production. You might want to also get to know someone who makes their living teaching English. They may be able to help you decide if it's the career for you. I also recommend that you try to have balance in your life. I'm a member of the ski team at my school. Whenever I come back from skiing and sit down to study, I feel like I'm more focused and I feel like my whole life isn't just studying. I'm more motivated that way. I also get a lot more done in a shorter time because I have more energy.

Your first year away from home can be a big adjustment. I can guarantee you, it will get better. You can help make it easier by exploring different professions, changing some of your normal routines, and trying classes that other students say are interesting or exciting.

team, composed of a center, a power forward, a small forward, a shooting guard, and a point guard. Each person has a different role and a different style of play, but only by combining their abilities can they achieve success. The more diverse the team members, the greater the chance that new ideas and solutions will find their way to the table, increasing the chances of solving any problem. As a member of any team, use these three strategies to maximize team success.

1. Open your mind and accept that different team members have valuable roles.
2. Consider the new information and ideas that others offer.
3. Evaluate contributions based on how they help solve the problem or achieve the goal instead of based on the identity of the person who had the idea. Successful teams use what works.

> *"He has not yet learned the lesson of life who does not every day surmount a fear."*
>
> Ralph Waldo Emerson

## Living Your Role

It's not always easy to open your mind to differences. However, doing so can benefit both you and others around you. You may consider actions like these as you define your role in the diverse world:

➤ **To accept diversity as a fact of life.** The world will only continue to diversify. The more you adapt to and appreciate this diversity, the more enriched your life will be. Diversity is an asset, not a deficiency.

➤ **To explore differences.** Open your mind and learn about what is unfamiliar around you.

➤ **To celebrate your own uniqueness as well as that of others.** It's natural to think that your own way is the best way. Expand your horizons by considering your way as one good way and seeking out different and useful ways to which other people can introduce you.

➤ **To consider new perspectives.** The wide variety of ideas and perspectives brought by people from all different groups and situations creates a wealth of thought from which the world can find solutions to tough and complex problems.

➤ **To continue to learn.** Education is one of the most productive ways to combat discrimination and become more open-minded about differences. Classes such as sociology and ethics can increase your awareness of the lives, choices, and values of people in other cultures. Even though your personal beliefs may be challenged in the process, facing how you feel about others is a positive step toward harmony among people.

Throughout this book you will find references to a diverse mixture of people in different life circumstances. Chapter 8 will go into more detail about communicating across lines of difference and addressing the problems that arise when people have trouble accepting each other's differences. Diversity is not a subject that you study at one point in the semester and then leave behind. It is a theme that touches every chapter in this book and every part of your life. Note especially the "Real World Perspective" feature in every chapter, which highlights people from different backgrounds who are striving to learn about themselves and their world.

In Chinese writing, this character has two meanings: One is "chaos"; the other is "opportunity." The character communicates the belief that every challenging, chaotic, demanding situation in life also presents an opportunity. By responding to challenges in a positive and active way, you can discover the opportunity that lies within the chaos.

Let this concept reassure you as you begin college. You may feel that you are going through a time of chaos and change. Remember that no matter how difficult the obstacles, you have the ability to persevere. You can create opportunities for yourself to learn, grow, and improve.

# Chapter 1: Applications

Name _____     Date _____

 Key Into Your Life: Opportunities to Apply What You Learn

## Exercise 1: Identify Yourself

Where do you fit in today's student population? Describe your particular circumstances, opinions, and needs in a short paragraph. Here are some questions to inspire thought:

➤ How do you describe yourself—your culture, ethnicity, gender, age, lifestyle?

➤ How long are you planning to spend in college?

➤ What do you expect out of your college experience?

➤ What resources do you plan to use?

➤ What is your work situation, if you work?

➤ What are your financial needs for college and living expenses?

➤ What are your career goals?

➤ How would you describe your family?

➤ What qualities make you special?

_____

_____

_____

_____

_____

_____

_____

_____

## Exercise 2: Brainstorm Your Ideal Life

Take some quiet time to think about your life. Spend a half-hour or so brainstorming everything that you wish you could be, do, have, or experience. List your wishes on a blank piece of paper, draw them, or depict them using cutouts from magazines—whatever you like best.

Here are some wish categories for you to consider, each with an example:

| CATEGORY | EXAMPLES |
|---|---|
| Career choices (job, perks, schedule, opportunities) | I want to teach elementary school. I want a job that's within 20 minutes' driving time of where I live. I want health benefits. |
| Lifestyle issues (what type of house, cars you want to own, hobbies and interests) | I want to own instead of rent. I want to finish paying off my car. I want to spend more time exercising. |
| Finances | I want to pay off my credit card debt. I want to provide at least part of my tuition. |
| Family and relationships | I want to keep in touch with my parents. I want to spend more time with my child. |
| Serving and helping others | I want to see what I can do at the senior center. |
| Creativity | I want to get my camera out and take pictures more often. |
| Experiences | I want to see Washington, D.C. I want to spend some time driving across the country. |
| Other important wishes | I want to work harder to keep myself organized. |

Now take a look at your list. You probably have a wide variety of details. To discover how your wishes relate to one another, group them in order of priority. Take four pieces of paper and label them *Priority 1*, *Priority 2*, *Priority 3*, and *Future Dreams*. Write each wish on the piece of paper where it fits, with *Priority 1* being the most important wishes, *Priority 2* the second most important, *Priority 3* the third most important, and *Future Dreams* the wishes that you would like to accomplish someday in the future.

Look at your priority lists. What do your lists tell you about what is most important to you? What wishes are you ready to work toward right now? Choose three high-priority wishes that you want to work on this semester. List them here.

_____

_____

_____

### Exercise 3: Who Can Help You?

Every school is unique and offers its own particular range of opportunities. Investigate your school. Use the resource table as a guide, and explore your student handbook. Make a check mark by the resources which you think will be most helpful to you.

| | | | |
|---|---|---|---|
| Advisors and counselors | _____ | Adult education center | _____ |
| Library/media center | _____ | Support groups/hotlines | _____ |
| Instructors | _____ | Career/job placement office | _____ |
| Clubs/organizations | _____ | Administration | _____ |
| Bulletin boards | _____ | Academic centers | _____ |
| Student health center | _____ | School publications | _____ |
| Housing and transportation | _____ | Tutoring | _____ |
| Wellness/fitness centers | _____ | Financial-aid office | _____ |

Gather in small groups; or, if you have a small class, work as one large group together. Each member of each group should choose one or more different resources (make sure no two people within a group explore the same resource). Make sure all resources on the following grid are accounted for. Then, each group member will investigate his or her resources and fill in the information on the grid, answering the questions listed across the top of the grid. The two blank spaces at the bottom are for you to use if you find resources not listed here.

After each person has completed his or her investigation, meet again to exchange information and fill in the information on the grid. You now have a resource guide that you can refer to any time. Write here how you will use the three resources that you feel will benefit you the most.

1. _____

_____

_____

2. _____

_____

_____

3. _____

_____

_____

| RESOURCE | WHO PROVIDES IT? | WHERE CAN YOU FIND IT? | WHEN IS IT AVAILABLE? | HOW CAN IT HELP YOU? | HOW DO YOU ASK FOR IT? | PHONE # OR OTHER KEY DETAILS? |
|---|---|---|---|---|---|---|
| Administrative help | | | | | | |
| Instructor advice | | | | | | |
| Academic advising | | | | | | |
| Personal counseling | | | | | | |
| Financial aid | | | | | | |
| Academic centers | | | | | | |
| Organizations and clubs | | | | | | |
| Bulletin boards | | | | | | |
| Housing and transportation | | | | | | |
| Career planning and placement | | | | | | |

| Resource | Who provides it? | Where can you find it? | When is it available? | How can it help you? | How do you ask for it? | Phone # or other key details? |
|---|---|---|---|---|---|---|
| Tutoring | | | | | | |
| Student health | | | | | | |
| Adult education center | | | | | | |
| Fitness | | | | | | |
| Support groups/ hotlines | | | | | | |
| Disabled-student services | | | | | | |
| English as a Second Language | | | | | | |
| | | | | | | |

## KEY TO SELF-EXPRESSION: DISCOVERY THROUGH JOURNAL WRITING

*To record your thoughts, use a separate journal or the lined page at the end of the chapter.*

**Your Diverse World**  Describe one particular person with whom you interact, a person who is different from you in some way. What have you learned from your relationship with this person? What is positive about spending time with him or her? What is negative? What is positive and negative about spending time with people who seem very similar to you?

Name _____ Date _____

## Journal Entry

Prentice Hall

2

# SELF-AWARENESS:

## Knowing Who You Are and How You Learn

Learning is not something you do just in college. Throughout your life, learning can help you keep up with the rapid pace at which the world is changing.

Technology, for example, is changing so fast that you cannot learn today about all of the computer operations that will be commonplace five years from now. However, you can learn how to be an effective learner in school and in the workplace so that you can keep pace with changes as they occur. In this chapter you will become aware of your learning style by completing three different learning style assessments. Each assessment will add a different dimension to the picture you are forming of yourself. You will then explore other important elements of self: your self-perception, your preferences, your habits, your abilities, and your attitudes.

In this chapter, you will explore answers to the following questions:

➤ Is there one best way to learn?

➤ How can you discover your learning styles?

➤ What are the benefits of knowing your learning styles?

➤ How do you explore who you are?

➤ How can you start thinking about choosing a major?

# IS THERE ONE BEST WAY TO LEARN?

Your mind is the most powerful tool you will ever possess. You are accomplished at many skills and can process all kinds of information. However, when you have trouble accomplishing a particular task, you may become convinced that you can't learn how to do anything new. You may feel that those who can do what you can't have the "right" kind of ability. Not only is this perception incorrect, it can also damage your belief in yourself.

Every individual is highly developed in some abilities and underdeveloped in others. Many famously successful people were brilliant in one area but functioned poorly in other areas. Winston Churchill failed the sixth grade. Abraham Lincoln was demoted to a private in the Black Hawk War. Louis Pasteur was a poor student in chemistry. Walt Disney was fired from a job and told he had no good ideas. What some might interpret as a deficiency or disability may be simply a different method of learning.

There is no one "best" way to learn. Instead, there are many different learning styles, and different styles are suited to different situations. Your individual learning profile is made up of a combination of learning styles. Each person's profile is unique. Just like personality traits, learning styles are part of your personal characteristics. Knowing how you learn is one of the first steps in discovering who you are.

**Learning style,**
A particular way in which the mind receives and processes information.

# HOW CAN YOU DISCOVER YOUR LEARNING STYLES?

Your brain is so complex that one inventory cannot give you all the information you need to maximize your learning skills. You will learn about and complete three assessments: the Learning Styles Inventory, the Pathways to Learning inventory based on the Multiple Intelligences Theory, and the Personality Spectrum. Each of these assessments evaluates your mind's abilities in a different way, although they often have related ideas. Your results will combine to form your learning-styles profile, consisting of the styles and types that best fit the ways that you learn and interact with others. After you complete the various learning-styles inventories, you will read about strategies that can help you make the most of particular styles and types, both in school and beyond. Your learning-styles profile will help you to improve your understanding of yourself, how you learn, and how you may function as a learner in the workplace.

## Learning Styles Inventory

One of the first instruments to measure psychological types, the Myers-Briggs Type Inventory (MBTI), was designed by Katharine Briggs and her daughter, Isabel Briggs Myers. Later David Keirsey and Marilyn Bates combined the sixteen Myers-Briggs types into four temperaments. Barbara

*"To be what we are, and to become what we are capable of becoming, is the only end of life."*
Robert Louis Stevenson

Soloman, Associate Director of the University Undesignated Student Program at North Carolina State University, has developed the following learning styles inventory based on these theories and on her work with thousands of students.[1]

"Students learn in many ways," says Professor Soloman. "Mismatches often exist between common learning styles and standard teaching styles. Therefore, students often do poorly and get discouraged. Some students doubt themselves and doubt their ability to succeed in the curriculum of their choice. Some settle for low grades and even leave school. If students understand how they learn most effectively, they can tailor their studying to their own needs."

"Learning effectively" and "tailoring studying to your own needs" means choosing study techniques that help you learn. For example, if a student responds more to visual images than to words, he or she may want to construct notes in a more visual way. Or, if a student learns better when talking to people than when studying alone, he or she may want to study primarily in pairs or groups.

# LEARNING STYLES INVENTORY

This inventory has four "dimensions," within each of which are two opposing styles. At the end of the inventory, you will have two scores in each of the four dimensions. The difference between your two scores in any dimension tells you which of the two styles in that dimension is dominant for you. A few people will score right in between the two styles, indicating that they have fairly equal parts of both styles. Following are brief descriptions of the four dimensions. You will learn more about them after you complete all three assessments, in the section on study strategies.

Active/Reflective.   *Active* learners learn best by experiencing knowledge through their own actions. *Reflective* learners understand information best when they have had time to reflect on it on their own.

Factual/Theoretical.   *Factual* learners learn best through specific facts, data, and detailed experimentation. *Theoretical* learners are more comfortable with big-picture ideas, symbols, and new concepts.

Visual/Verbal.   *Visual* learners remember best what they see: diagrams, flowcharts, time lines, films, and demonstrations. *Verbal* learners gain the most learning from reading, hearing spoken words, participating in discussion, and explaining things to others.

Linear/Holistic.   *Linear* learners find it easiest to learn material presented step by step in a logical, ordered progression. *Holistic* learners progress in fits and starts, perhaps feeling lost for a while, but eventually seeing the big picture in a clear and creative way.

Holistic,
Relating to the wholes of complete systems rather than the analysis of parts.

Please complete this inventory by circling **a** or **b** to indicate your answer to each question. Answer every question and choose only one answer for each question. If both answers seem to apply to you, choose the answer that applies more often.

1. I study best
   a. in a study group.
   b. alone or with a partner.

2. I would rather be considered
   a. realistic.
   b. imaginative.

3. When I recall what I did yesterday, I am most likely to think in terms of
   a. pictures/images.
   b. words/verbal descriptions.

4. I usually think new material is
   a. easier at the beginning and then harder as it becomes more complicated.
   b. often confusing at the beginning but easier as I start to understand what the whole subject is about.

5. When given a new activity to learn, I would rather first
   a. try it out.
   b. think about how I'm going to do it.

6. If I were an instructor, I would rather teach a course
   a. that deals with real-life situations and what to do about them.
   b. that deals with ideas and encourages students to think about them.

7. I prefer to receive new information in the form of
   a. pictures, diagrams, graphs, or maps.
   b. written directions or verbal information.

8. I learn
   a. at a fairly regular pace. If I study hard I'll "get it" and then move on.
   b. in fits and starts. I might be totally confused and then suddenly it all "clicks."

9. I understand something better after
   a. I attempt to do it myself.
   b. I give myself time to think about how it works.

10. I find it easier
    a. to learn facts.
    b. to learn ideas/concepts.

11. In a book with lots of pictures and charts, I am likely to
    a. look over the pictures and charts carefully.
    b. focus on the written text.

12. It's easier for me to memorize facts from
    a. a list.
    b. a whole story/essay with the facts embedded in it.

13. I will more easily remember
    a. something I have done myself.
    b. something I have thought or read about.

14. I am usually
    a. aware of my surroundings. I remember people and places and usually recall where I put things.
    b. unaware of my surroundings. I forget people and places. I frequently misplace things.

15. I like instructors
    a. who put a lot of diagrams on the board.
    b. who spend a lot of time explaining.

16. Once I understand
    a. all the parts, I understand the whole thing.
    b. the whole thing, I see how the parts fit.

17. When I am learning something new, I would rather
    a. talk about it.
    b. think about it.

18. I am good at
    a. being careful about the details of my work.
    b. having creative ideas about how to do my work.

19. I remember best
    a. what I see.
    b. what I hear.

20. When I solve problems that involve some math, I usually
    a. work my way to the solutions one step at a time.
    b. see the solutions but then have to struggle to figure out the steps to get to them.

21. In a lecture class, I would prefer occasional in-class
    a. discussions or group problem-solving sessions.
    b. pauses that give opportunities to think or write about ideas presented in the lecture.

22. On a multiple-choice test, I am more likely to
    a. run out of time.
    b. lose points because of not reading carefully or making careless errors.

23. When I get directions to a new place, I prefer
    a. a map.
    b. written instructions.

24. When I'm thinking about something I've read,
    a. I remember the incidents and try to put them together to figure out the themes.
    b. I just know what the themes are when I finish reading and then I have to back up and find the incidents that demonstrate them.

25. When I get a new computer or VCR, I tend to
    a. plug it in and start punching buttons.
    b. read the manual and follow instructions.

26. In reading for pleasure, I prefer
    a. something that teaches me new facts or tells me how to do something.
    b. something that gives me new ideas to think about.

27. When I see a diagram or sketch in class, I am most likely to remember
    a. the picture.
    b. what the instructor said about it.

28. It is more important to me that an instructor
    a. lay out the material in clear, sequential steps.
    b. give me an overall picture and relate the material to other subjects.

---

SCORING SHEET: Use Table 2-1 to enter your scores.

1. Put 1's in the appropriate boxes in the table (e.g., if you answered **a** to Question 3, put a 1 in the column headed **a** next to the number 3).

2. Total the 1's in the columns and write the totals in the indicated spaces at the base of the columns.

## TABLE 2-1   LEARNING STYLES INVENTORY SCORES

| ACTV/REFL | | | FACT/THEO | | | VISL/VRBL | | | LINR/HOLS | | |
|---|---|---|---|---|---|---|---|---|---|---|---|
| Q # | a | b | Q# | a | b | Q# | a | b | Q# | a | b |
| 1 | | | 2 | | | 3 | | | 4 | | |
| 5 | | | 6 | | | 7 | | | 8 | | |
| 9 | | | 10 | | | 11 | | | 12 | | |
| 13 | | | 14 | | | 15 | | | 16 | | |
| 17 | | | 18 | | | 19 | | | 20 | | |
| 21 | | | 22 | | | 23 | | | 24 | | |
| 25 | | | 26 | | | 27 | | | 28 | | |

Write Totals for Each Column in the Spaces Below

3. For each of the four dimensions, circle your two scores on the bar scale and then fill in the bar between the scores. For example, if under "ACTV/REFL" you had 2 **a** and 5 **b** responses, you would fill in the bar between those two scores, as this sample shows:

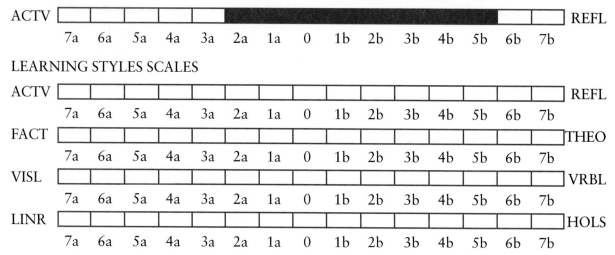

## LEARNING STYLES SCALES

If your filled-in bar has the 0 close to its center, you are well balanced on the two dimensions of that scale. If your bar is drawn mainly to one side, you have a strong preference for that one dimension and may have difficulty learning in the other dimension.

Continue on to the next assessment. After you complete all three, the next section of the chapter will help you understand and make use of your results from each assessment.

---

# Multiple Intelligences Theory

Howard Gardner, a Harvard University professor, has developed a theory called Multiple Intelligences. He believes there are at least eight distinct intelligences possessed by all people, and that every person has developed some intelligences more fully than others. Most people have experienced a time when they learned something very quickly and comfortably. Most have also had the opposite experience when, no matter how hard they tried, something they wanted to learn just would not sink in. According to the Multiple Intelligences Theory, when you find a task or subject easy, you are probably using a more fully developed intelligence; when you have more trouble, you may be using a less developed intelligence.[2]

Following are brief descriptions of the focus of each of the intelligences. Study skills that reinforce each intelligence will be described later in the chapter.

> **Verbal-Linguistic Intelligence**—ability to communicate through language (listening, reading, writing, speaking)

> **Logical-Mathematical Intelligence**—ability to understand logical reasoning and problem solving (math, science, patterns, sequences)

> **Bodily-Kinesthetic Intelligence**—ability to use the physical body skillfully and to take in knowledge through bodily sensation (coordination, working with hands)

> **Visual-Spatial Intelligence**—ability to understand spatial relationships and to perceive and create images (visual art, graphic design, charts and maps)

**Intelligence,**

As defined by H.Gardner, an ability to solve problems or fashion products that are useful in a particular cultural setting or community.

**Kinesthetic,**

Coming from physical sensation caused by body movements and tensions.

➤ **Interpersonal Intelligence**—ability to relate to others, noticing their moods, motivations, and feelings (social activity, cooperative learning, teamwork)

➤ **Intrapersonal Intelligence**—ability to understand one's own behavior and feelings (independence, time spent alone)

➤ **Musical Intelligence**—ability to comprehend and create meaningful sound (music, sensitivity to sound)

➤ **Naturalistic Intelligence**—ability to understand features of the environment (interest in nature, environmental balance, ecosystem, stress relief brought by natural environments)

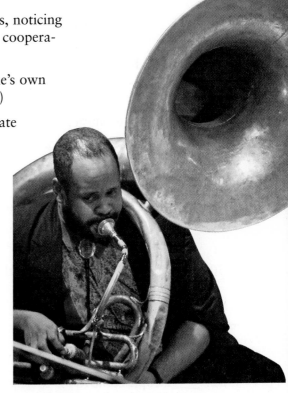

Please complete the following assessment of your multiple intelligences, called Pathways to Learning, developed by Joyce Bishop. It will help you determine which of your intelligences are most fully developed. Don't be concerned if some of your scores are low. That is true of most people, even your instructors and your authors!

# PATHWAYS TO LEARNING[3]

Developed by Joyce Bishop, Ph.D. and based upon Howard Gardner. (Frames of Mind: The Theory of Multiple Intelligences.)

**Directions:** Rate each statement as follows: Write the number of your response (1-4) on the line next to the statement and total each set of six questions.

| rarely | sometimes | usually | always |
|--------|-----------|---------|--------|
| 1 | 2 | 3 | 4 |

| | |
|---|---|
| 1. ____ I enjoy physical activities. | 13. ____ I enjoy telling stories. |
| 2. ____ I am uncomfortable sitting still. | 14. ____ I like to write. |
| 3. ____ I prefer to learn through doing. | 15. ____ I like to read. |
| 4. ____ When sitting I move my legs or hands. | 16. ____ I express myself clearly. |
| 5. ____ I enjoy working with my hands. | 17. ____ I am good at negotiating. |
| 6. ____ I like to pace when I'm thinking or studying. | 18. ____ I like to discuss topics that interest me. |
| ____ **TOTAL for Bodily-Kinesthetic** | ____ **TOTAL for Verbal-Linguistic** |
| 7. ____ I use maps easily. | 19. ____ I liked math in high school. |
| 8. ____ I draw pictures/diagrams when explaining ideas. | 20. ____ I like science. |
| 9. ____ I can assemble items easily from diagrams. | 21. ____ I problem-solve well. |
| | 22. ____ I question how things work. |
| 10. ____ I enjoy drawing or photography. | 23. ____ I enjoy planning or designing something new. |
| 11. ____ I do not like to read long paragraphs. | |
| 12. ____ I prefer a drawn map over written directions. | 24. ____ I am able to fix things. |
| ____ **TOTAL for Visual-Spatial** | ____ **TOTAL for Logical-Mathematical** |

# PATHWAYS TO LEARNING (continued)

**Directions:** Rate each statement as follows:
Write the number of your response (1-4) on the line
next to the statement and total each set of six questions.

| rarely | sometimes | usually | always |
|:---:|:---:|:---:|:---:|
| 1 | 2 | 3 | 4 |

25. _____ I listen to music.

26. _____ I move my fingers or feet when I hear music.

27. _____ I have good rhythm.

28. _____ I like to sing along with music.

29. _____ People have said I have musical talent.

30. _____ I like to express my ideas through music.

_____ **TOTAL for Musical**

37. _____ I need quiet time to think.

38. _____ I think about issues before I want to talk.

39. _____ I am interested in self-improvement.

40. _____ I understand my thoughts and feelings.

41. _____ I know what I want out of life.

42. _____ I prefer to work on projects alone.

_____ **TOTAL for Intrapersonal**

31. _____ I like doing a project with other people.

32. _____ People come to me to help settle conflicts.

33. _____ I like to spend time with friends.

34. _____ I am good at understanding people.

35. _____ I am good at making people feel comfortable.

36. _____ I enjoy helping others.

_____ **TOTAL for Interpersonal**

43. _____ I enjoy nature whenever possible.

44. _____ I think about having a career involving nature.

45. _____ I enjoy studying plants, animals, or oceans.

46. _____ I avoid being indoors except when I sleep.

47. _____ As a child I played with bugs and leaves.

48. _____ When I feel stressed I want to be out in nature.

_____ **TOTAL for Naturalistic**

Write each of your eight intelligences in the column where it fits below. For each, choose the column that corresponds with your total in that intelligence.

| SCORES OF 20–24 HIGHLY DEVELOPED | | SCORES OF 14–19 MODERATELY DEVELOPED | | SCORES BELOW 14 UNDERDEVELOPED | |
|---|---|---|---|---|---|
| Scores | Intelligences | Scores | Intelligences | Scores | Intelligences |
| | | | | | |

Learning styles and multiple intelligences are gauges to help you understand yourself. Instead of labeling yourself narrowly using one category or another, learn as much as you can about your preferences and how you can maximize your learning. Most people are a blend of styles and preferences, with one or two being dominant. In addition, you may change preferences depending on the situation. For example, a student might find it easy to take notes in outline style when the instructor lectures in an organized way. However, if another instructor jumps from topic to topic, the student might choose to use the Cornell system or a think link (Chapter 6 goes into detail about note-taking styles).

The final assessment, through its evaluation of personality types, focuses on how you relate to others.

## Personality Spectrum

A system that simplifies learning styles into four personality types has been developed by Joyce Bishop (1997). Her work is based on the Myers-Briggs and Keirsey theories discussed earlier in the chapter. The Personality Spectrum will give you a personality perspective on your learning styles. Please complete the following assessment.

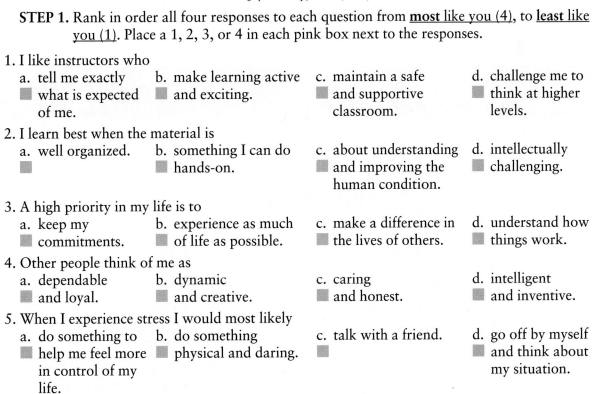

# PERSONALITY SPECTRUM

Joyce Bishop, Ph.D. (1997)

**STEP 1.** Rank in order all four responses to each question from **most** like you (4), to **least like you (1)**. Place a 1, 2, 3, or 4 in each pink box next to the responses.

1. I like instructors who
   - a. tell me exactly what is expected of me.
   - b. make learning active and exciting.
   - c. maintain a safe and supportive classroom.
   - d. challenge me to think at higher levels.

2. I learn best when the material is
   - a. well organized.
   - b. something I can do hands-on.
   - c. about understanding and improving the human condition.
   - d. intellectually challenging.

3. A high priority in my life is to
   - a. keep my commitments.
   - b. experience as much of life as possible.
   - c. make a difference in the lives of others.
   - d. understand how things work.

4. Other people think of me as
   - a. dependable and loyal.
   - b. dynamic and creative.
   - c. caring and honest.
   - d. intelligent and inventive.

5. When I experience stress I would most likely
   - a. do something to help me feel more in control of my life.
   - b. do something physical and daring.
   - c. talk with a friend.
   - d. go off by myself and think about my situation.

6. The greatest flaw someone can have is to be
   a. irresponsible.   b. unwilling to try new     c. selfish and          d. an illogical thinker.
   ▪                    ▪ things.                   ▪ unkind to others.     ▪

7. My vacations could be best described as
   a. traditional.     b. adventuresome.          c. pleasing to others.  d. a new learning
   ▪                    ▪                           ▪                       ▪ experience.

8. One word that best describes me is
   a. sensible.        b. spontaneous.            c. giving.              d. analytical.
   ▪                    ▪                           ▪                       ▪

**STEP 2.** Add up the total points for each column.

| TOTAL | TOTAL | TOTAL | TOTAL |
|-------|-------|-------|-------|
| ▪ | ▪ | ▪ | ▪ |
| Organizer | Adventurer | Giver | Thinker |

**STEP 3.** Plot these numbers on the brain diagram on the next page.

When you have tallied your scores, plot them on Figure 2-1 to create a visual representation of your spectrum.

Your Personality Spectrum assessment can help you maximize your functioning at school and at work. Each personality type has its own abilities that improve work and school performance, suitable learning techniques, and ways of relating in interpersonal relationships. Table 2-2 explains what suits each type.

**TABLE 2-2   PERSONALITY SPECTRUM AT SCHOOL AND WORK**

| PERSONALITY | STRENGTHS AT WORK AND SCHOOL | INTERPERSONAL RELATIONSHIPS |
|---|---|---|
| **ORGANIZER** | • Can efficiently manage heavy work loads<br>• Good organizational skills<br>• Natural leadership qualities | • Loyal<br>• Dependable<br>• Traditional |
| **ADVENTURER** | • Adaptable to most changes<br>• Creative and skillful<br>• Dynamic and fast-paced | • Free<br>• Exciting<br>• Intense |
| **GIVER** | • Always willing to help others<br>• Honest and sincere<br>• Good people skills | • Giving<br>• Romantic<br>• Warm |
| **THINKER** | • Good analytical skills<br>• Can develop complex designs<br>• Is thorough and exact | • Quiet<br>• Good problem solver<br>• Inventive |

FIGURE 2-1

# Personality Spectrum –Thinking Preferences & Learning Styles

Place a dot on the appropriate number line for each of your 4 scores and connect the dots. A new shape will be formed inside each square. Color each shape in a different color.

**Thinker**
Technical
Scientific
Mathematical
Dispassionate
Rational
Analytical
Logical
Problem solving
Theoretical
Intellectual
Objective
Quantitative
Explicit
Realistic
Literal
Precise
Formal

**Giver**
Interpersonal
Emotional
Caring
Sociable
Giving
Spiritual
Musical
Romantic
Feeling
Peacemaker
Trusting
Adaptable
Passionate
Harmonious
Idealistic
Talkative
Honest

Left Brain     Right Brain

**Organizer**
Systematic
Administrative
Procedural
Organized
Conservative
Confident
Structured
Safekeeping
Disciplined
Practical
Sequential
Predictable
Detailed
Tactical
Controlled
Dependable
Planning

**Adventurer**
Imaginative
Adventuresome
Open-minded
Fast-paced
Metaphoric
Original
Simultaneous
Visual
Impulsive
Experimental
Risking
Divergent
Artistic
Spatial
Skillful
Competitive
Active

# WHAT ARE THE BENEFITS OF KNOWING YOUR LEARNING STYLES?

Determining your learning-styles profile takes work and self-exploration. For it to be worth your while, you need to understand what knowing your profile can do for you. The following sections will discuss benefits specific to study skills as well as more general benefits.

## Study Benefits

Most students aim to maximize learning while minimizing frustration and time spent studying. If you know your particular learning style, you can use techniques that complement it. Such techniques take advantage of your highly developed areas while helping you through your less developed ones. For example, say you perform better in smaller, discussion-based classes. When you have the opportunity, you might choose a course section that is smaller or that is taught by an instructor who prefers group discussion. You might also apply specific strategies to improve your retention in a lecture situation.

This section describes the techniques that tend to complement the strengths and shortcomings of each style. Students in Professor Soloman's program made many of these suggestions according to what worked for their own learning styles. Concepts from different assessments that benefit from similar strategies are grouped together. In Figure 2-2 on p. 38, you can see which styles tend to be dominant among students.

Remember that you may have characteristics from many different styles, even though some are dominant. Therefore, you may see suggestions for styles other than your dominant ones that may apply to you. What's important is that you use what works. Note the boxes next to the names of each style or type. In order to spot your best suggestions quickly, mark your most dominant styles or types by making check marks in the appropriate boxes.

### Are You Active or Reflective?

<u>Active learners</u> ☐ include <u>Bodily-Kinesthetic</u> ☐ and <u>Interpersonal</u> ☐ learners as well as <u>Adventurers</u> ☐.   They like to apply the information to the real world, experience it in their own actions, or discuss or explain to others what they have learned.

Student-suggested strategies for active learners:

➤ Study in a group in which members take turns explaining topics to each other and then discussing them.

➤ Think of practical uses of the course material.

➤ Pace and recite while you learn.

➤ Act out material or design games.

➤ Use flash-cards with other people.

➤ Teach the material to someone else.

Reflective learners ☐ include Intrapersonal ☐ and Logical/Mathematical ☐ learners as well as Thinkers ☐.   They retain and understand information better after they have taken time to think about it.

Student-suggested strategies for reflective learners:

➤ Study in a quiet setting.

➤ When you are reading, stop periodically to think about what you have read.

➤ Don't just memorize material; think about why it is important and what it relates to, considering the causes and effects involved.

➤ Write short summaries of what the material means to you.

## Are You Factual or Theoretical?

Factual learners ☐ and Organizers ☐ prefer concrete and specific facts, data, and detailed experimentation.   They like to solve problems with standard methods and are patient with details. They don't respond well to surprises and unique complications that upset normal procedure. They are good at memorizing facts.

Student-suggested strategies for factual learners:

➤ Ask the instructor how ideas and concepts apply in practice.

➤ Ask for specific examples of the ideas and concepts.

➤ Brainstorm specific examples with classmates or by yourself.

➤ Think about how theories make specific connections with the real world.

Theoretical learners ☐ are often also logical/mathematical and prefer innovation and theories.   They are good at grasping new concepts and big-picture ideas. They dislike repetition and fact-based learning. They are comfortable with symbols and abstractions, often connecting them with prior knowledge and experience. Most classes are aimed at theoretical learners.

Student-suggested strategies for theoretical learners:

➤ If a class deals primarily with factual information, try to think of concepts, interpretations, or theories that link the facts together.

➤ Because you become impatient with details, you may be prone to careless mistakes on tests. Read directions and entire questions before answering, and be sure to check your work.

➤ Look for systems and patterns that arrange facts in a way that makes sense to you.

➤ Spend time analyzing the material.

## Are You Visual/Spatial or Verbal/Linguistic?

Visual/Spatial learners ☐ remember best what they see: diagrams, flow-charts, time lines, films, and demonstrations. They tend to forget spoken words and ideas. Classes generally don't include that much visual information. Note that although words written on paper or shown with an overhead projector are something you see, visual learners learn most easily from visual cues that don't involve words.

Student-suggested strategies for visual/spatial learners:

➤ Add diagrams to your notes whenever possible. Dates can be drawn on a time line; math functions can be graphed; percentages can be drawn in a pie chart.

➤ Organize your notes so that you can clearly see main points and supporting facts and how things are connected. You will learn more about different styles of note-taking in Chapter 6.

➤ Connect related facts in your notes by drawing arrows.

➤ Color-code your notes using different colored highlighters so that everything relating to a particular topic is the same color.

Verbal/Linguistic learners ☐ (often also interpersonal) remember much of what they hear and more of what they hear and then say. They benefit from discussion, prefer verbal explanation to visual demonstration, and

FIGURE 2-2  PERCENTAGES OF STUDENTS WITH PARTICULAR LEARNING STYLES

Visual 80%    Verbal 20%

Active 80%    Reflective 20%

Factual 70%    Theoretical 30%

Linear 85%    Holistic 15%

*Source:* Barbara Soloman, North Carolina State University

learn effectively by explaining things to others. Because written words are processed as verbal information, verbal learners learn well through reading. The majority of classes, since they present material through the written word, lecture, or discussion, are geared to verbal learners.

Student-suggested strategies for verbal learners:

➤ Talk about what you learn. Work in study groups so that you have an opportunity to explain and discuss what you are learning.

➤ Read the textbook and highlight no more than 10 percent.

➤ Rewrite your notes.

➤ Outline chapters.

➤ Recite information or write scripts and debates.

## Are You Linear or Holistic?

Linear learners ☐ find it easiest to learn material presented in a logical, ordered progression.  They solve problems in a step-by-step manner. They can work with sections of material without yet fully understanding the whole picture. They tend to be stronger when looking at the parts of a whole rather than understanding the whole and then dividing it up into parts. They learn best when taking in material in a progression from easiest to more complex to most difficult. Many courses are taught in a linear fashion.

Student-suggested strategies for linear learners:

➤ If you have an instructor who jumps around from topic to topic, spend time outside of class with the instructor or a class-mate who can help you fill the gaps in your notes.

➤ If class notes are random, rewrite the material according to whatever logic helps you understand it best.

➤ Outline the material.

Holistic learners ☐ learn in fits and starts.  They may feel lost for days or weeks, unable to solve even the simplest problems or show the most basic understanding, until they suddenly "get it." They may feel discouraged when struggling with material which many other students seem to learn easily. Once they understand, though, they tend to see the big picture to an extent that others may not often achieve. They are often highly creative.

Student-suggested strategies for the holistic learner:

➤ Recognize that you are not slow or stupid. Don't lose faith in yourself. You will get it!

➤ Before reading a chapter, preview it by reading all the subheadings, summaries, and any margin glossary terms. The chapter may also start with an outline and overview of the entire chapter.

➤ Instead of spending a short time on every subject every night, try setting aside evenings for specific subjects and immerse yourself in just one subject at a time.

➤ Try taking difficult subjects in summer school when you are handling fewer courses.

➤ Try to relate subjects to other things you already know. Keep asking yourself how you could apply the material.

### Study Techniques for Additional Multiple Intelligences

People who score high in the <u>Musical/Rhythmic</u> ☐ intelligence have strong memories for rhymes and can be energized by music.   They often have a song running through their minds and find themselves tapping a foot or their fingers when they hear music.

Student-suggested strategies for musical/rhythmic people:

➤ Create rhymes out of vocabulary words.

➤ Beat out rhythms when studying.

➤ Play instrumental music while studying if it does not distract you, but first determine what type of music improves your concentration the most.

➤ Take study breaks and listen to music.

➤ Write a rap about your topic.

<u>Naturalistic learners</u> ☐ feel energized when they are connected to nature. Their career choices and hobbies reflect their love of nature.

Student-suggested strategies for naturalistic people:

➤ Study outside whenever practical but only if it is not distracting.

➤ Explore subject areas that reflect your love for nature. Learning is much easier when you have a passion for it.

➤ Relate abstract information to something concrete in nature.

➤ Take breaks with something you love from nature—a walk, watching your fish, or a nature video. Use nature as a reward for getting other work done.

### Study Techniques for Different Personality Types

The different personality types of the Personality Spectrum combine the learning styles and multiple intelligences you have explored. Table 2-3 shows learning techniques that benefit each type.

## General Benefits

Although schools have traditionally favored verbal-linguistic students, there is no general advantage to one style over another. The only advantage is in discovering your profile through accurate and honest analysis. Following are three general benefits of knowing your learning styles.

1. You will have a better chance of avoiding problematic situations. If you don't explore what works best for you, you risk

forcing yourself into career or personal situations that stifle your creativity, development, and happiness. Knowing how you learn and how you relate to the world can help you make smarter choices.

2. You will be more successful on the job. Your learning style is essentially your working style. If you know how you learn, you will be able to look for an environment that suits you best and you'll be able to work effectively on work teams. This will prepare you for successful employment in the twenty-first century.

3. You will be more able to target areas that need improvement. The more you know about your learning styles, the more you will be able to pinpoint the areas that are more difficult for you. That has two advantages. One, you can begin to work on difficult areas, step by step. Two, when a task comes up requiring a skill that is tough for you, you can either take special care with it or suggest someone else whose style may be better suited to it.

Your learning-style profile is one important part of self-knowledge. Next you will explore other important factors that help to define you.

## TABLE 2-3  TYPES AND LEARNING TECHNIQUES

| PERSONALITY TYPE | RELATED LEARNING STYLES | LEARNING TECHNIQUES TO USE |
|---|---|---|
| **ORGANIZER** | Factual, Linear | • Organize material before studying.<br>• Whenever possible, select instructors who have well-planned courses.<br>• Keep a daily planner and to-do list. |
| **ADVENTURER** | Active, Bodily-Kinesthetic | • Keep study sessions moving quickly.<br>• Make learning fun and exciting.<br>• Study with other Adventurers but also with Organizers. |
| **GIVER** | Interpersonal | • Form study groups.<br>• Help someone else learn.<br>• Pick classes that relate to your interest in people. |
| **THINKER** | Reflective, Intrapersonal, Logical-Mathematical, Theoretical | • Study alone.<br>• Allow time to think about material.<br>• Pick classes and instructors who are intellectually challenging. |

## How can I adjust my learning style to my instructors' teaching styles?

### Patti Reed-Zweiger, South Puget Sound Community College, Tacoma, Washington

This last year I took a class in math that left me extremely stressed and exhausted. The way the teacher presented the material just didn't work for me. He threw out way too much information in a short period of time with little or no tools for completing the tasks. I really think he was unprepared. When he'd get to class, he'd fum-  ble through his book for awhile until he latched onto something to share. Sometimes, he'd spend the whole class answering a question or two about the previous homework and then, at the very last minute, give us a new assignment for the next class. We'd leave without any understanding of what we were to accomplish. It seems to me this teacher did very little teaching.

I'm a state trooper, so I'm used to handling enormous pressure, but in this case, nothing seemed to work. I'd leave in tears, class after class. This is frustrating for me. I'm forty years old and very confident and yet in this class I felt like I was back in grade school again. I felt inadequate, foolish and out of control. So much so that I would become sick to my stomach—nauseous. I wouldn't wish this experience on my worst enemy. What can I do to succeed in math and still maintain my self-esteem? At this point, I'm ready to drop it altogether.

### Jacque Hall, University of Georgia, Terry College of Business

You're not alone. Math is frightening to most people. When I began taking math classes, I felt like a total failure. In fact, I dropped out of my Math 102 class. I just couldn't handle it. That's the first thing I'd recommend to you. Get out of the class if the teacher is not what you need. But make sure you talk with the teacher first and see if  there's something the two of you can do to make the class successful for you. If you feel that it just won't work, let it go and try to find a better situation for yourself. Math is hard enough without subjecting yourself to inadequate teaching. I found that networking with other students on what classes and instructors to take really helped. The younger students always seem to know who the best teachers are.

If you can afford the additional time, I recommend you audit a class. If that isn't an option, hire a math tutor or take advantage of the math lab on a regular basis. Most importantly, remember that you are not a failure. And you're also not alone. I have felt a great deal of despair over math myself. I have seen people cry in class and others leave in total frustration. At some time or other, every student is going to run into a teacher or a classroom situation that leaves them feeling dissatisfied. Do your part by communicating with the teacher. If that doesn't work, move on. I'm glad I did.

# HOW DO YOU EXPLORE WHO YOU ARE?

You are an absolutely unique individual. Although you may share individual characteristics with others, your combination of traits is one-of-a-kind. It could take a lifetime to learn everything there is to know about yourself, because you are constantly changing. However, you can start by exploring these facets of yourself: self-perception, interests, habits, abilities, and limitations.

## Self-Perception

Having an accurate image of yourself is difficult. Unfortunately, many people err on the side of negativity. Feeling inadequate from time to time is normal, but a constantly negative self-perception can have destructive effects. Look at people you know who think that they are less intelligent, capable, or attractive than they really are. Observe how that shuts down their confidence and motivation. You do the same to yourself when you perceive yourself negatively.

**Self-perception,** How one views oneself, one's opinion of oneself.

Negative self-perception has a series of effects that lead to a self-fulfilling prophecy, meaning, something that comes true because you have convinced yourself it will: First you believe that you are incapable of being or doing something, then you neglect to try, and finally, you most likely don't do or become what you had already decided was impossible.

For example, say you think you can't pass a certain course. Since you feel you don't have a chance, you don't put as much effort into the work for that course. Sure enough, at the end of the semester, you don't pass. The worst part is that you may see your failure as proof of your incapability, instead of realizing that you didn't allow yourself to try. This chain of events can occur in many situations. When it happens in the workplace, people lose jobs. When it happens in personal life, people lose relationships.

Refine your self-image so that it reflects more of your true self. These strategies might help.

> **Believe in yourself.**  If you don't believe in yourself, others may have a harder time believing in you. Work to eliminate negative self-talk. Have faith in your abilities. When you set your goals, stick to them. Know that your mind and will are very powerful.

> **Talk to other people whom you trust.**  People who know you well often have a more realistic perception of you than you do of yourself.

> **Take personal time.**  Stress makes having perspective on your life more difficult. Take time out to clear your mind and think realistically about who you are and who you want to be.

> **Look at all of the evidence.**  Mistakes can loom large in your mind. Consider what you do well and what you have accomplished as carefully as you consider your stumbles.

Building a positive self-perception is a lifelong challenge. If you maintain a bright but realistic vision of yourself, it will take you far along the road toward achieving your goals.

## Interests

Taking some time now to explore your interests will help you later when you select a major and a career. You may be aware of many of your general interests already. For example, you can ask yourself:

➤ What areas of study do I like?

➤ What activities make me happy?

➤ What careers seem interesting to me?

➤ What kind of daily schedule do I like to keep (early riser, night owl)?

➤ What type of home and work environment do I prefer?

Interests play an important role in the workplace. Many people, however, do not take their interests seriously when choosing a career. Some make salary or stability their first priority. Some feel they have to take the first job that comes along. Some may not realize they can do better. Not considering what you are interested in may lead to an area of study or a job that leaves you unhappy, uninterested, or unfulfilled.

Choosing to consider your interests and happiness takes courage but brings benefits. Think about your life. You spend hours of time both attending classes and studying outside of class. You will spend at least eight hours a day, five or more days a week, up to fifty or more weeks a year as a working contributor to the world. Although your studies and work won't always make you deliriously happy, it is possible to spend your school and work time in a manner that suits you.

Here are three positive effects of focusing on your interests.

1. **You will have more energy.** Think about how you feel when you are looking forward to seeing a special person, participating in a favorite sports activity, or enjoying some entertainment. When you're doing something you like, time seems to pass very quickly. You will be able to get much more done in a subject or career area that you enjoy.

2. **You will perform better.** When you were in high school, you probably got your best grades in your favorite classes and excelled in your favorite activities. That doesn't change as you get older. The more you like something, the harder you work at it—and the harder you work, the more you will improve.

3. **You will have a positive attitude.** A positive attitude creates a positive environment and might even make up for areas in which you lack ability or experience. Because businesses currently emphasize teamwork to such a great extent, your ability to maintain a positive attitude might mean the difference between success and failure.

> "The greatest discovery of any generation is that human beings can alter their lives by altering their attitudes of mind."
>
> Albert Schweitzer

**Attitude,**
A state of mind or feeling toward something.

# Habits

A preference for a particular action that you do a certain way, and often on a regular basis or at certain times, is a habit. You might have a habit of showering in the morning, eating raisins, channel surfing with the TV remote control, hitting the snooze button on your clock, talking for hours on the phone, or studying late at night. Your habits reveal a lot about you. Some habits you consider to be good habits, and some may be bad habits.

Bad habits   earn that title because they can prevent you from reaching important goals. Some bad habits, such as chronic lateness, cause obvious problems. Other habits, such as renting movies three times a week, may not seem bad until you realize that you needed to spend those hours studying. People maintain bad habits because they offer immediate, enjoyable rewards, even if later effects are negative. For example, going out to eat frequently may drain your budget, but at first it seems easier than shopping for food, cooking, and washing dishes.

Good habits   are those that have positive effects on your life. You often have to wait longer and work harder to see a reward for good habits, which makes them harder to maintain. If you cut out fattening foods, you wouldn't lose weight in two days. If you reduced your nights out to gain study time, your grades wouldn't improve in a week. When you strive to maintain good habits, trust that the rewards are somewhere down the road. Changing a habit can be a long process.

> "To fall into a habit is to begin to cease to be."
>
> Miguel de Unamuno

Take time to evaluate your habits. Look at the positive and negative effects of each, and decide which are helpful and which harmful to you. Here are steps you can take to change a habit that has more negative effects than positive ones.

1. Be honest about your habits. Admitting negative or destructive habits can be hard to do. You can't change a habit until you admit that it is a habit.

2. Recognize the habit as troublesome. Sometimes the trouble may not seem to come directly from the habit. For example, spending every weekend working on the house may seem important, but you may be overdoing it and ignoring friends and family members.

3. Decide to change. You might realize what your bad habits are but do not yet care about their effects on your life. Until you are convinced that you will receive something positive and useful from changing, your efforts will not get you far.

4. Start today. Don't put it off until after this week, after the family reunion, or after the semester. Each day lost is a day you haven't had the chance to benefit from a new lifestyle.

5. Change one habit at a time. Changing and breaking habits is difficult. Trying to spend more time with your family, reduce TV time, increase studying, and save more money all at once can bring on a fit of deprivation, sending you scurrying back to all your old habits. Easy does it.

6. Reward yourself appropriately for positive steps taken. If you earn a good grade, avoid slacking off on your studies the following week. Choose a reward that will not encourage you to stray from your target.

7. Keep it up. To have the best chance at changing a habit, be consistent for at least three weeks. Your brain needs time to become accustomed to the new habit. If you go back to the old habit during that time, you may feel like you're starting all over again.

8. Don't get too discouraged. Rarely does someone make the decision to change and do so without a setback or two. Being too hard on yourself might cause frustration that tempts you to give up and go back to the habit.

## Abilities

Everyone's abilities include both strengths and limitations. Both are part of you. Examining both strengths and limitations is part of establishing the kind of clear vision of yourself that will help you maximize your potential.

### Strengths

As you think about your preferences, your particular strengths will come to mind, because you often like best the things you can do well. Some strengths seem to be natural—things you learned to do without ever having to work too hard. Others you struggled to develop and continue to work hard to maintain. Asking yourself these questions may help you define more clearly what your abilities are:

➤ What have I always been able to do well?

➤ What have others often praised about me?

➤ What do I like most about myself, and why?

➤ What is my learning-style profile?

➤ What are my accomplishments—at home, at school, at work?

As with your preferences, knowing your abilities will help you find a job that makes the most of them. When your job requires you to do work you like, you are more likely to perform to the best of your ability. Keep that in mind as you explore career areas. Assessments and inventories that will help you further assess your abilities may be available at your school's career center or library. Once you know yourself, you will be more able to set appropriate goals.

### Limitations

Nobody is perfect, and no one is good at everything. Everyone has limitations. However, that doesn't mean they are any easier to take. Limitations can make you feel frustrated, stressed, or angry. You may feel as though no one else has the limitations you have, or that no one else has as many.

There are three ways to deal with your limitations. The first two—ignoring them or dwelling on them—are the most common. Both are natural, but neither is wise. The third way is to face them and to work to improve them while keeping the strongest focus on your abilities.

Ignoring your limitations can cause you to be unable to accomplish your goals. For example, say you are an active, global learner with a well-developed interpersonal intelligence. You have limitations in logical-mathematical intelligence and in linear thought. Ignoring that fact, you decide that you can make good money in computer programming, and you sign up for math and programming courses. You certainly won't fail automatically. However, if you ignore your limited ability in those courses and don't seek extra help, you may have more than a few stumbles.

Dwelling on your limitations can make you forget you have any strengths at all. This results in negative self-talk and a poor self-perception. Continuing the example, if you were to dwell on your limitations in math, you might very likely stop trying altogether.

Facing limitations and working to improve them is the best response. A healthy understanding of your limitations can help you avoid troublesome situations. In the example, you could face your limitations in math and explore other career areas that use your more well-developed abilities and intelligences. If you decided to stick with computer technology, you could study an area of the field that focuses on management and interpersonal relationships. Or you could continue to aim for a career as a programmer, taking care to seek special help in areas that give you trouble.

# HOW CAN YOU START THINKING ABOUT CHOOSING A MAJOR?

While many students come to college knowing what they want to study, many do not. That's completely normal. College is a perfect time to begin exploring your different interests. In the process, you may discover talents and strengths you never realized you had. For example, taking an environmental class may teach you that you have a passion for finding solutions to pollution problems. You may discover a talent for public speaking and decide to explore on-camera journalism.

While some of your explorations may take you down paths that don't resonate with your personality and interests, each experience will help to clarify who you really are and what you want to do with your life. Thinking about choosing a major involves exploring potential majors, being open to changing majors, and linking majors to career areas.

**Major,**
A subject of academic knowledge chosen as a field of specialization, requiring a specific course of study.

## Exploring Potential Majors

Here are some steps to help you explore majors that may interest you.

Take a variety of classes. Although you will generally have core requirements to fulfill, use your electives to branch out. Try to take at least one class in each area that sparks your interest.

**Don't rule out subject areas that aren't classified as "safe."** Friends or parents may have warned you against pursuing certain careers, encouraging you to stay with "safe" careers that pay well. Even though financial stability is important, following your heart's dreams and desires is equally important. Choosing between the "safe" path and the path of the heart can be challenging. Only you can decide which is the best for you.

**Spend time getting to know yourself, your interests, and your abilities.** The more you know about yourself, the more ability you will have to focus on areas that make the most of who you are and what you can do. Pay close attention to which areas inspire you to greater heights and which areas seem to deaden your initiative.

**Work closely with your advisor.** Begin discussing your major early on with your advisor, even if you don't intend to declare a major right away. For any given major, your advisor may be able to tell you about both the corresponding department at your school and the possibilities in related career areas. You may also discuss with your advisor the possibility of a double major (completing the requirements for two different majors) or designing your own major, if your school offers an opportunity to do so.

**Take advantage of other resources.** Seek opinions from instructors, friends, and family members. Talk to students who have declared majors that interest you. Explore the course materials your college gives you in order to see what majors your college offers.

**Develop your critical-thinking skills.** Working toward any major will help you develop your most important skill—knowing how to use your mind. Critical thinking is the most crucial ingredient in any recipe for school and career success. More than anything, your future career and employer will depend on your ability to think clearly, effectively, creatively, and wisely, and to contribute to the workplace by truly making a difference.

## Changing Majors

Some people may change their minds several times before honing in on a major that fits. Although this may add to the time you spend in college, being happy with your decision is important. For example, an education major may begin student teaching only to discover that he really didn't feel comfortable in front of students. Or, a student may declare English as a major only to realize that her passion was in religion.

If this happens to you, don't be discouraged. You're certainly not alone. Changing a major is much like changing a job. Skills and experiences from one job will assist you in your next position, and some of the courses from your first major may apply—

or even transfer as credits—to your next major. Talk with your academic advisor about any desire to change majors. Sometimes an advisor can speak to department heads in order to get the maximum number of credits transferred to your new major.

Whatever you decide, realize that you do have the right to change your mind. Continual self-discovery is part of the journey. No matter how many detours you make, each interesting class you take along the way helps to point you toward a major that feels like home.

## Linking Majors to Career Areas

The point of declaring and pursuing a major is to help you reach a significant level of knowledge in one subject, often in preparation for a particular career area. Before you discard a major as not practical enough, consider where it might be able to take you. Thinking through the possibilities may open doors that you never knew existed. Besides finding an exciting path, you may discover something highly marketable and beneficial to humankind as well.

For each major there are many career options that aren't obvious right away. For example, a student working toward a teaching certification doesn't have to teach public school. This student could develop curricula, act as a consultant for businesses, develop an on-line education service, teach overseas for the Peace Corps, or create a public television program. The sky's the limit.

Explore the educational requirements of any career area that interests you. Your choice of major may be more or less crucial depending on the career area. For example, pursuing a career in medicine almost always requires a major in some area of the biological sciences, while aspiring lawyers may have majored in anything from political science to philosophy. Many employers are more interested in your ability to think than in your specific knowledge, and therefore may not pay as much attention to your major as they do to your critical-thinking skills. Ask advisors or people in your areas of interest what educational background is necessary or helpful to someone pursuing a career in that area.

## Sabiduría

In Spanish, the term *sabiduría* represents the two sides of learning—both knowledge and wisdom. Knowledge—building what you know about how the world works—is the first part. Wisdom—deriving meaning and significance from knowledge, and deciding how to use that knowledge—is the second. As you continually learn and experience new things, the *sabiduría* you build will help you make knowledgeable and wise choices about how to lead your life.

Think of this concept as you discover more about how you learn and receive knowledge in all aspects of your life—in school, work, and personal situations. As you learn how your unique mind works and how to use it, you can more confidently assert yourself. As you expand your ability to use your mind in different ways, you can create lifelong advantages for yourself.

# Chapter 2: Applications

Name _____ Date _____

 Key Into Your Life: Opportunities to Apply What You Learn

## Exercise 1: How Do You Learn Best?

Start by writing your scores next to each term.

| LEARNING STYLES INVENTORY | PATHWAYS TO LEARNING | PERSONALITY SPECTRUM |
|---|---|---|
| ___ Active | ___ Bodily-Kinesthetic | ___ Organizer |
| ___ Reflective | ___ Visual-Spatial | ___ Adventurer |
| ___ Factual | ___ Verbal-Linguistic | ___ Giver |
| ___ Theoretical | ___ Logical-Mathematical | ___ Thinker |
| ___ Visual | ___ Musical | |
| ___ Verbal | ___ Interpersonal | |
| ___ Linear | ___ Intrapersonal | |
| ___ Holistic | ___ Naturalist | |

Circle your highest preferences (largest numbers) for each assessment. What positive experiences have you had at work and school that you can link to the strengths you circled? _____

_____

_____

_____

What negative experiences have you had that may be related to your least developed learning styles or intelligences? _____

_____

_____

_____

_____

_____

_____

## Exercise 2: Making School More Enjoyable

List two required classes that you are not necessarily looking forward to taking. Discuss what parts of your learning-style profile may relate to your lack of enthusiasm. Name learning-styles-related study techniques that may help you get the most out of the class and enjoy it more.

| CLASS | REASON FOR LACK OF ENTHUSIASM | LEARNING OR STUDY TECHNIQUES |
|-------|-------------------------------|------------------------------|
| 1. | | |
| 2. | | |

## Exercise 3: Your Habits

You have the power to change your habits. List three habits that you want to change. Discuss the effects of each and how those effects keep you from reaching your goals.

| HABIT | EFFECTS THAT PREVENT YOU FROM REACHING GOALS |
|-------|----------------------------------------------|
| 1. | |
| 2. | |
| 3. | |

Out of these three, put a star by the habit you want to change first. Write down a step you can take today toward overcoming that habit.

_____

_____

_____

What helpful habit do you want to develop in its place? For example, if your problem habit were a failure to express yourself when you are angry, a replacement habit might be to talk calmly about situations that upset you as soon as they arise. If you have a habit of cramming for tests at the last minute, you could replace it with a regular study schedule that allows you to cover your material bit by bit over a longer period of time.

_____

_____

One way to help yourself abandon your old habit is to think about how your new habit will improve your life. List two benefits of your new habit.

1. _____

2. _____

Give yourself one month to complete your habit shift. Set a specific deadline. Keep track of your progress by indicating on a chart or calendar how well you did each day. If you avoided the old habit, write an X below the day. If you used the new one, write an N. Therefore, a day when you only avoided the old habit will have an X; a day when you did both will have both letters; a day when you did neither will be left blank. You can use the chart below or mark your own calendar. Try pairing up with another student and arranging to check up on each other's progress.

| 1 | 2 | 3 | 4 | 5 | 6 | 7 | 8 | 9 | 10 | 11 | 12 | 13 | 14 | 15 | 16 |
|---|---|---|---|---|---|---|---|---|----|----|----|----|----|----|----|
|   |   |   |   |   |   |   |   |   |    |    |    |    |    |    |    |
| 17 | 18 | 19 | 20 | 21 | 22 | 23 | 24 | 25 | 26 | 27 | 28 | 29 | 30 | 31 | |
|    |    |    |    |    |    |    |    |    |    |    |    |    |    |    | |

Don't forget to reward yourself for your hard work. Write here what your reward will be when you feel you are on the road to a new and beneficial habit.

_____

_____

_____

### Exercise 4: Interests, Majors, and Careers

Start by listing activities and subjects you like.

1. _____

2. _____

3. _____

4. _____

5. _____

6. _____

Name three majors that might relate to your interests and help you achieve your career goals.

1. _____

2. _____

3. _____

For each major, name a corresponding career area you may want to explore.

1. _____

2. _____

3. _____

Keep these majors and career areas in mind as you gradually narrow your course choices in the time before you declare a major.

## KEY TO SELF-EXPRESSION: DISCOVERY THROUGH JOURNAL WRITING

*To record your thoughts, use a separate journal or the lined pages at the end of the chapter.*

**Your Learning Style Profile**   Discuss the insights you have gained, through exploring your learning-style profile, about your strengths and struggles at school and work. What new strengths have come to your attention? What struggles have you become aware of that you couldn't explain before? Talk about how your insights may have changed the way you see yourself.

Name _____ Date _____

# Journal Entry

Prentice Hall

Name _____ Date _____

# Journal Entry

# GOAL SETTING AND TIME MANAGEMENT:

## Mapping Your Course

People dream of what they want out of life, but not everyone knows how to turn dreams into reality. Often dreams seem far off in time, too difficult, or even completely unreachable. You can build paths to your dreams, however, by identifying the goals you need to achieve, one by one, to arrive at your destination. When you set goals, prioritize, and manage your time effectively, you increase your ability to take those steps to achieve your long-term goals.

This chapter explains how taking specific steps toward goals can help you turn your dreams into reality. You will explore how your values relate to your goals, how to create a framework for your life's goals, how to set long-term and short-term goals, and how to set priorities. The section on time management will discuss how to translate those goals into daily, weekly, monthly, and yearly steps. Finally, you will explore the effects of procrastination.

In this chapter, you will explore answers to the following questions:

➤ What defines your values?

➤ How do you set and achieve goals?

➤ What are your priorities?

➤ How can you manage your time?

➤ Why is procrastination a problem?

# WHAT DEFINES YOUR VALUES?

**Values,**
Principles or qualities that one considers important, right, or good.

Your personal values are the beliefs that guide your choices. Examples of values include family togetherness, a good education, caring for others, and worthwhile employment. The sum total of all your values is your *value system.* You demonstrate your particular value system in the priorities you set, how you communicate with others, your family life, your educational and career choices, and even the material things with which you surround yourself.

## Choosing and Evaluating Values

Examining the sources of your values can help you define those values, trace their origin, and question the reasons why you have adopted them. Value sources, however, aren't as important as the process of considering each value carefully to see if it makes sense to you. Some of your current values may have come from television or other media but still ring true. Some may come from what others have taught you. Some you may have constructed from your own personal experience and opinion. You make the final decision about what to value, regardless of the source.

Each individual value system is unique, even if many values come from other sources. Your value system is yours alone. Your responsibility is to make sure that your values are your own choice, and not the choice of others. Make value choices for yourself based on what feels right for you, for your life, and for those who are touched by your life.

You can be more sure of making choices that are right for you if you try to always question and evaluate your values. Before you adopt a value, ask yourself: Does it feel right? What effects might it have on my life? Am I choosing it to please someone else, or is it truly my choice? Values are a design for life, and you are the one who has to live the life you design.

Because life change and new experiences may bring a change in values, try to continue to evaluate values as time goes by. Periodically evaluate the effects that having each value has on your life, and see if a shift in values might suit your changing circumstances. For example, losing your sight may cause you to value your hearing intensely. The difficulty of a divorce may have a positive result: a new value of independence and individuality. After growing up in a homogeneous community, a student who meets other students from unfamiliar backgrounds may learn a new value of living in a diverse community. Your values will grow and develop as you do if you continue to think them through.

> "Obstacles are what people see when they take their eyes off the goal."
>
> New York City Subway bulletin board

## How Values Relate to Goals

Understanding your values will help you set career and personal goals, because the most ideal goals help you achieve what you value. If you value spending time with your family, related goals may include living near your parents or writing to your grandmother every week. A value of financial independence may generate goals, such as working while going to school and keeping credit-card debt low, that reflect the value. If you value helping others, try to make time for volunteer work.

Goals enable you to put values into practice. When you set and pursue goals that are based on values, you demonstrate and reinforce values through taking action. The strength of those values, in turn, reinforces your goals. You will experience a much stronger drive to achieve if you build goals around what is most important to you.

# HOW DO YOU SET AND ACHIEVE GOALS?

A goal can be something as concrete as buying a health insurance plan or as abstract as working to control your temper. When you set goals and work to achieve them, you engage your intelligence, abilities, time, and energy in order to move ahead. From major life decisions to the tiniest day-to-day activities, setting goals will help you define how you want to live and what you want to achieve.

> Goal,
> An end toward which effort is directed; an aim or intention.

Paul Timm, a best-selling author and teacher who is an expert in self-management, feels that focus is a key ingredient in setting and achieving goals. "Focus adds power to our actions. If somebody threw a bucket of water on you, you'd get wet, and probably get mad. But if water was shot at you through a high-pressure nozzle, you might get injured. The only difference is focus."[1] Each part of this section will explain ways to focus your energy through goal-setting. You can set and achieve goals by defining a personal mission statement, placing your goals in long-term and short-term time frames, evaluating goals in terms of your values, and linking your goals to five life areas.

## Identifying Your "Personal Mission Statement"

Some people go through their lives without ever really thinking about what they can do or what they want to achieve. If you choose not to set goals or explore what you want out of life, you may look back on your past with a sense of emptiness. You may not know what you've done or why you did it. However, you can avoid that emptiness by periodically taking a few steps back and thinking about where you've been and where you want to be.

One helpful way to determine your general direction is to write a *personal mission statement*. Dr. Stephen Covey, author of the best-seller *The Seven Habits of Highly Effective People*, defines a mission statement as a philosophy that outlines what you want to be (character), what you want to do (contributions and achievements), and the principles by which you live. Dr. Covey compares the personal mission statement to the Constitution of the United States, a statement of principles that gives this country guidance and standards in the face of constant change.[2]

Your personal mission isn't written in stone. It should change as you move from one phase of life to the next—from single person to spouse, from parent to single parent to caregiver of an older parent. Stay flexible and reevaluate your personal mission from time to time.

Here is an example of author Carol Carter's personal mission statement:

My mission is to use my talents and abilities to help people of all ages, stages, backgrounds, and economic levels achieve their human potential through fully developing their minds and their talents. I also aim to balance work with people in my life, understanding that my family and friends are a priority above all else.

A company, like a person, needs to establish standards and principles that guide its many activities. Companies often have mission statements so that each member of the organization, from the custodian to the president, clearly understands what to strive for. If a company fails to identify its mission, a million well-intentioned employees might focus their energies in just as many different directions, creating chaos and low productivity.

Here is a mission statement from Northwest Airlines. It is displayed inside their company buildings and on the back of every employee's business card. Notice how it reinforces the company's goals of teamwork, leadership, and excellence.

To build together the world's most preferred airline with the best people; each committed to exceeding our customer's expectations every day.

Another example is from Prentice Hall, the company that publishes this text:

To provide the most innovative resources—books, technology, programs—to help students of all ages and stages achieve their academic and professional goals inside the classroom and out.

You will have an opportunity to write your own personal mission statement at the end of this chapter. Writing a mission statement is much more than an in-school exercise. It is truly for you. Thinking through your personal mission can help you begin to take charge of your life. It helps to put you in control instead of allowing circumstances and events to control you. If you frame your mission statement carefully so that it truly reflects your goals, it can be your guide in everything you do.

## Placing Goals in Time

Everyone has the same twenty-four hours in a day, but it often doesn't feel like enough. Have you ever had a busy day flash by so quickly that it seems you accomplished nothing? Have you ever felt that way about a longer period of time, like a month or even a year? Your commitments can overwhelm you unless you decide how to use time to plan your steps toward goal achievement.

If developing a personal mission statement establishes the big picture, placing your goals within particular time frames allows you to bring individual areas of that picture into the foreground. Planning your progress step by step will help you maintain your efforts over the extended time period often needed to accomplish a goal. Goals fall into two categories: long-term and short-term.

## Setting Long-Term Goals

Establish first the goals that have the largest scope, the *long-term goals* that you aim to attain over a lengthy period of time, up to a few years or more. As a student, you know what long-term goals are all about. You have set yourself a goal to attend school and earn a degree or certificate. Becoming educated is an admirable goal that takes a good number of years to reach.

Some long-term goals are lifelong, such as a goal to continually learn more about yourself and the world around you. Others have a more definite end, such as a goal to complete a course successfully. To determine your long-term goals, think about what you want out of your professional, educational, and personal life. Here is Carol Carter's long-term goal statement.

<u>Carol's Goals:</u>   To accomplish my mission through writing books, giving seminars, and developing programs that create opportunities for students to learn and develop. To create a personal, professional, and family environment that allows me to manifest my abilities and duly tend to each of my responsibilities.

For example, you may establish long-term goals such as these:

> ➤ I will graduate from school and know that I have learned all that I could, whether my grade point average shows it or not.
> ➤ I will build my leadership and teamwork skills by forming positive, productive relationships with classmates, instructors, and co-workers.

Long-term goals don't have to be lifelong goals. Think about your long-term goals for the coming year. Considering what you want to accomplish in a year's time will give you clarity, focus, and a sense of what needs to take place right away. When Carol thought about her long-term goals for the coming year, she came up with the following:

1. Develop programs to provide internships, scholarships, and other quality initiatives for students.
2. Allow time in my personal life to eat well, run five days a week, and spend quality time with family and friends. Allow time daily for quiet reflection and spiritual devotion.

In the same way that Carol's goals are tailored to her personality and interests, your goals should reflect who you are. Personal missions and goals are as unique as each individual. Continuing the example above, you might adopt these goals for the coming year:

> ➤ I will earn passing grades in all my classes.
> ➤ I will join two clubs and make an effort to take leadership roles in each.

### Setting Short-Term Goals

When you divide your long-term goals into smaller, manageable goals that you hope to accomplish within a relatively short time, you are setting *short-term goals*. Short-term goals narrow your focus, helping you to maintain your progress toward your long-term goals. They are the steps that take you where you want to go. Say you have set the two long-term goals you just read in the previous section. To stay on track toward those goals, you may want to accomplish these short-term goals in the next six months:

➤ I will pass Business Writing I so that I can move on to Business Writing II.

➤ I will attend four of the monthly meetings of the Journalism Club.

These same goals can be broken down into even smaller parts, such as one month.

➤ I will complete five of the ten essays for Business Writing.

➤ I will write an article for next month's Journalism Club newsletter.

In addition to monthly goals, you may have short-term goals that extend for a week, a day, or even a couple of hours in a given day. Take as an example the article you have planned to write for the next month's Journalism Club newsletter. Such short-term goals may include the following:

➤ Three weeks from now: Have a final draft ready. Submit it to the editor of the newsletter.

➤ Two weeks from now: Have a second draft ready, and give it to one more person to review.

➤ One week from now: Have a first draft ready. Ask my writing instructor if he will review it.

➤ Today by the end of the day: Freewrite about the subject of the article, and narrow it down to a specific topic.

➤ By 3 P.M. today: Brainstorm ideas and subjects for the article (more on brainstorming and freewriting in Chapter 6).

As you consider your long-term and short-term goals, notice how all of your goals are linked to one another. As Figure 3-1 shows, your long-term goals establish a context for the short-term goals. In turn, your short-term goals make the long-term goals seem clearer and more reachable. The whole system works to keep you on track.

## Linking Goals With Values

If you are not sure how to start formulating your mission, look to your values to guide you. Define your mission and goals based on what is important to you.

If you value physical fitness, your mission statement might emphasize your commitment to staying in shape throughout your life. Your long-

> *"Even if you're on the right track, you'll get run over if you just sit there."*
>
> Will Rogers

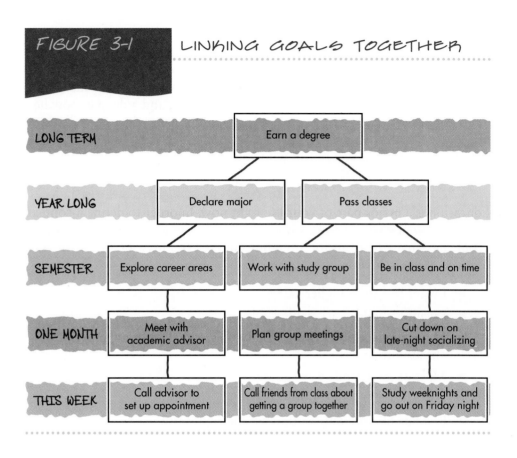

FIGURE 3-1    LINKING GOALS TOGETHER

| LONG TERM | Earn a degree |
| YEAR LONG | Declare major / Pass classes |
| SEMESTER | Explore career areas / Work with study group / Be in class and on time |
| ONE MONTH | Meet with academic advisor / Plan group meetings / Cut down on late-night socializing |
| THIS WEEK | Call advisor to set up appointment / Call friends from class about getting a group together / Study weeknights and go out on Friday night |

term goal might be to run a marathon, while your short-term goals might involve your weekly exercise and eating plan. Similarly, if you value a close family, your personal mission might emphasize how you want to maintain family ties and stability. In this case, your long-term goals might involve finding a job that allows for family time or living in a town close to your parents. Your short-term goals may focus on helping your son learn a musical instrument or having dinner with your family at least twice a week.

## Current and Personal Values Mean Appropriate Goals

When you use your values as a compass for your goals, make sure the compass is pointed in the direction of your real feelings. Watch out for the following two pitfalls that can occur.

**Setting goals according to other peoples' values.**    Friends or family may encourage you to strive for what they think you should value, rather than what is right for you. If you follow their advice without believing in it, you may have a harder time sticking to your path. For example, someone who attends school primarily because a parent or spouse thought it was right may have less motivation and initiative than someone who made an independent decision to become a student. Look hard at what you really want, and why. Staying in tune with your own values will help you make decisions that are right for you.

Setting goals that reflect values you held in the past. What you felt yesterday may no longer apply, because life changes can alter your values. The best goals reflect what you believe today. For example, a person who has been through a near-fatal car accident may experience a dramatic increase in how he or she values time with friends and family, and a drop in how he or she values material possessions. Someone who survives a serious illness may value healthy living above all else. Keep in touch with your life's changes so your goals can reflect who you are.

## Values Can Help You Identify Educational Goals

Education is a major part of your life right now. In order to define a context for your school goals, explore what you value about pursuing an education. People have many reasons for attending college. You may identify with one or more of the following possible reasons.

- ➤ I want to earn a higher salary.
- ➤ I want to build marketable skills.
- ➤ My supervisor at work says that a degree will help me move ahead in my career.
- ➤ Most of my friends were going.
- ➤ I want to be a student and learn all that I can.
- ➤ It seems like the only option for me right now.
- ➤ I am recently divorced and need to find a way to earn money.
- ➤ Everybody in my family goes to college; it's expected.
- ➤ I don't feel ready to jump into the working world yet.
- ➤ I got a scholarship.
- ➤ My friend loves her job and encouraged me to take courses in the field.
- ➤ My parent (or a spouse or partner) pushed me to go to college.
- ➤ I am pregnant and need to increase my skills so I can provide for my baby.
- ➤ I am studying for a specific career.
- ➤ I don't really know.

All of these answers are legitimate, even the last one. Being honest with yourself is crucial if you want to discover who you are and what life paths make sense for you. Whatever your reasons are for being in school, you are at the gateway to a journey of discovery.

It isn't easy to enroll in college, pay tuition, decide what to study, sign up for classes, gather the necessary materials, and actually get yourself to the school and into the classroom. Many people drop out at different places along the way, but somehow your reasons have been compelling enough for you to have arrived at this point. Thinking about why you value your education will help you stick with it.

Achieving goals becomes easier when you are realistic about what is possible. Setting priorities will help you make that distinction.

# WHAT ARE YOUR PRIORITIES?

When you set a priority, you identify what's important at any given moment. *Prioritizing* helps you focus on your most important goals, even when they are difficult to achieve. If you were to pursue your goals in no particular order, you might tackle the easy ones first and leave the tough ones for later. The risk is that you might never reach for goals that are important to your success. Setting priorities helps you focus your plans on accomplishing your most important goals.

To explore your priorities, think about your personal mission and look at your goals in the five life areas: personal, family, school/career, finances, and lifestyle. These five areas may not all be equally important to you right now. At this stage in your life, which two or three are most critical? Is one particular category more important than others? How would you prioritize your goals from most important to least important?

You are a unique individual, and your priorities are yours alone. What may be top priority to someone else may not mean that much to you, and vice versa. You can see this in Figure 3-2, which compares the priorities of two very different students. Each student's priorities are listed in order, with the first priority at the top and the lowest priority at the bottom.

First and foremost, your priorities should reflect your personal goals. In addition, they should reflect your relationships with others. For example, if you are a parent, your children's needs will probably be high on the priority list. You may decide to go back to school so you can get a better job, earn

**Priority,**
An action or intention that takes precedence in time, attention, or position.

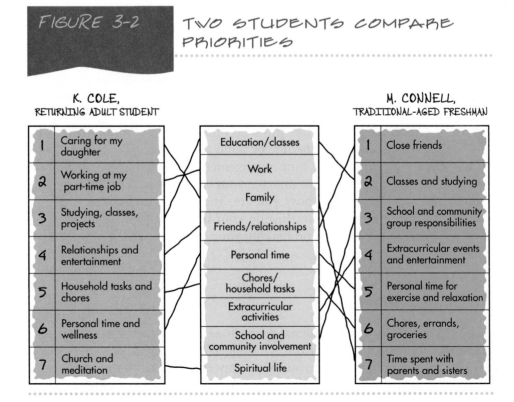

**FIGURE 3-2**   TWO STUDENTS COMPARE PRIORITIES

K. COLE, RETURNING ADULT STUDENT

| | |
|---|---|
| 1 | Caring for my daughter |
| 2 | Working at my part-time job |
| 3 | Studying, classes, projects |
| 4 | Relationships and entertainment |
| 5 | Household tasks and chores |
| 6 | Personal time and wellness |
| 7 | Church and meditation |

Education/classes
Work
Family
Friends/relationships
Personal time
Chores/household tasks
Extracurricular activities
School and community involvement
Spiritual life

M. CONNELL, TRADITIONAL-AGED FRESHMAN

| | |
|---|---|
| 1 | Close friends |
| 2 | Classes and studying |
| 3 | School and community group responsibilities |
| 4 | Extracurricular events and entertainment |
| 5 | Personal time for exercise and relaxation |
| 6 | Chores, errands, groceries |
| 7 | Time spent with parents and sisters |

more money, and give them a better life. If you are in a committed relationship, you may consider the needs of your partner. You may schedule your classes so that you and your partner are home together as often as possible. Even as you consider the needs of others, though, never lose sight of your personal goals. Be true to your goals and priorities so that you can make the most of who you are.

Setting priorities moves you closer to accomplishing specific goals. It also helps you begin planning to achieve your goals within specific time frames. Being able to achieve your goals is directly linked to effective time management.

# HOW CAN YOU MANAGE YOUR TIME?

Time is one of your most valuable and precious resources. Unlike money, or opportunity, or connections, time doesn't discriminate—everyone has the same twenty-four hours in a day, every day. Your responsibility, and your potential for success, lie in how you use yours. You cannot manipulate or change how time passes, but you can spend it taking steps to achieve your goals. Efficient time management helps you achieve your goals in a steady, step-by-step process.

People have a variety of different approaches to time management. Your learning style (explained in more detail in Chapter 2) can help you identify the particular way you currently use your time. For example, factual and linear learners tend to organize activities within a framework of time. Because they stay aware of how long it takes them to do something or travel somewhere, they are usually prompt. Theoretical and holistic learners tend to miss the passing of time while they are busy thinking of something else. Because they focus on the big picture, they may neglect details such as structuring their activities within available time. They frequently lose track of time and can often be late without meaning to be.

Time management, like physical fitness, is a lifelong pursuit. No one can plan a perfect schedule or build a terrific physique and then be "done." You'll work at time management throughout your life, and it can be tiring. Your ability to manage your time will vary with your mood, your stress level, how busy you are, and other factors. You're human; don't expect perfection. Just do your best. Time management involves building a schedule and making your schedule work through lists and other strategies.

## Building a Schedule

Being in control of how you manage your time is a key factor in taking responsibility for yourself and your choices. When you plan your activities with an eye toward achieving your most important goals, you are taking personal responsibility for how you live. Building a schedule helps you be responsible.

Just as a road map helps you travel from place to place, a *schedule* is a time-and-activity map that helps you get from the beginning of the day (or week, or month) to the end as smoothly as possible. A written schedule helps you gain control of your life. Schedules have two major advantages: They allocate segments of time for the fulfillment of your daily, weekly, monthly, and longer-term goals, and they serve as a concrete reminder of tasks, events, due dates, responsibilities, and deadlines. Few moments are more stressful than suddenly realizing you have forgotten to pick up a prescription, take a test, or be on duty at work. Scheduling can help you avoid events like these.

## Keep a Date Book

Gather the tools of the trade: a pen or pencil and a *date book* (sometimes called a planner). Some of you already have date books and may have used them for years. Others may have had no luck with them or have never tried. Even if you don't feel you are the type of person who would use one, give it a try. A date book is indispensable for keeping track of your time. Paul Timm says, "Most time management experts agree that rule number one in a thoughtful planning process is: Use some form of a planner where you can write things down."

There are two major types of date books. The *day-at-a-glance* version devotes a page to each day. While it gives you ample space to write the day's activities, this version makes it difficult to see what's ahead. The *week-at-a-glance* book gives you a view of the week's plans, but has less room to write per day. If you write out your daily plans in detail, you might like the day-at-a-glance version. If you prefer to remind yourself of plans ahead of time, try the book that shows a week's schedule all at once. Some date books contain additional sections that allow you to note plans and goals for the year as a whole and for each month. You can also create your own sheets for yearly and monthly notations in a notepad section, if your book has one, or on plain paper that you can then insert into the book.

Another option to consider is an *electronic planner*. These are compact mini-computers that can hold a large amount of information. You can use them to schedule your days and weeks, make to-do lists, and create and store an address book. Electronic planners are powerful, convenient, and often fun. On the other hand, they certainly cost more than the paper version, and you can lose a lot of important data if something goes wrong with the computer inside. Evaluate your options and decide what you like best.

## Set Weekly and Daily Goals

The most ideal time management starts with the smallest tasks and builds to bigger ones. Setting short-term goals that tie in to your long-term goals lends the following benefits:

➤ Increased meaning for your daily activities

➤ Shaping your path toward the achievement of your long-term goals

➤ A sense of order and progress

For college students as well as working people, the week is often the easiest unit of time to consider at one shot. Weekly goal-setting and planning allows you to keep track of day-to-day activities while giving you the larger perspective of what is coming up during the week. Take some time before each week starts to remind yourself of your long-term goals. Keeping long-term goals in mind will help you determine related short-term goals you can accomplish during the week to come.

Figure 3-3 shows parts of a daily schedule and a weekly schedule.

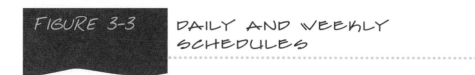

FIGURE 3-3    DAILY AND WEEKLY SCHEDULES

| | | 1997 |
|---|---|---|
| **MONDAY, MARCH 24** | | **PRIORITY** |
| **TIME** | **TASKS** | |
| 7:00 AM | | ☆ |
| 8:00 | Up at 8am — finish homework | |
| 9:00 | | |
| 10:00 | Business Administration | ☆ |
| 11:00 | Renew driver's license @ DMV | |
| 12:00 PM | | |
| 1:00 | Lunch | ☆ |
| 2:00 | Writing Seminar (peer editing today) | |
| 3:00 | | |
| 4:00 | check on Ms. Schwartz's office hrs. | |
| 5:00 | 5:30 work out | |
| 6:00 | ↳6:30 | |
| 7:00 | Dinner | |
| 8:00 | Read two chapters for Business Admin. | |
| 9:00 | | |
| 10:00 | | |
| 11:00 | | |

**Monday, March 24**

| | | | |
|---|---|---|---|
| 8 | | | |
| 9 | BIO 212 | CALL: Maggie Blair | |
| 10 | | Financial Aid Office | 1 |
| 11 | CHEM 203 | EMS 262 ☆ Paramedic role-play ☆ | 2 |
| 12 | | | 3 |
| Evening | 6pm yoga class | | 4 |

**Tuesday, March 25**

| | | | |
|---|---|---|---|
| 8 | Finish reading assignment! | | 5 |
| 9 | | Work @ library | |
| 10 | ENG 112 | | 1 |
| 11 | ↓ | | |
| 12 | | (study for quiz) | 2 |
| Evening | | | 3 |

**Wednesday, March 26**

| | | | |
|---|---|---|---|
| 8 | | ↓ until 7pm | 5 |
| 9 | BIO 212 | Meet w/advisor | |
| 10 | | | 1 |
| 11 | CHEM 203 ☆ QUIZ ☆ | EMS 262 | 2 |
| 12 | | | 3 |
| Evening | 6pm Aerobics | ☆ Pick up photos | 4 |
| | | | 5 |

## Link Daily and Weekly Goals With Long-Term Goals

After you evaluate what you need to accomplish in the coming year, semester, month, week, and day in order to reach your long-term goals, use your schedule to record those steps. Write down the short-term goals that will enable you to stay on track. Here is how a student might map out two different goals over a year's time.

| | |
|---|---|
| This year: | Complete enough courses to graduate. |
| | Improve my physical fitness. |
| This semester: | Complete my accounting class with a B average or higher. |
| | Lose 10 pounds and exercise regularly. |
| This month: | Set up study-group schedule to coincide with quizzes. |
| | Begin walking and weight lifting. |
| This week: | Meet with study group; go over material for Friday's quiz. |
| | Go for a fitness walk three times; go to weight room twice. |
| Today: | Go over Chapter 3 in accounting text. |
| | Walk for 40 minutes. |

## Prioritize Goals

Prioritizing enables you to use your date book with maximum efficiency. On any given day, your goals will have varying degrees of importance. Record your goals first, and then label them according to level of importance, using these categories: Priority 1, Priority 2, and Priority 3. Identify these categories using any code that makes sense to you. Some people use numbers, as above. Some use letters (A, B, C). Some write activities in different colors according to priority level. Some use symbols (*, +, -).

Priority 1 activities are the most important things in your life. They may include attending class, picking up a child from day care, putting gas in the car, and paying bills.

Priority 2 activities are part of your routine. Examples include grocery shopping, working out, participating in a school organization, or cleaning. Priority 2 tasks are important but more flexible than priority 1's.

Priority 3 activities are those you would like to do but can reschedule without much sacrifice. Examples might be a trip to the mall, a visit to a friend, a social phone call, a sports event, a movie, or a hair appointment. As much as you would like to accomplish them, you don't consider them urgent. Many people don't enter priority 3 tasks in their date books until they are sure they have time to get them done. You may want to list Priority 3 tasks separately and refer to the list when you have some extra time.

Prioritizing your activities is essential for two reasons. First, some activities are more important than others, and effective time management requires that you focus most of your energy on priority 1 items. Second, looking at all your priorities helps you plan when you can get things done. Often, it's not possible to get all your priority 1 activities done early in the day, especially if these activities involve scheduled classes or meetings. Prioritizing helps you set priority 1 items and then schedule priority 2 and 3 items around them as they fit.

*"The right time is any time that one is still so lucky as to have. . . .Live!"*

Henry James

# REAL WORLD PERSPECTIVE

## How can I stay focused on my goals?

### Karin Lounsbury, Gonzaga University, Spokane, Washington, Bachelor of General Studies in Human Resources

I decided to return to school when I had just turned forty. I didn't like feeling dependent on my husband for my financial security so I thought that I'd do something about it. I also did it for my two children. My marriage had been shaky for quite a few years and I was scared to death that I wouldn't be able to provide for them on my own. Even though I'd worked in the business  world for a long time, the salary was never very good. I was over-experienced and underpaid. I thought that by completing my education, I could find a great job that allowed me to support my family. Although I knew that college would be challenging, I wasn't concerned with the work load—I'm used to carrying a lot of responsibilities. In fact, probably more than most people. Besides my two young children, I'm married to a man who lost both his legs in the Vietnam war. He's in a wheelchair, which means a lot of extra work falls on my shoulders.

This last few months everything seems to be falling apart. My husband and I decided to get a divorce; my son has been struggling at school; my mother was just diagnosed with cancer; and I feel like I can hardly keep my head above water. All of this is taking a toll on my grades. I'm usually so emotionally and physically exhausted by the end of the day, I just don't have the energy to put into my work. When I'm at school, I'm distracted thinking about the future. I don't want to drop out of school but I also don't want my kids to suffer when they need me so badly. How can I get through this difficult time and still accomplish my educational goals?

### Shirley Williamson, University of Georgia

To begin with, I want to encourage you to hold onto your dream of finishing your education. Even though there are probably going to be some very cloudy days ahead, don't give up. The long-term rewards are worth all the extra effort it's going to take for a while. If you could lighten your academic load in any way, I think it would be wise to do so. It might take you a little longer to graduate, but you and  your children will appreciate the extra time you get with one another. Right now, maintaining your family life is extremely important. It's healthy for children to learn that you have goals and that they may have to make compromises some times, but they should never suffer at the expense of those goals. If that means putting off your studies until after they're in bed, then that's what you should do. You might even try studying at the same time they are doing their homework. Make it a family activity. But whatever you do, try and keep your family structure consistent.

My heart goes out to you. You really have a lot on your plate right now. I would also suggest you find some time to care for yourself. I think the greatest stress reducer is exercise. It gets your adrenalin going and keeps your body and mind healthy. You may have to get up a little earlier or work out on your lunch hour like I do, but it's work the extra effort.

### Keep Track of Events

Your date book also enables you to schedule *events*. Rather than thinking of events as separate from goals, tie them to your long-term goals just as you would your other tasks. For example, attending a wedding in a few months contributes to your commitment to spending time with your family. Being aware of quiz dates, due dates for assignments, and meeting dates will aid your goals to achieve in school and become involved.

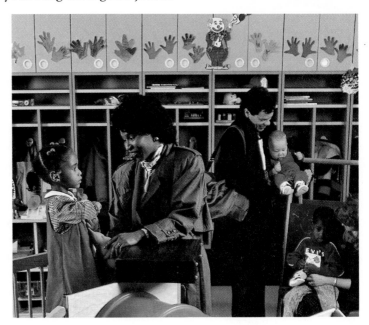

Note events in your date book so that you can stay aware of them ahead of time. Write them in daily, weekly, monthly, or even yearly sections, where a quick look will remind you that they are approaching. Writing them down will also help you see where they fit in the context of all your other activities. For example, if you have three big tests and a presentation all in one week, you'll want to take time in the weeks before to prepare for them all.

Following are some kinds of events worth noting in your date book:

➤ Due dates for papers, projects, presentations, and tests

➤ Important meetings, medical appointments, or due dates for bill payments

➤ Birthdays, anniversaries, social events, holidays, and other special occasions

➤ Benchmarks for steps toward a goal, such as due dates for sections of a project or a deadline for losing five pounds on your way to twenty

## Time Management Strategies

Managing time takes thought and energy. Here are some additional strategies to try.

1. Plan your schedule each week. Before each week starts, note events, goals, and priorities. Look at the map of your week to decide where to fit activities like studying and priority 3 items. For example, if you have a test on Thursday, you can plan study sessions on the days up until then. If you have more free time on Tuesday and Friday than on other days, you can plan workouts or priority 3 activities at those times. Looking at the whole week will help you avoid being surprised by something you had forgotten was coming up.

*FIGURE 3-4* MONTHLY CALENDAR

**APRIL**
**1997**

| Sunday | Monday | Tuesday | Wednesday | Thursday |
|---|---|---|---|---|
| | | 1 Turn in English paper topic | 2 Dentist 2pm | 3 |
| 6 Frank's Birthday | 7 9am PSYCH TEST WORK | 8 6:30pm Meeting @ Student Ctr. | 9 | |
| 13 | 14 ENGLISH PAPER DUE! WORK | 15 | | |
| 20 | 21 | | | |
| 27 | | | | |

2. Make and use to-do lists. Use a *to-do list* to record the things you want to accomplish. If you generate a daily or weekly to-do list on a separate piece of paper, you can look at all tasks and goals at once. This will help you consider time frames and priorities. You might want to prioritize your tasks and transfer them to appropriate places in your date book. Some people create daily to-do lists right on their date book pages. You can tailor a to-do list to an important event such as exam week or an especially busy day when you have a family gathering or a presentation to make. This kind of specific to-do list can help you prioritize and accomplish an unusually large task load.

3. Post monthly and yearly calendars at home. Keeping a calendar on the wall will help you stay aware of important events. You can purchase one or draw it yourself, month by month, on plain paper. Use a yearly or a monthly version (Figure 3-4 shows part of a monthly calendar) and keep it where you can refer to it often. If you live with family or friends, make the calendar a group project so that you stay aware of each other's plans. Knowing each other's schedules can also help you avoid scheduling problems such as two people needing the car at the same time or one partner scheduling a get-together when the other has to work.

4. Schedule down time. When you're wiped out from too much activity, you don't have the energy to accomplish much with your time. A little down time will refresh you and improve your attitude. Even half an hour a day will help. Fill the time with whatever relaxes you—having a snack, reading, watching TV, playing a game or sport, walking, writing, or just doing nothing. Make down time a priority.

5. Be flexible. Since priorities determine the map of your day, week, month, or year, any priority shift can jumble your schedule. Be ready to reschedule your tasks as your priorities change. On Monday, a homework assignment due in a week might be priority 2. By Saturday, it has become priority 1. On some days a surprise priority such as a medical emergency or a family situation may pop up and force you to cancel everything else on your schedule. Other days a class may be canceled and you will have extra time on your hands. Adjust to whatever each day brings.

**Down time,**
Quiet time set aside for relaxation and low-key activity.

No matter how well you schedule your time, you will have moments when it's hard to stay in control. Knowing how to identify and avoid procrastination and other time traps will help you get back on track.

# WHY IS PROCRASTINATION A PROBLEM?

Procrastination occurs when you postpone unpleasant or burdensome tasks. People procrastinate for different reasons. Having trouble with goal setting is one reason. People may project goals too far into the future, set unrealistic goals that are too frustrating to reach, or have no goals at all. People also procrastinate because they don't believe in their ability to complete a task or don't believe in themselves in general. As natural as these tendencies are, they can also be extremely harmful. If continued over a period of time, procrastination can develop into a habit that will dominate a person's behavior. Following are some ways to face your tendencies to procrastinate and *just do it!*

**Procrastination,**
The act of putting off something that needs to be done.

## Strategies to Fight Procrastination

**Weigh the benefits (to you and others) of completing the task versus the effects of procrastinating.**   What rewards lie ahead if you get it done? What will be the effects if you continue to put it off? Which situation has better effects? Chances are you will benefit more in the long term from facing the task head-on.

**Set reasonable goals.**   Plan your goals carefully, allowing enough time to complete them. Unreasonable goals can be so intimidating that you do nothing at all. "Pay off the credit-card bill next month" could throw you. However, "Pay off the credit-card bill in six months" might inspire you to take action.

**Get started.**   Going from doing nothing to doing something is often the hardest part of avoiding procrastination. Once you start, you may find it easier to continue.

**Break the task into smaller parts.**   If it seems overwhelming, look at the task in terms of its parts. How can you approach it step by step? If you can concentrate on achieving one small goal at a time, the task may become less of a burden.

**Ask for help with tasks and projects at school, work, and home.**   You don't always have to go it alone. For example, if you have put off an intimidating assignment, ask your instructor for guidance. If you need accommodations due to a disability, don't assume that others know about it. Once you identify what's holding you up, see who can help you face the task.

Don't expect perfection.   No one is perfect. Most people learn by starting at the beginning and wading through plenty of mistakes and confusion. It's better to try your best than to do nothing at all.

Procrastination is natural, but it can cause you problems if you let it get the best of you. When it does happen, take some time to think about the causes. What is it about this situation that frightens you or puts you off? Answering that question can help you address what causes lie underneath the procrastination. These causes might indicate a deeper problem that needs to be solved.

In Hebrew, the word *chai* means "life," representing all aspects of life—spiritual, emotional, family, educational, and career. Individual Hebrew characters have number values. Because the characters in the word *chai* add up to 18, the number 18 has come to be associated with good luck. The word *chai* is often worn as a good-luck charm. As you plan your goals, think about your view of luck. Many people feel that a person can create his or her own luck by pursuing goals persistently and staying open to possibilities and opportunities. Canadian novelist Robertson Davies once said, "What we call luck is the inner man externalized. We make things happen to us."

Consider that your vision of life may largely determine how you live. You can prepare the way for luck by establishing a personal mission and forging ahead toward your goals. If you believe that the life you want awaits you, you will be able to recognize and make the most of luck when it comes around. *L'Chaim*—to life, and good luck.

# Chapter 3: Applications

Name _____   Date _____

 *Key Into Your Life: Opportunities to Apply What You Learn*

### Exercise 1: Your Values

Begin to explore your values by rating the following values on a scale from 1 to 4, 1 being least important to you, and 4 being most important. If you have values that you don't see in the chart, list them in the blank spaces and rate them.

| Value | Rating | Value | Rating |
|---|---|---|---|
| Knowing yourself | | Mental health | |
| Physical health | | Fitness and exercise | |
| Spending time with your family | | Close friendships | |
| Helping others | | Education | |
| Being well-paid | | Being employed | |
| Being liked by others | | Free time/vacations | |
| Enjoying entertainment | | Time to yourself | |
| Spiritual/religious life | | Reading | |
| Keeping up with the news | | Staying organized | |
| Being financially stable | | Having an intimate relationship | |
| Creative/artistic pursuits | | Self-improvement | |
| Lifelong learning | | Facing your fears | |
| | | | |
| | | | |
| | | | |

Considering your priorities, write your top five values here:

1. _____

2. _____

3. _____

4. _____

5. _____

## Exercise 2: Why Are You Here?

Why did you decide to enroll in school? Do any of the reasons listed in the chapter fit you? Do you have other reasons all your own? Many people have more than one answer. Write up to five here.

_____

_____

_____

_____

_____

Take a moment to think about your reasons. Which reasons are most important to you? Why? Prioritize your reasons above by writing 1 next to the most important, 2 next to the second most important, etc.

How do you feel about your reasons? You may be proud of some. On the other hand, you may not feel comfortable with others. Which do you like or dislike and why?

_____

_____

_____

_____

_____

## Exercise 3: Short-Term Scheduling

Take a close look at your schedule for the coming month, including events, important dates, and steps toward goals. On the calendar layout on p. 78, fill in the name of the month and appropriate numbers for the days. Then record what you hope to accomplish, including the following:

➤ Due dates for papers, projects, and presentations
➤ Test dates
➤ Important meetings, medical appointments, and due dates for bill payments
➤ Birthdays, anniversaries, and other special occasions
➤ Steps toward long-term goals

This kind of chart will help you see the big picture of your month. To stay on target from day to day, check these dates against the entries in your date book and make sure that they are indicated there as well.

### Exercise 4: To-Do Lists

Make a to-do list for what you have to do tomorrow. Include all tasks —priority 1, 2, and 3—and events.

TOMORROW'S DATE:_____

1. _____
2. _____
3. _____
4. _____
5. _____
6. _____
7. _____
8. _____
9. _____
10. _____

Use a coding system of your choice to indicate priority level of both tasks and events. Place a check by the items that are important enough to note in your date book. Use this list to make your schedule for tomorrow in the date book, making a separate list for priority 3 items. At the end of the day, evaluate this system. Did the to-do list help you? How did it make a difference? If you liked it, use this exercise as a guide for using to-do lists regularly.

_____

_____

_____

_____

MONTH CHART

*Key to Self-Expression:*
*Discovery Through Journal*
*Writing*

*To record your thoughts, use a separate journal or the*
*lined page at the end of the chapter.*

Using the personal mission statement examples in the chapter as a guide,
consider what you want out of your life and create your own personal
mission statement. You can write it in paragraph form, in a list of long-
term goals, or in the form of a think link. Take as much time as you
need in order to be as complete as possible.

Name _____ Date _____

Journal Entry

# CRITICAL AND CREATIVE THINKING:

## Tapping the Power of Your Mind

Your mind's powers show in everything you do, from the smallest chores (comparing prices on cereals at the grocery store) to the most complex situations (figuring out how to earn money after being laid off). Your mind is able to process, store, and create with the facts and ideas it encounters. Critical and creative thinking are what enable those skills to come alive.

Understanding how your mind works is the first step toward critical thinking. When you have that understanding, you can perform the essential critical thinking task: asking important questions about ideas and information. This chapter will show you both the mind's basic actions and the thinking processes that use those actions. You will explore what it means to be an open-minded critical and creative thinker, able to ask and understand questions that promote your success in college, career, and life.

In this chapter, you will explore answers to the following questions:

➤ What is critical thinking?
➤ How does your mind work?
➤ How does critical thinking help you solve problems and make decisions?
➤ Why shift your perspective?
➤ Why plan strategically?
➤ How can you develop your creativity?

# WHAT IS CRITICAL THINKING?

Critical thinking is thinking that goes beyond the basic recall of information. If the word *critical* sounds negative to you, consider that the dictionary defines its meaning as "indispensable" and "important." Critical thinking is important thinking that involves asking questions. Using critical thinking, you question established ideas, create new ideas, turn information into tools to solve problems and make decisions, and take the long-term view as well as the day-to-day view.

A critical thinker asks as many kinds of questions as possible. The following are examples of possible questions about a given piece of information: *Where did it come from? What could explain it? In what ways is it true or false, and what examples could prove or disprove it? How do I feel about it, and why? How is this information similar to or different from what I already know? Is it good or bad? What causes led to it, and what effects does it have?* Critical thinkers also try to transform information into something they can use. They ask themselves whether the information can help them solve a problem, make a decision, create something new, or anticipate the future. Such questions help the critical thinker learn, grow, and create.

Not thinking critically means not asking questions about information or ideas. A person who does not think critically tends to accept or reject information or ideas without examining them. Table 4-1 compares how a critical thinker and a non-critical thinker might respond to particular situations.

Asking questions (the focus of the table), considering without judgment as many responses as you can, and choosing responses that are as complete and accurate as possible are some primary ingredients that make up the skill of critical thinking.

## Critical Thinking Is a Skill

Anyone can develop the ability to think critically. Critical thinking is a skill that can be taught to students at all different levels of ability. One of the most crucial components of this skill is learning information. For instance, part of the skill of critical thinking is comparing new information with what you already know. Your prior knowledge provides a framework within which to ask questions about and evaluate a new piece of information. Without a solid base of knowledge, critical thinking is harder to achieve. For example, thinking critically about the statement "Shakespeare's character King Richard III is like an early version of Adolf Hitler" is impossible without basic knowledge of World War II and Shakespeare's play *Richard III*.

The skill of critical thinking focuses on generating questions about statements and information. To examine potential critical-thinking responses in more depth, explore the different questions that a critical thinker may have about one particular statement.

**TABLE 4-1   NOT THINKING CRITICALLY VS. THINKING CRITICALLY**

| YOUR ROLE | SITUATION | NON-QUESTIONING RESPONSE | QUESTIONING RESPONSE |
|---|---|---|---|
| **STUDENT** | Instructor is lecturing on the causes of the Vietnam War. | You assume that everything your instructor tells you is true. | You consider what the instructor says, write down questions about issues you want to clarify, initiate discussion with the professor or other classmates. |
| **PARENT** | Instructor discovers your child lying about something at school. | You're mad at your child and believe the instructor, or you think the instructor is lying. | You ask both instructor and child about what happened, and you compare their answers, evaluating who you think is telling the truth. You discuss the concepts of lying/honesty with your child. |
| **SPOUSE/PARTNER** | Your partner feels that he or she no longer has quality time with you. | You think he or she is wrong and defend yourself. | You ask how long he/she has felt this way, ask your partner and yourself why this is happening, and explore how you can improve the situation. |
| **EMPLOYEE** | Your supervisor is angry at you. | You ignore or avoid your supervisor, or you deny responsibility for what the supervisor is angry about. | You are willing to discuss the situation; you ask what you could have done better; you ask what changes you can make in the future. |
| **NEIGHBOR** | People different from you move in next door. | You ignore or avoid them; you think their way of living is weird. | You introduce yourself; you offer to help if they need it; you respectfully explore what's different about them. |
| **CITIZEN** | You encounter a homeless person. | You avoid the person and the issue. | You examine whether the community has a responsibility to the homeless and, if you find that it does, you explore how to fulfill that responsibility. |
| **CONSUMER** | You want to buy a car. | You decide on a brand-new car and don't think through how you will handle the payments. | You consider the different effects of buying a new car vs. buying a used car; you examine your money situation to see what kind of payment you can handle each month. |

## A Critical-Thinking Response to a Statement

Consider the following statement of opinion: *"My obstacles are keeping me from succeeding in school. Other people make it through school because they don't have to deal with the obstacles that I have."*

Non-questioning thinkers may accept an opinion such as this as an absolute truth, believing that their obstacles will hinder their success. As a result, on the road to achieving their goals, they may lose motivation to overcome those obstacles. In contrast, critical thinkers would take the opportunity to examine the opinion through a series of questions. Here are some examples of questions one student might ask (the type of each question is indicated in parentheses):

*"What exactly are my obstacles?* Examples of my obstacles are a heavy work schedule, single parenting, being in debt, and returning to school after ten years out." (**recall**)

*"Are there other cases different from mine?* I do have one friend who is going through problems worse than mine, and she's getting by. I also know another guy who doesn't have too much to deal with that I can tell, and he's struggling just like I am." (**difference**)

*"Who has problems similar to mine?* Well, if I consider my obstacles specifically, I might be saying that single parents and returning adult students will all have trouble in school. That is not necessarily true. People in all kinds of situations may still become successful." (**similarity**)

*"Why do I think this?* Maybe I am scared of returning to school and adjusting to a new environment. Maybe I am afraid to challenge myself, which I haven't done in a long time. Whatever the cause, the effect is that I feel bad about myself and don't work to the best of my abilities, and that can hurt both me and my family who depends on me." (**cause and effect**)

*"What is an example of someone who has had success despite having to overcome obstacles?* What about Oseola McCarty, the cleaning woman who saved money all her life and raised $150,000 to create a scholarship at the University of Southern Mississippi? She didn't have what anyone would call advantages, such as a high-paying job or a college education." (**idea to example**)

*"What conclusion can I draw from my questions?* From thinking about my friend and about Oseola McCarty, I would say that people can successfully overcome their obstacles by working hard, focusing on their abilities, and concentrating on their goals." (**example to idea**)

*"How do I evaluate the effects of this statement?* I think it's harmful. When we say that obstacles equal difficulty, we can damage our desire to try to overcome those obstacles. When we say that successful people don't have obstacles, we might overlook that some very successful people have to deal with hidden disadvantages such as learning disabilities or abusive families." (**evaluation**)

Remember these types of questions. When you explore the seven mind actions later in the chapter, refer to these questions to see how they illustrate the different actions your mind performs.

## The Value of Critical Thinking

Critical thinking has many important advantages. Following are some of the positive effects, or benefits, of putting energy into critical thinking.

**You will increase your ability to perform thinking processes that help you reach your goals.**    Critical thinking is a learned skill, just like shooting a basketball or using a word-processing program on the computer. As with any other skill, the more you use it, the better you become. The more you ask questions, the better you think. The better you think, the more effective you will be when completing schoolwork, managing your personal life, and performing on the job.

**You can produce knowledge, rather than just reproduce it.**    The interaction of new information with what you already know creates new knowledge. The usefulness of such knowledge can be judged by how you apply it to new situations. For instance, it won't mean much for an early-childhood-education student to quote the stages of child development on an exam unless he or she can make judgments about children's needs when on the job.

**You can be a valuable employee.**    You certainly won't be a failure in the workplace if you follow directions. However, you will be even more valuable if you think critically and ask strategic questions about how to make improvements, large or small. Questions could range from "Is there a better way to deliver phone messages?" to "How can we increase business to keep from going under?" An employee who shows the initiative to think critically will be more likely to earn responsibility and promotions.

**You can increase your creativity.**    You cannot be a successful critical thinker without being able to come up with new and different questions to ask, possibilities to explore, and ideas to try. Creativity is essential in producing what is new. Being creative generally improves your outlook, your sense of humor, and your perspective as you cope with problems. Later in this chapter, you will look at ways to awaken and increase your natural creativity.

In the next section, you will read about the seven basic actions your mind performs when asking important questions. These actions are the basic blocks you will use to build the critical-thinking processes you will explore later in the chapter.

> "We do not live to think but, on the contrary, we think in order that we may succeed in surviving."
> José Ortega y Gassett

# HOW DOES YOUR MIND WORK?

Critical thinking depends on a thorough understanding of the workings of the mind. Your mind has some basic moves, or actions, that it uses to understand relationships among ideas and concepts. Sometimes it uses one action by itself, but most often it uses two or more in combination.

## Mind Actions: The Thinktrix

You can identify your mind's actions using a system called the Thinktrix, originally conceived by educators Frank Lyman, Arlene Mindus, and Charlene Lopez[1] and developed by numerous other instructors. They studied how students think and named seven mind actions that are the basic building blocks of thought. These actions are not new to you, although some of their names may be. They represent the ways in which you think all the time.

Through exploring these actions, you can go beyond just thinking and learn *how* you think. This will help you take charge of your own thinking. The more you know about how your mind works, the more control you will have over thinking processes such as problem solving, decision making, creating, and strategic planning.

Following are explanations of each of the mind actions. Each explanation names the action, defines it, and explains it with examples. As you read, write your own examples in the blank spaces provided. Each action is also represented by an picture or *icon* that helps you visualize and remember it.

**Recall:** ***Facts, sequence, and description.*** This is the simplest action. When you **recall** you describe facts, objects, or events, or put them into sequence. *Examples:*

➤ Naming the steps of a geometry proof, in order

➤ Remembering your best friends' phone numbers

*Your example:* Recall some important events this month. _____

_____

_____

*The icon:* A string tied around a finger is a familiar image of recall or remembering.

**Similarity:** ***Analogy, likeness, comparison.*** This action examines what is **similar** about one or more things. You might compare situations, ideas, people, stories, events, or objects. *Examples:*

➤ Comparing notes with another student to see what facts and ideas you have both considered important

➤ Analyzing the arguments you've had with your partner this month and seeing how they all seem to be about the same problem

*Your example:* Tell what is similar about two of your best friends. _____

_____

_____

*The icon:* Two alike objects, in this case triangles, indicate similarity.

**Difference:** *Distinction, contrast.* This action examines what is **different** about one or more situations, ideas, people, stories, events, or objects, contrasting them with one another. *Examples:*

➤ Seeing how two instructors differ in style—one divides the class into small groups and encourages discussion; the other keeps desks in straight lines and lectures for most of the class

➤ Contrasting a weekday where you work half day and go to school half day with a weekday when you attend class and then have the rest of the day to study

*Your example:* Explain how your response to a course you like differs from how you respond to a course you don't like as much. _____

_____

_____

*The icon:* Two differing objects, in this case a triangle and a square, indicate difference.

**Cause and effect:** *Reasons, consequences, prediction.* Using this action, you look at what has **caused** a fact, situation, or event, and/or what **effects**, or consequences, come from it. In other words, you examine both what led up to something and what will follow because of it. *Examples:*

➤ You see how staying up late at night causes you to oversleep, which has the effect of your being late to class. This causes you to miss some of the material, which has the further effect of your having problems on the test.

➤ When you pay your phone and utility bills on time, you create effects such as a better credit rating, uninterrupted service, and a better relationship with your service providers.

*Your example:* Name what causes you to like your favorite class, and the effects that liking the class has on you._____

_____

_____

*The icon:* The water droplets making ripples indicate causes and their resulting effects.

**Example to Idea:** *Generalization, classification, conceptualization.* From one or more **examples** (facts or events), you develop a general **idea** or ideas. Grouping facts or events into patterns may allow you to make a general statement about several of them at once. Classifying a fact or event helps you build knowledge. This mind action moves from the specific to the general. *Examples:*

➤ You have had trouble finding a baby sitter who can match your schedule. A classmate even brought her child to class once. Your brother has had to drop off his daughter at your mom's and doesn't like being unable to see her all day. From these examples, you derive the idea that your school needs an on-campus day-care program.

➤ You see a movie and you decide it is mostly about pride.

*Your example:* Name examples of activities you enjoy, and from them, come up with an idea of your choice of vacation. _____

_____

*The icon:* The arrow and "Ex" pointing to a light bulb on their right indicate how an example or examples lead to the idea (the light bulb, lit up).

Idea to Example: *Categorization, substantiation, proof.* In a reverse of the previous action, you take an **idea** or ideas and think of **examples** (events or facts) that support or prove that idea. This mind action moves from the general to the specific. *Examples:*

➤ When you write a paper, you start with a thesis statement, which communicates the central idea: "Men are favored over women in the modern workplace." Then you gather examples to back up that idea: Men make more money on average than women in the same jobs; there are more men in upper management positions than there are women; women can be denied advancement when they make their families a priority.

➤ You talk to your instructor about changing your major, giving examples that support your idea: You have worked in the field you want to change to, you have fulfilled some of the requirements for that major already, and you are unhappy with your current course of study.

*Your example:* Name a person whom you consider to be admirable. Give three examples that show how that person is admirable. _____

_____

*The icon:* In a reverse of the previous icon, this one starts with the light bulb and has an arrow pointing to "Ex". This indicates that you start with the idea, the lit bulb, and then branch into the example or examples that support the idea.

Evaluation: *Value, judgment, rating.* Here you **judge** whether something is useful or not useful, important or unimportant, good or bad, or right or wrong by identifying and weighing its positive and negative effects (pros and cons). Be sure to consider the specific situation at hand (a cold drink might be good on the beach in August, not so good in the snowdrifts in January). With the facts you have gathered, you determine the value of something in terms of both predicted effects and your own needs. Cause and effect analysis always accompanies evaluation. *Examples:*

➤ You decide to try taking later classes for a semester. You schedule classes in the afternoons and spend your nights on the job. You find that instead of getting up early to use the morning time, you tend to sleep in and then get up not too long before you have to be at school. From those harmful effects, you evaluate that it doesn't work for you. You decide to schedule earlier classes next time.

➤ Someone offers you a chance to cheat on a test. You evaluate the potential effects if you are caught. You also evaluate the long-term effects on you of not actually learning the material. You decide that it isn't worth your while to participate in the plan to cheat.

*Your example:* Evaluate your mode of transportation to school. _____

*The icon:* A set of scales out of balance indicates how you weigh positive and negative effects to arrive at an evaluation.

You may want to use a *mnemonic device*—a memory tool, explained in more detail in Chapter 7—to remember the seven mind actions. Try recalling them using the word DECRIES—each letter is the first letter of a mind action. You can also make a sentence of words that each start with a mind action's first letter. Here's an example: "Really Smart Dogs Cook Eggs In Enchiladas" (the first letter of each word stands for one of the mind actions).

## How Mind Actions Build Thinking Processes

The seven mind actions are the fundamental building blocks that your mind uses every day. Note that you will rarely use them one at a time in a step-by-step process, as they are presented here. You will usually combine them, overlap them, and repeat them more than once, using different actions for different situations. For example, when you want to say something nice at the end of a date, you might consider past comments that had an effect *similar* to what you want now. When a test question asks you to explain what prejudice is, you might name similar *examples* that show your *idea* of what prejudice means.

When you combine mind actions in working toward a specific goal, you are performing a thinking process. The next few sections will explore some of the most important critical-thinking processes: solving problems, making decisions, shifting your perspective, and planning strategically. Each thinking process helps you succeed by directing your critical thinking toward the achievement of your goals. Figure 4-3, appearing later in the chapter, shows all of the mind actions and thinking processes together and reminds you that the mind actions form the core of the thinking processes.

# HOW DOES CRITICAL THINKING HELP YOU SOLVE PROBLEMS AND MAKE DECISIONS?

Problem solving and decision making are probably the two most crucial and common thinking processes. Each one requires various mind actions. They overlap somewhat, because every problem that needs solving requires you to make a decision. However, not every decision requires that you solve a problem (for example, not many people would say that deciding what to order in a restaurant is a problem). Each process will be considered separately here. You will notice similarities in the steps involved in each.

Although both of these processes have multiple steps, you will not always have to work your way through each step. As you become more comfortable with solving problems and making decisions, your mind will automatically click through the steps you need whenever you encounter a problem or decision. Also, you will become more adept at evaluating which problems and decisions need serious consideration and which can be taken care of more quickly and simply.

> "I have always thought that one man of tolerable abilities may work great changes, and accomplish great affairs among mankind, if he first forms a good plan."
>
> Benjamin Franklin

## Problem Solving

Life constantly presents problems to be solved, ranging from average daily problems (how to manage study time or learn not to misplace your keys) to life-altering situations (how to care for a sick elderly relative or design a custody plan during a divorce). Choosing a solution without thinking critically may have negative effects. For example, if you decide to move a sick elderly relative into your home without considering the effects of your work schedule, the relative may be alone in the evenings with no one to help should a medical emergency arise. However, if you use the steps of the following problem-solving process to think critically, you have the best chance of coming up with a favorable solution.

You can apply this problem-solving plan to any situation or issue that you want to resolve. Using the following steps will maximize the number of possible solutions you generate and will allow you to explore each one as fully as possible.

1. State the problem clearly. What are the facts? *Recall* the details of the situation. Be sure to name the problem specifically, without focusing on causes or effects. For example, a student might state this as a problem: "I'm not understanding the class material." However, that may be a *cause* of the actual problem at hand: "I'm failing my economics quizzes."

2. Analyze the problem. What is happening that, in your opinion, needs to change? In other words, what *effects* does the situation have that cause a problem for you? What *causes* these effects? Look at the *causes and effects* that surround the problem. Continuing the example of the economics student, if some effects of failing quizzes include poor grades in the course and disinter-

est, some causes may include poor study habits, poor test-taking skills, lack of sleep, or not understanding the material.

3.  Brainstorm possible solutions. Brainstorming will help you think of examples of other similar problems and how you solved them. Consider what is different about this problem, and see if the thoughts you generate might lead you to new possible solutions. You will find more about brainstorming on p. 101 of this chapter. *It's very important to base your possible solutions upon causes rather than effects*. Getting to the heart of a problem requires addressing the cause rather than putting a bandage on the effect. If the economics student were to aim for better assignment grades to offset the low quiz grades, that might raise his GPA but wouldn't address the cause of not understanding the material. Looking at this cause, on the other hand, might lead him to work on study habits or seek help from his instructor, a study group, or a tutor.

4.  Explore each solution. Why might your solution work? Why not? Might a solution work partially, or in a particular situation? *Evaluate* ahead of time the pros and cons, or the positive and negative effects, of each plan. Create a chain of causes and effects in your head, as far into the future as you can, to see where you think this solution would lead. The economics student might consider the effects of improved study habits, more sleep, tutoring, or dropping the class.

5.  Choose and execute the solution you decide is best. Decide how you will put your solution to work. Then, execute your solution. The economics student could decide on a combination of improved study habits and tutoring.

6.  Evaluate the solution that you acted upon, looking at its *effects*. What are the positive and negative effects of what you did? In terms of your needs, was it a useful solution or not? Could the solution use any adjustments or changes in order to be more useful? Would you do the same again or not? Evaluating his choice, the economics student may decide that the effects are good but that his fatigue still causes a problem.

7.  Continue to refine the solution. Problem solving is always a process. You may have opportunities to apply the same solution over and over again. Evaluate repeatedly, making changes that you decide make the solution better. The economics student may decide to continue to study more regularly but, after a few weeks of tutoring, could opt to trade in the tutoring time for some extra sleep. He may decide to take what he has learned from the tutor so far and apply it to his increased study efforts.

Using this process will enable you to solve personal, educational, and workplace problems in a thoughtful, comprehensive way. Figure 4-1 is a think link that demonstrates a way to visualize the flow of problem solving. Figure 4-2 contains a sample of how one person used this plan to solve a problem. Figure 4-2 represents the same plan as 4-1 but gives room to write so that it can be used in the problem-solving process.

**Brainstorming,**

The spontaneous, rapid generation of ideas or solutions, undertaken by a group or an individual, often as part of a problem-solving process.

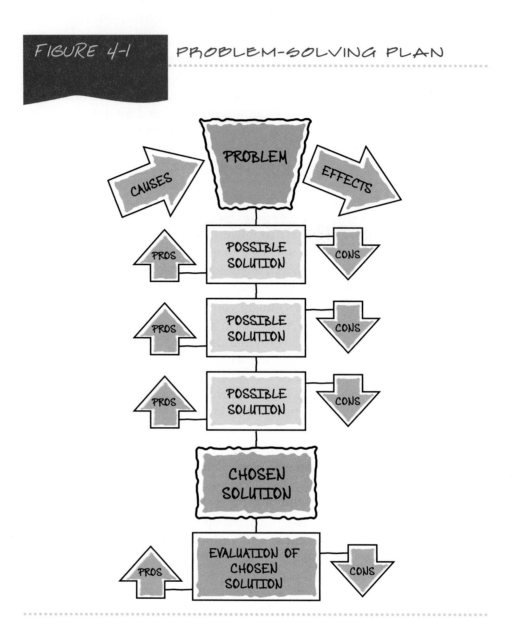

*FIGURE 4-1* PROBLEM-SOLVING PLAN

## Decision Making

Although every problem-solving process involves making a decision (when you decide which solution to try), not all decisions involve solving problems. Decisions are choices. Making a choice, or decision, requires thinking critically through all of the possible choices and evaluating which will work best for you and for the situation. Decisions large and small come up daily, hourly, even every few minutes. Do you call your landlord when the heat isn't coming on? Do you drop a course? Should you stay in a relationship? Can you work part time without interfering with school?

Before you begin the decision-making process, evaluate the level of the decision you are making. Do you have to decide what to have for lunch (usually a minor issue), or whether to quit a good job (often a major life change)? Some decisions are little, day-to-day considerations that you can take care of quickly on your own. Others require thoughtful evaluation,

FIGURE 4-2    HOW ONE STUDENT WORKED THROUGH A PROBLEM

**LIST CAUSES OF PROBLEM:**

Must go to school to take classes

Can't have child with me in class

No one else at home to watch child

**STATE PROBLEM HERE:**

Need some way to provide child-care while I'm at school

**LIST EFFECTS OF PROBLEM:**

Missed exams and classes sometimes

Logistics take extra time, transport

Stress created for me and child

Lack of routine & comfort

**List potential POSITIVE effects for each solution:**

Care is consistent

Reliable and familiar setting

Doesn't matter if child is sick

Use boxes below to list possible solutions:

**SOLUTION #1**

Have a nanny at home

**List potential NEGATIVE effects for each solution:**

Expensive

Hard to find someone to trust

Person must follow my schedule

Meet parents like myself

Child has playmates

Inexpensive

**SOLUTION #2**

Join child-care co-op

Must trust other parents

Sick child might get others sick

Close by to classes

Reliable care

No extra transport time

**SOLUTION #3**

Get school to provide child-care on campus

Costs school money

Need to find space and create facility

Restrictions & waiting lists

Now choose the solution you think is best—and try it.

**CHOSEN SOLUTION**

Join child-care co-op

**List the actual POSITIVE effects of the solution:**

Met some helpful people who understand me

My child likes the other three children

Low cost helps my budget

**List the actual NEGATIVE effects of the solution:**

When it's my turn, I have to care for four children

Sometimes our schedules clash

Can't let a sick child participate

**FINAL EVALUATION: was it a good or bad choice?**

All in all, I think this is the best I could do on my budget. There are times when I have to stay home with a sick child, but I'm mostly able to stay committed to both parenting and school.

*Source:* Adapted from a heuristic developed by Frank T. Lyman Jr., Ph.D., University of Maryland, 1983.

time, and perhaps the input of others you trust. The following is a list of steps to take in order to think critically through a decision.

1. Decide on a goal. Why is this decision necessary? In other words, what result do you want from this decision, and what is its value? Considering the *effects* you want can help you formulate your goal. For example, say a student currently attends a small private college. Her goal is to become a physical therapist. The school has a good program, but her financial situation has changed and has made this school too expensive for her.

2. Establish needs. *Recall* the needs of everyone (or everything) involved in the decision. The student needs a school with a full physical therapy program; she and her parents need to cut costs (her father changed jobs and her family cannot continue to afford the current school); she needs to be able to transfer credits.

3. Name, investigate, and evaluate available options. Brainstorm possible choices, and then look at the facts surrounding each. *Evaluate* the good and bad effects of each possibility. Weigh these effects and judge which is the best course of action. Here are some possibilities that the student in the college example might consider:

   ➤ *Continue at the current college.* **Positive effects:** I wouldn't have to adjust to a new place or to new people. I could continue my course work as planned. **Negative effects:** I would have to find a way to finance most of my tuition and costs on my own, whether through loans, grants, or work. I'm not sure I could find time to work as much as I would need to, and I don't think I would qualify for as much aid as I now need.

   ➤ *Transfer to the state college.* **Positive effects:** I could reconnect with people there that I know from high school. Tuition and room costs would be cheaper than at my current school. I could transfer credits. **Negative effects:** I would still have to work some or find minimal financial aid. The physical therapy program is small and not very strong.

   ➤ *Transfer to the community college.* **Positive effects:** They have many of the courses I need to continue with the physical therapy curriculum. The school is twenty minutes from my parents' house, so I could live at home and avoid paying housing costs. Credits will transfer. The tuition is extremely reasonable. **Negative effects:** I don't know anyone there. I would be less independent. The school doesn't offer a bachelor's degree.

4. Decide on a plan of action and pursue it. Make a choice based on your evaluation, and act on your choice. In this case the student might decide to go to the community college for two

years and then transfer back to a four-year school to earn a bachelor's degree in physical therapy. Although she might lose some independence and contact with friends, the positive effects are money saved, opportunity to spend time on studies rather than working to earn tuition money, and the availability of classes that match the physical therapy program requirements.

5. Evaluate the result. Was it useful? Not useful? Some of both? Weigh the positive and negative effects. The student may find with her transfer decision that it can be hard living at home, although her parents are adjusting to her independence and she is trying to respect their concerns as parents. Fewer social distractions result in her getting more work done. The financial situation is much more favorable. All things considered, she evaluates that this decision was a good one.

Making important decisions can take time. Think through your decision thoroughly, considering your own ideas as well as those of others you trust, but don't hesitate to act once you have your plan. You cannot benefit from your decision until you act upon it and follow through.

# WHY SHIFT YOUR PERSPECTIVE?

Seeing the world only from your perspective, or point of view, is inflexible, limiting, and frustrating to both you and others. You probably know how hard it can be to relate to someone who cannot understand where you are coming from—a co-worker who's annoyed that you leave early on Thursdays for physical therapy, a parent who doesn't see why you can't take a study break to visit, a friend who can't understand why you would date someone of a different race. Seeing beyond one's own perspective can be difficult, especially when life problems and fatigue take their toll.

On the other hand, when you shift your own perspective to consider someone else's, you open the lines of communication. Trying to understand what other people feel, need, and want makes you more responsive to them. They then may feel respected by you and respond to you in turn. For example, if you want to add or drop a course and your advisor says it's impossible, not waiting to hear you out, the last thing you may feel like doing is pouring your heart out. On the other hand, if your advisor asks to hear your point of view, you may sense that your needs are respected. Because the advisor wants to hear from you, you feel valued; that may encourage you to respond, or even to change your mind.

Every time you shift your perspective, you can also learn something new. There are worlds of knowledge and possibilities outside your individual existence. You may learn that what you eat daily may be against someone else's religious beliefs. You may discover people who don't fit a stereotype. You may find different and equally valid ways of getting an education, living as a family, relating to one another, having a spiritual life, or spending free time. Above all else, you may see that each person is entitled to his or her own perspective, no matter how foreign it may be to you.

**Perspective,**
A mental point of view or outlook, based on a cluster of related assumptions, incorporating values, interests, and knowledge.

# REAL WORLD PERSPECTIVE

## How can I find a satisfactory solution to my problem?

### Chelsea Phillips, Hampshire College, Massachusetts, Environmental Science Major

I attend Hampshire College in Massachusetts. This year I'm involved in a field study program called Earth Lands. The college gives me credits but the program is not affiliated with Hampshire. I live and work in a sustainable community and study ecological issues. There are nine of us that live together. All of us are environmental activists and we agree to live by  certain principles. The lodge we live in is run by solar power. We use kerosene and flashlights, too. Our food is entirely vegan, which means we not only don't eat meat, we also don't eat other foods that come from animals, like milk and butter.

Five of the participants in the program, including myself, are here as paying students. The other members are brought in to live with us and support us as we learn about the environment and community living. When we got involved, we believed the program was an entirely collaborative effort—at least that's what the brochure said. We're coming to find out there is a subtle power structure that exists between the five of us and the group called the "centering Team." We don't have as much input as we'd like into the schedule or decisions that need to be made. Because we're learning how to build community and resolve problems, I'd like to find a way to resolve this feeling of separation between the two groups. I'd like to see much more dialogue and collaboration so that we're all equal participants. What process could I initiate that would address this problem and allow for more equality within our community?

### Raymond Reyes, Community and Organizational Consultant

There seems to be a "tale of two cities" where there are two distinct groups of people. I would recommend that you revisit and "reclaim" the core principles that you have said were agreed upon by everyone in the community. There is an obvious gap between what has been said and reality. As a community, you need to journey into the gap, or  what Plato called, "the fertile void." You may want to give serious consideration to identifying and inviting an individual who can guide you through a process to establish a greater level of trust and authenticity and to do some team building.

Communities and other "learning organizations" need to address what I often refer to as the "other three R's" of education: relationship, relevance, and respect. First, address the need for honest and healthy relationships by specifically identifying and working through the trust and power issues. Secondly, make the core principles upon which your community is based more relevant so that the members truly "own" them whether they are paying students or part of the "centering Team." Lastly, your community needs to establish a social culture which has "wake up" calls that remind everyone to practice respect. Just as you are practicing respect for our Earth Mother, your community needs to have the daily fellowship behaviors which are likewise respectful.

Asking questions like these will help you maintain flexibility and openness in your perspective.

➤ What is similar and different about this person/belief/method and me/my beliefs/my methods?

➤ What positive and negative effects come from this different way of being/acting/believing? Even if this perspective seems to have negative effects for me, how might it have positive effects for others, and therefore have value?

➤ What can I learn from this different perspective? Is there anything I could adopt for my own life—something that would help me improve who I am or what I do? Is there anything I wouldn't do myself but that I can still respect and learn from?

Shifting your perspective is at the heart of all successful communication. Each person is unique. Even within a group of people similar to yourself, there will be a great variety of perspectives. Whether you see that each world community has different customs or you understand that a friend can't go out on weekends because he spends that time with his mother, you have increased your wealth of knowledge and shown respect to others. Being able to shift perspective and communicate more effectively may mean the difference between success and failure in today's diverse working world.

# WHY PLAN STRATEGICALLY?

If you've ever played a game of chess or checkers, participated in a wrestling or martial arts match, or had a drawn-out argument, you have had experience with strategy. In those situations and many others, you continually have to think through and anticipate the moves the other person is about to make. Often you have to think about several possible options that person could put into play, and you consider what you would counter with should any of those options occur. In competitive situations, you try to outguess the other person with your choices. The extent of your strategic skills can determine whether you will win or lose.

**Strategy,**
A plan of action designed to accomplish a specific goal.

Strategy is the plan of action, the method, the "how" behind any goal you want to achieve. Specifically, strategic planning means having a plan for the future, whether you are looking at the next week, month, year, ten years, or fifty years. It means exploring the future positive and negative effects of the choices you make and actions you take today. You are planning strategically right now just by being in school. You made a decision that the requirements of attending college are a legitimate price to pay for the skills, contacts, and opportunities that will help you in the future. As a student, you are challenging yourself to achieve. You are learning to set goals for the future, analyze what you want in the long term, and prepare for the job market to increase your career options. Being strategic with yourself means challenging yourself as you would challenge a competitor, urging yourself to work toward your goals with conviction and determination.

What are the benefits, or positive effects, of strategic planning?

**Strategy is an essential skill in the workplace.** A food company that wants to develop a successful health-food product needs to examine the anticipated trends in health consciousness. A lawyer needs to think through every aspect of the client's case, anticipating how to respond to any allegation the opposing side will bring up in court. Strategic planning creates a vision into the future that allows the planner to anticipate all kinds of possibilities and, most importantly, to be prepared for them.

**Strategic planning powers your short-term and long-term goal setting.** Once you have set goals, you need to plan the steps that will help you achieve those goals over time. For example, a strategic thinker who wants to own a home in five years' time might drive a used car and cut out luxuries, put a small amount of money every month into a mutual fund, and keep an eye on current mortgage percentages. In class, a strategic planner will think critically about the material presented, knowing that information is most useful later on if it is clearly understood.

FIGURE 4-3    THE WHEEL OF THINKING

**Strategic planning helps you keep up with technology.** As technology develops more and more quickly, jobs become obsolete. It's possible to spend years in school training for a career area that will be drying up when you are ready to enter the work force. When you plan strategically, you can take a broader range of courses or choose a major and career that are expanding. This will make it more likely that your skills will be in demand when you graduate.

Effective critical thinking is essential to strategic planning. If you aim for a certain goal, what steps will move you toward that goal? What positive effects do you anticipate these steps will have? How do you evaluate your past experiences with planning and goal setting? What can you learn from similar or different previous experiences in order to take different steps today? Critical thinking runs like a thread through all of your strategic planning.

Here are some tips for becoming a strategic planner:

**Develop an appropriate plan.** What approach will best achieve your goal? What steps toward your goal will you need to take one year, five years, ten years or twenty years from now?

**Anticipate all possible outcomes of your actions.** What are the positive and negative effects that may occur?

**Ask the question "how?"** How do you achieve your goals? How do you learn effectively and remember what you learn? How do you develop a productive idea on the job? How do you distinguish yourself at school and at work?

**Use human resources.** Talk to people who are where you want to be, whether professionally or personally. What caused them to get there? Ask them what they believe are the important steps to take, degrees to have, training to experience, knowledge to gain.

In each thinking process, you use your creativity to come up with ideas, examples, causes, effects, and solutions. You have a capacity to be creative, whether you are aware of it or not. Open up your mind and awaken your creativity. It will enhance your critical thinking and make life more enjoyable.

# HOW CAN YOU DEVELOP YOUR CREATIVITY?

Everyone is creative. Although the word "creative" may seem to refer primarily to artists, writers, musicians, and others who work in fields whose creative aspects are in the forefront, creativity comes in many other forms. It is the power to create anything, whether it is a solution, idea, approach, tangible product, work of art, system, program—anything at all. To help you expand your concept of creativity, here are some examples of day-to-day creative thinking:

**Creativity,**
The ability to produce something new through imaginative skill.

➤ Figuring out an alternative plan when your baby sitter unexpectedly cancels on you

➤ Planning how to coordinate your work and class schedules

➤ Talking through a problem with an instructor, and finding a way to understand each other

Creative innovations introduced by all kinds of people continually expand and change the world. Here are some that have had an impact:

➤ Susan B. Anthony and other women fought for and won the right for women to vote.

➤ Art Fry and Spencer Silver invented the Post-It™ note in 1980, enabling people to save paper and protect documents by using removable notes.

➤ Henry Ford introduced the assembly-line method of automobile construction, making cars cheap enough to be available to the average citizen.

➤ Rosa Parks refused to give up her seat on the bus to a white person, thus setting off a chain of events that gave rise to the civil rights movement.

➤ Alicia Diaz, director of the Center of Hispanic Policy, Research, and Development, developed corporate partnerships and internship programs that have become models for small, efficient government.

Even though these particular innovations had wide-ranging effects, the characteristics of these influential innovators can be found in all people who exercise their creative capabilities.

## Characteristics of Creative People

Creative people think in fresh new ways that improve the world and increase productivity, consistently responding to change with new ideas. Roger van Oech, an expert on creativity, highlights this kind of flexibility.[2] "I've found that the hallmark of creative people is their mental flexibility," he says. "Like race-car drivers who shift in and out of different gears depending on where they are on the course, creative people are able to shift in and out of different types of thinking depending on the needs of the situation at hand. . . . they're doggedly persistent in striving to reach their goals."

Creative people combine ideas and information in ways that form completely new solutions, ideas, processes, uses, or products. Children often can tap into this creative freedom more easily than adults. Whether they make up a new game, wear a bowl as a hat, or create forts from chairs and blankets, they create naturally without worrying that their ideas might not be "right." See if you can retrieve some of that creative freedom from your childhood when you use the following creative technique.

# Brainstorming Toward a Creative Answer

You are brainstorming when you approach a problem by letting your mind free-associate and come up with as many possible ideas, examples, or solutions as you can, without immediately evaluating them as good or bad. Brainstorming is also referred to as divergent thinking—you start with the issue or problem and then let your mind diverge, or go in as many different directions as it wants, in search of ideas or solutions. You can use brainstorming for problem solving, decision making, preparing to write an essay, or any time you want to open your mind to new possibilities. Here are some rules for successful brainstorming:[3]

**Don't evaluate or criticize an idea right away.** Write down your ideas so that you remember them. Evaluate later, after you have had a chance to think about them. Try to avoid criticizing other people's ideas as well. Students often become stifled when their ideas are evaluated during brainstorming.

**Focus on quantity; don't worry about quality until later.** Try to generate as many ideas or examples as you can. The more thoughts you generate, the better the chance that one may be useful. Brainstorming works well in groups. Group members can become inspired by, and make creative use of, one another's ideas.

**Let yourself consider wild and wacky ideas.** Trust yourself to fall off the edge of tradition when you explore your creativity. Sometimes the craziest ideas end up being the most productive, positive, workable solutions around.

Remember, creativity can be developed if you have the desire and patience. Be gentle with yourself in the process. Most people are harsher with themselves and their ideas than is necessary. Your creative expression will become more free with practice.

# Creativity and Critical Thinking

Critical thinking and creativity work hand in hand. Critical thinking is inherently creative, because it requires you to take the information you are given and come up with original ideas or solutions to problems. For example, you can brainstorm to generate possible causes of a certain effect. If the effect you were examining was fatigue in afternoon classes, you might come up with possible causes such as lack of sleep, too much morning caffeine, a diet heavy in carbohydrates, a natural tendency toward low energy at that time, or an instructor who doesn't inspire you. Through your consideration of causes and solutions, you have been thinking both creatively and critically.

Creative thinkers and critical thinkers have similar characteristics—both consider new perspectives, ask questions, don't hesitate to question accepted assumptions and traditions, and persist in the search for answers. Only through thinking critically and creatively can you freely question, brain-

> "The world of reality has its limits. The world of imagination is boundless."
>
> Jean Jacques Rousseau

storm, and evaluate in order to come up with the most fitting ideas, solutions, decisions, arguments, and plans.

You use critical-thinking mind actions throughout everything you do in school and in your daily life. In this chapter and in some of the other study skills chapters, you will notice mind-action icons placed where they can help you to label your thinking.

# Κριvειv

The word "critical" is derived from the Greek word *krinein*, which means to separate in order to choose or select. To be a mindful, aware critical thinker, you need to be able to separate, evaluate, and select ideas, facts, and thoughts.

Think of this concept as you apply critical thinking to your reading, writing, and interaction with others. Be aware of the information you take in and of your thoughts, and be selective as you process them. Critical thinking gives you the power to make sense of life by deliberately selecting how to respond to the information, people, and events that you encounter.

# Chapter 4: Applications

Name                            Date

 *Key Into Your Life: Opportunities to Apply What You Learn*

## Exercise 1: Making a Decision

In this series of exercises you will make a personal decision using the seven mind actions and the decision-making steps described in this chapter. Before you proceed through each of the steps, write here an important personal decision you have to make. Choose a decision that you want to act on and will be able to address soon.

_____

_____

*Step 1   Name Your Goal*

    Be specific: What goal, or desired effects, do you seek from this decision? For example, if your decision is a choice between two jobs, the effects you want might be financial security, convenience, experience, or anything else that is a priority to you. It could also be a combination of these effects. Write down the desired effects that together make up your goal. Note priorities by numbering the effects in order of importance.

_____

_____

_____

*Step 2   Establish Needs*

    Who and what will be affected by your decision? If you are deciding how to finance your education and you have a family to support, you must take into consideration their financial needs as well as your own when exploring options.

    List here the people/things/situations that may be affected by your decision and indicate how your decision will affect them.

_____

_____

_____

_____

### Step 3   Check Out Your Options

Look at all the options you can imagine. Consider options even if they seem impossible or unlikely—you can evaluate them later. Some decisions only have two options (to move to a new apartment or not, to get a new roommate or not); others have a wider selection of choices. For example, if you are a full-time student and the parent of a child you must coordinate your class schedule with the child's needs. Options could be the following: (1) put the child in day care, (2) ask a relative to care for the child, (3) hire a full-time nanny, or (4) arrange your class schedule so that you can balance the duties with another parent.

First, list the possible options for your own personal decision. Then evaluate the good and bad effects of each.

Option 1 _____

Positive effects _____

Negative effects _____

Option 2 _____

Positive effects _____

Negative effects _____

Option 3 _____

Positive effects _____

Negative effects _____

Option 4 _____

Positive effects _____

Negative effects _____

Have you or someone else ever made a decision similar to the one you are about to make? What can you learn from that decision that may help you?

_____

_____

### Step 4   Make Your Decision and Pursue It to the Goal

Taking your entire analysis into account, decide what to do. Write your decision here.

_____

_____

Next is perhaps the most important step: Act on your decision.

### Step 5   Evaluate the Result

After you have acted on your decision, evaluate how everything turned out. Did you achieve the effects you wanted to achieve? What were the effects on you? On others? On the situation? To what extent were they positive, negative, or some of both?

List four effects here. Name each effect, circle *Positive* or *Negative*, and explain that evaluation.

Effect _____
      *Positive*                                           *Negative*

Why? _____

Effect _____
      *Positive*                                            *Negative*

Why? _____

Effect _____
      *Positive*                                           *Negative*

Why? _____

Effect _____
      *Positive*                                           *Negative*

Why? _____

*Final evaluation:* Write one statement in reaction to the decision you made. Indicate whether you feel the decision was useful or not useful, and why. Indicate any adjustments that could have made the effects of your decision more positive.

_____

_____

_____

_____

## Exercise 2: Brainstorming on the Idea Wheel

Your creative mind can solve problems when you least expect it. Many people report having sudden ideas while exercising, driving, showering, upon waking, or even when dreaming. When the pressure is off, the mind is often more free to roam through uncharted territory and bring back treasures.

To make the most of this mind-float, grab ideas right when they surface. If you don't, they roll back into your subconscious as if on a wheel. Since you never know how big the wheel is, you can't be sure when that particular idea will roll to the top again. That's one of the reasons why writers carry notebooks—they need to grab thoughts when they come to the top of the wheel.

Name a problem, large or small, to which you haven't yet found a satisfactory solution. Do a brainstorm without the time limit. Be on the lookout for ideas, causes, effects, solutions, or similar problems coming to the top of your wheel. The minute it happens, grab this book and write your idea next to the problem. Take a look at your ideas later and see how your creative mind may have pointed you toward some original and workable solutions. You may want to keep a book by your bed to catch ideas that pop up before, during, or after sleep.

Problem: _____

Ideas: _____

_____

_____

_____

_____

_____

_____

_____

### Exercise 3: Group Problem Solving

As a class, brainstorm a list of problems in your lives. Write the problems on the board or on a large piece of paper attached to an easel. Include any problems you feel comfortable discussing with others. Such problems may be in the categories of schoolwork, relationships, job stress, discrimination, parenting, housing, procrastination, and others. Divide into groups of two to four with each group choosing or being assigned one problem to work on. Use the empty problem-solving flowchart on the next page to fill in your work.

1. **Identify the problem.** As a group, state your problem specifically, without causes ("I'm not attending all of my classes" is better than "lack of motivation"). Then, look at the causes and effects that surround it. Record the effects that the problem has on your lives. List what causes the problem. Remember to look for "hidden" causes (you may perceive that traffic makes you late to school, but the hidden cause might be that you don't get up early enough to have adequate commuting time in the morning).
2. **Brainstorm possible solutions.** Determine the most likely causes of the problem; from those causes, derive possible solutions. Record all the ideas that group members offer. After ten minutes or so, each group member should choose one possible solution to explore independently.
3. **Explore each solution.** In thinking independently through the assigned solution, each group member should (a) weigh the positive and negative effects, (b) consider similar problems, (c) determine whether the problem requires a different strategy from other problems like it, and (d) describe how the solution affects the causes of the problem. Evaluate your assigned solution. Is it a good one? Will it work?

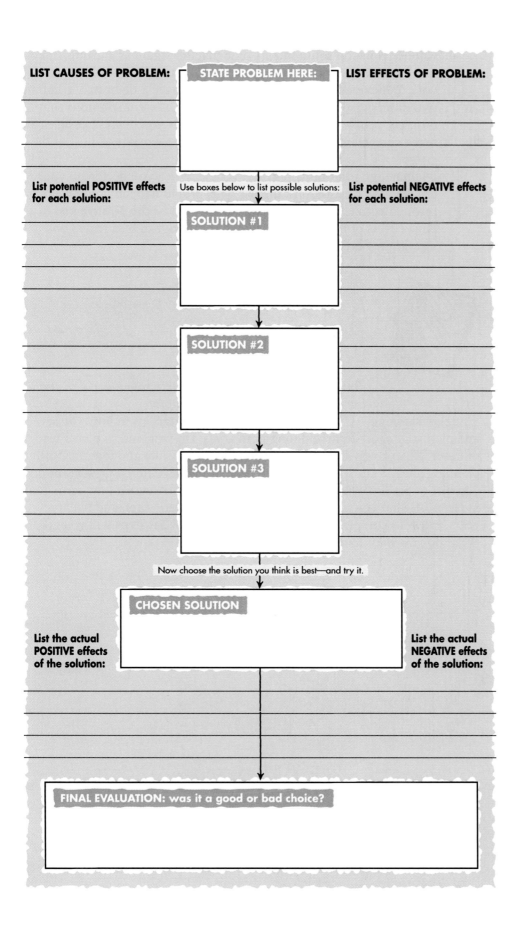

**LIST CAUSES OF PROBLEM:**

**STATE PROBLEM HERE:**

**LIST EFFECTS OF PROBLEM:**

**List potential POSITIVE effects for each solution:**

Use boxes below to list possible solutions:

**List potential NEGATIVE effects for each solution:**

**SOLUTION #1**

**SOLUTION #2**

**SOLUTION #3**

Now choose the solution you think is best—and try it.

**CHOSEN SOLUTION**

**List the actual POSITIVE effects of the solution:**

**List the actual NEGATIVE effects of the solution:**

**FINAL EVALUATION: was it a good or bad choice?**

4. **Choose your top solution(s).** Come together again as a group. Take turns sharing your observations and recommendations, then take a vote: Which solution is the best? You may have a tie or may combine two different solutions. Either way is fine. Different solutions suit different people and situations. Although it's not always possible to reach agreement, try to find the solution that works for most of the group.

5. **Evaluate the solution you decide is best.** When you decide on your top solution or solutions, discuss what would happen if you went through with it. What do you predict would be the positive and negative effects of this solution? Would it turn out to be a truly good solution for everyone?

## KEY TO SELF-EXPRESSION: DISCOVERY THROUGH JOURNAL WRITING

*To record your thoughts, use a separate journal or the lined pages at the end of the chapter.*

**Strategic Planning**   Discuss your abilities and limitations in how you set and plan your short-term and long-term goals. Do you tend to plan ahead of time? Why or why not? What do you like and dislike about strategically planning ahead? Do you have a hard time seeing beyond the present, or do you like to predict what will happen in the future? Discuss a long-term goal in terms of what you want in one year, five years, ten years, and twenty years. How do you plan to accomplish this goal? What steps will you take? What do you want to achieve?

Name _____ Date _____

# Journal Entry

Name _____ Date _____

Journal Entry

# READING AND STUDYING:
## Maximizing Written Resources

The society you live in revolves around the written word. As the Condition of Education 1996 report states, "In recent years, literacy has been viewed as one of the fundamental tools necessary for successful economic performance in industrialized societies. Literacy is no longer defined merely as a basic threshold of reading ability, but rather as the ability to understand and use printed information in daily activities, at home, at work, and in the community."[1]

If you read thoroughly and understand what you read, and if you achieve your study goals, you can improve your capacity to learn and understand. In this chapter you will learn how you can overcome barriers to successful reading and benefit from defining a purpose each time you read. You will explore the PQ3R study technique and see how critical reading can help you maximize your understanding of any text. Finally, the chapter will provide an overview of your library's resources.

In this chapter, you will explore answers to the following questions:

➤ What are some challenges of reading?

➤ Why define your purpose for reading?

➤ How can PQ3R help you study?

➤ How can you read critically?

➤ What resources does your library offer?

# WHAT ARE SOME CHALLENGES OF READING?

Whatever your skill level, you will encounter challenges that make reading more difficult, such as an excess of reading assignments, difficult texts, distractions, a lack of speed and comprehension, and insufficient vocabulary. Following are some ideas about how to meet these challenges. Note that if you have a reading disability, if English is not your primary language, or if you have limited reading skills, you may need additional support and guidance. Most colleges provide services for students through a reading center or tutoring program. Take the initiative to seek help if you need it. Many accomplished learners have benefited from help in specific areas.

## Dealing With Reading Overload

Reading overload is part of almost every college experience. On a typical day, you may be faced with reading assignments that look like this:

➤ An entire textbook chapter on the causes of the Civil War (American history).

➤ An original research study on the stages of sleep (psychology).

➤ Pages 1–50 in Arthur Miller's play *Death of a Salesman* (American literature).

Reading all this and more leaves little time for anything else unless you read selectively and skillfully. You can't control your reading load. You can, however, improve your reading skills. The material in this chapter will present techniques that can help you read and study as efficiently as you possibly can, while still having time left over for other things.

## Working Through Difficult Texts

While many textbooks are useful teaching tools, some can be poorly written and organized. Students using texts that aren't well written may blame themselves for the difficulty they're experiencing. Because texts are often written with the purpose of challenging the intellect, even well-written and organized texts may be difficult and dense to read. Generally, the further you advance in your education, the more complex your required reading is likely to be. For example, your sociology professor may assign a chapter on the dynamics of social groups, including those of dyads and triads. When is the last time you heard the terms *dyads* and *triads* in normal conversation? You may feel at times as though you are reading a foreign language as you encounter new concepts, words, and terms.

Assignments can also be difficult when the required reading is from primary sources rather than from texts. *Primary sources* are original documents rather than another writer's interpretation of these documents. They include:

➤ historical documents

➤ works of literature (novels, poems, and plays)

➤ scientific studies, including lab reports and accounts of experiments

➤ journal articles

The academic writing found in journal articles and scientific studies is different from other kinds of writing. Some academic writers assume that readers understand sophisticated concepts. They may not define basic terms, provide background information, or supply a wealth of examples to support their ideas. As a result, concepts may be difficult to understand.

Making your way through poorly written or difficult reading material is hard work that can be accomplished through focus, motivation, commitment, and skill. The following strategies may help.

**Approach your reading assignments head-on.**   Be careful not to prejudge them as impossible or boring before you even start to read.

**Accept the fact that some texts may require some extra work and concentration.**   Set a goal to make your way through the material and learn, whatever it takes.

**When a primary source discusses difficult concepts that it does not explain, put in some extra work to define such concepts on your own.**   Ask your instructor or other students for help. Consult reference materials in that particular subject area, other class materials, dictionaries, and encyclopedias. You may want to make this process more convenient by creating your own mini-library at home. Collect reference materials that you use often, such as a dictionary, a thesaurus, a writer's style handbook, and maybe an atlas or computer manual. You may also benefit from owning reference materials in your particular areas of study. "If you find yourself going to the library to look up the same reference again and again, consider purchasing that book for your personal or office library," advises library expert Sherwood Harris.[2]

**Look for order and meaning in seemingly chaotic reading materials.**   The information you will find in this chapter on the PQ3R reading technique and on critical reading will help you discover patterns and achieve a greater depth of understanding. Finding order within chaos is an important skill, not just in the mastery of reading, but also in life. This skill can give you power by helping you "read" (think through) work dilemmas, personal problems, and educational situations.

> " No barrier of the senses shuts me out from the sweet, gracious discourse of my book friends. They talk to me without embarrassment or awkwardness. "
>
> Helen Keller

## Managing Distractions

With so much happening around you, it's often hard to keep your mind on what you are reading. Distractions take many forms. Some are external: the sound of a telephone, a friend who sits next to you at lunch and wants to talk, a young child who asks for help with homework. Other distractions come from within. As you try to study, you may be thinking about your parent's health, an argument you had with a friend or partner, a paper due in art History, or a site on the Internet that you want to visit.

## How can I cope with a learning disability?

### Clacy Albert, Washington State University—Pullman, Washington, Communications Major

All my life I've felt different. I just couldn't seem to learn the way other kids did. I felt stupid and afraid that other people would think I couldn't do any-thing right. I wouldn't raise my hand in class because I was afraid of being laughed at. I wouldn't volunteer for games because I was afraid I'd let my team down. Study groups were impossible for me. I  didn't want anyone to know that I was dif-ferent. Because of this, my self-esteem really suffered. I became very quiet.

It wasn't until I was a sophomore in high school that a teacher recognized something was wrong with the way I learned. It was my math teacher who saw that I couldn't recog-nize certain patterns. I would see things in reverse or not be able to recognize a pattern at all. He sat down with my parents and helped them understand something was wrong. Unfortunately, the school I attended didn't have any testing for learning disabili-ties, so I let it go until I was in college. When I enrolled at WSU they told us about the learning disability resource center. My mom suggested I finally get the testing I needed. I'm glad I did, because now I know that I have dyslexia and need special assistance to handle my studies. I wish there was manda-tory testing for this disability in grade school. If there had been I wouldn't have suf-fered so deeply all these years. What sugges-tions do you have for helping me cope with this disability?

### Edith Hall, Senior Sales Representative—Prentice Hall

I have a different disability but one that causes similar problems. I have Attention Deficit Hyperactivity Disorder and the fact that it was undiagnosed and untreated for many years has caused lots of problems in my life. It wasn't until I was six years out of college that I was diag-nosed ADHD. And the great thing about it is I don't feel crazy any-more. Now I know why I can't sit still for  long periods and why I can't complete large and/or long projects like other non-ADHD people can.

I think acknowledging that I had a dis-order and then accepting it were the biggest steps to coping and living with this disorder. The other thing I have done is to get educat-ed. I have read almost anything I can get my hands on. I am also involved in a support group. Having other people I can talk with about how my brain affects my behavior and my life truly is one of the best coping strategies I know.

Having a disability or disorder is not a bad thing. Ennis Cosby, slain son of comedi-an Bill Cosby, said of his dyslexia, "The day I found out I had dyslexia was the best day of my life." Finding out he had dyslexia relieved him of the belief that he was dumb or stupid or slow. For me, like Ennis Cosby, finding out I had ADHD was a great day in my life because I now had tools and help to be different . . . and I no longer felt alone.

### Identify the Distraction and Choose a Suitable Action

Pinpoint what's distracting you before you decide what kind of action to take. If the distraction is *external* and *out of your control*, such as construction outside your building or a noisy group in the library, try to move away from it. If the distraction is *external* but *within your control*, such as the television, telephone, or children, take action. For example, if the television or phone is a problem, turn off the TV or unplug the phone for an hour.

If the distraction is *internal*, there are a few strategies to try that may help you clear your mind. You may want to take a break from your studying and tend to one of the issues that you are worrying about. Physical exercise may relax you and bring back your ability to focus. For some people, studying while listening to music helps to quiet a busy mind. For others, silence may do the trick. If you need silence to read or study and cannot find a truly quiet environment, consider purchasing sound-muffling headphones or even earplugs.

### Find the Best Place and Time to Read

Any reader needs focus and discipline in order to concentrate on the material. Finding a place and time that minimize outside distractions will help you achieve that focus. Here are some suggestions:

*Read alone unless you are working with other readers.*　Family members, friends, or others who are not in study mode may interrupt your concentration. If you prefer to read alone, establish a relatively interruption-proof place and time, such as an out-of-the-way spot at the library or an after-class hour in an empty classroom. If you study at home and live with other people, you may want to place a "Quiet" sign on the door. Some students benefit from reading with one or more other students. If this helps you, plan to schedule a group reading meeting where you read sections of the assigned material and then break to discuss them.

*Find a comfortable location.*　Many students study in the library on a hard-backed chair. Others prefer a library easy chair, a chair in their room, or even the floor. The spot you choose should be comfortable enough for hours of reading, but not so comfortable that you fall asleep. Also, make sure that you have adequate lighting and aren't too hot or too cold.

*Choose a regular reading place and time.*　Choose a spot or two you like and return to them often. Also, choose a time when your mind is alert and focused. Some students prefer to read just before or after the class for which the reading is assigned. Eventually, you will associate preferred places and times with focused reading.

*If it helps you concentrate, listen to soothing background music.*　The right music can drown out background noises and relax you. However, the wrong music can make it impossible to concentrate; for some people, silence is better. Experiment to learn what you prefer; if music helps, stick with the type that works best. A personal headset makes listening possible no matter where you are.

*Turn off the television.*　For most people, reading and TV don't mix.

## Building Comprehension and Speed

Most students lead busy lives, carrying heavy academic loads while perhaps working a job or even caring for a family. It's difficult to make time to study at all, let alone handle the enormous reading assignments for your different classes. Increasing your reading comprehension and speed will save you valuable time and effort.

Rapid reading won't do you any good if you can't remember the material or answer questions about it. However, reading too slowly can be equally inefficient because it often eats up valuable study time and gives your mind space to wander. Your goal is to read for maximum speed *and* comprehension. Focus on comprehension first, because greater comprehension is the primary goal and also promotes greater speed.

### Methods for Increasing Reading Comprehension

Following are some specific strategies for increasing your understanding of what you read:

**Continually build your knowledge through reading and studying.** More than any other factor, what you already know before you read a passage will determine your ability to understand and remember important ideas. Previous knowledge, including vocabulary, facts, and ideas, gives you a context for what you read.

> **Context,**
> Written or spoken knowledge that can help to illuminate the meaning of a word or passage.

**Establish your purpose for reading.** When you establish what you want to get out of your reading, you will be able to determine what level of understanding you need to reach and, therefore, on what you need to focus.

**Remove the barriers of negative self-talk.** Instead of telling yourself that you cannot understand, think positively. Tell yourself: *I can learn this material. I am a good reader.*

**Think critically.** Ask yourself questions. Do you understand the sentence, paragraph, or chapter you just read? Are ideas and supporting examples clear to you? Could you clearly explain what you just read to someone else?

### Methods for Increasing Reading Speed

The following suggestions will help increase your reading speed.

> ➤ Try to read groups of words rather than single words.
> ➤ Avoid pointing your finger to guide your reading, since this will slow your pace.
> ➤ Try swinging your eyes from side to side as you read a passage, instead of stopping at various points to read individual words.
> ➤ When reading narrow columns, focus your eyes in the middle of the column and read down the page. With practice, you'll be able to read the entire column width.
> ➤ Avoid vocalization when reading.

> **Vocalization,**
> The practice of speaking the words and/or moving your lips while reading.

➤ Avoid thinking each word to yourself as you read it, a practice known as *subvocalization*. Subvocalization is one of the primary causes of slow reading speed.

Facing the challenges of reading is only the first step. The next important step is to examine why you are reading any given piece of material.

# WHY DEFINE YOUR PURPOSE FOR READING?

As with all other aspects of your education, asking important questions will enable you to make the most of your efforts. When you define your purpose, you ask yourself *why* you are reading a particular piece of material. One way to do this is by completing this sentence: "In reading this material, I intend to define/learn/answer/achieve . . . " With a clear purpose in mind, you can decide how much time and what kind of effort to expend on various reading assignments. Nearly 375 years ago, Francis Bacon, the English philosopher, recognized that . . .

Some books are to be tasted, others to be swallowed, and some few to be chewed and digested; that is, some books are to be read only in parts, others to be read but not curiously; and some few to be read wholly, and with diligence and attention.

Achieving your reading purpose requires adapting to different types of reading materials. Being a flexible reader—adjusting your reading strategies and pace—will help you to adapt successfully.

## Purpose Determines Reading Strategy

With purpose comes direction; with direction comes a strategy for reading. Following are four reading purposes, examined briefly. You may have one or more for each piece of reading material you approach.

**Purpose 1: Read to Evaluate Critically.** Critical evaluation involves approaching the material with an open mind, examining causes and effects, evaluating ideas, and asking questions that test the strength of the writer's argument and that try to identify assumptions. Critical reading is essential for you to demonstrate an understanding of material that goes beyond basic recall of information. You will read more about critical reading later in the chapter.

**Purpose 2: Read for Comprehension.** Much of the studying you do involves reading for the purpose of comprehending the material. The two main components of comprehension are *general ideas* and *specific facts/examples*. These components depend on one another. Facts and examples help to explain or support ideas, and ideas provide a framework that helps the reader to remember facts and examples.

*General Ideas.* General-idea reading is rapid reading that seeks an overview of the material. You may skip entire sections as you focus on headings, subheadings, and summary statements in search of general ideas.

*Specific Facts/Examples.* At times, readers may focus on locating specific pieces of information—for example, the stages of intellectual development in young children. Often, a reader may search for examples that support or explain more general ideas—for example, the causes of economic recession. Because you know exactly what you are looking for, you can skim the material at a rapid rate. Reading your texts for specific information may help before taking a test.

**Purpose 3: Read for Practical Application.**   A third purpose for reading is to gather usable information which you can apply toward a specific goal. When you read a computer software manual, an instruction sheet for assembling a gas grill, or a cookbook recipe, your goal is to learn how to do something. Reading and action usually go hand in hand.

**Purpose 4: Read for Pleasure.**   Some materials you read for entertainment, such as *Sports Illustrated* magazine or the latest John Grisham courtroom thriller. Entertaining reading may also go beyond materials that seem obviously designed to entertain. Whereas some people may read a Jane Austen novel for comprehension, as in a class assignment, others may read Austen books for pleasure.

## Purpose Determines Pace

George M. Usova, senior education specialist and graduate professor at The Johns Hopkins University, explains: "Good readers are flexible readers. They read at a variety of rates and adapt them to the reading *purpose* at hand, the *difficulty* of the material, and their *familiarity* with the subject area."[3] As Table 5-1 shows, good readers link the pace of reading to their reading purpose.

So far, this chapter has focused on reading. Recognizing obstacles to effective reading and defining the various purposes for reading lay the groundwork for effective *studying*—the process of mastering the concepts and skills contained in your texts.

> "In books, I could travel anywhere, be anybody, understand worlds long past and imaginary colonies in the future."
>
> Rita Dove

## TABLE 5-1 LINKING PURPOSE TO PACE

| TYPE OF MATERIAL | READING PURPOSE | PACE |
|---|---|---|
| **ACADEMIC READINGS**<br>• textbooks<br>• original sources<br>• articles from scholarly journals<br>• on-line publications for academic readers<br>• lab reports<br>• required fiction | • Critical analysis<br>• Overall mastery<br>• Preparation for tests | • Slow, especially if the material is new and unfamiliar |
| **MANUALS**<br>• instructions<br>• recipes | • Practical application | • Slow to medium |
| **JOURNALISM AND NONFICTION FOR THE GENERAL READER**<br>• nonfiction books<br>• newspapers<br>• magazines<br>• on-line publications for the general public | • Understanding of general ideas, key concepts, and specific facts for personal understanding and/or practical application | • Medium to fast |
| **NONREQUIRED FICTION** | • Understanding of general ideas, key concepts, and specific facts for enjoyment | • Variable, but tending toward the faster speeds |

*Source:* Adapted from Nicholas Reid Schaffzin, *The Princeton Review Reading Smart*. New York: Random House, 1996, p. 15.

*Source:* CALVIN AND HOBBES © 1987 Bill Watterson. Dist. by UNIVERSAL PRESS SYNDICATE. All rights reserved.

# How Can PQ3R Help You Study Reading Materials?

When you study, you take ownership of the material you read. You learn it well enough to apply it to what you do. For example, by the time students studying to be computer-hardware technicians complete their coursework, they should be able to assemble various machines and analyze hardware problems that lead to malfunctions.

Studying also gives you mastery over *concepts*. For example, a dental hygiene student learns the causes of gum disease, a biology student learns what happens during photosynthesis, and a business student learns about marketing research.

This section will focus on a technique that will help you learn and study more effectively as you read your college textbooks.

## PREVIEW-QUESTION-READ-RECITE-REVIEW (PQ3R)

**Skimming,**

Rapid, superficial reading of material that involves glancing through to determine central ideas and main elements.

**Scanning,**

Reading material in an investigative way, searching for specific information.

PQ3R is a technique that will help you grasp ideas quickly, remember more, and review effectively and efficiently for tests. The symbols P-Q-3-R stand for *preview, question, read, recite,* and *review* — all steps in the studying process. Developed more than 55 years ago by Francis Robinson, the technique is still being used today because it works.[4] It is particularly helpful for studying texts. When reading literature, read the work once from beginning to end to appreciate the story and language. Then, reread it using PQ3R to master the material.

Moving through the stages of PQ3R requires that you know how to skim and scan. Skimming involves rapid reading of various chapter elements, including introductions, conclusions, and summaries; the first and last lines of paragraphs; boldface or italicized terms; pictures, charts, and diagrams. In contrast, scanning involves the careful search for specific facts and examples. You will probably use scanning during the *review* phase of PQ3R when you need to locate and remind yourself of particular information. In a chemistry text, for example, you may scan for examples of how to apply a particular formula.

### Preview

The best way to ruin a "whodunit" novel is to flip through the pages to find out how everything turned out. However, when reading textbooks, previewing can help you learn and is encouraged. *Previewing* refers to the process of surveying, or pre-reading, a book before you actually study it. Most textbooks include devices that give students an overview of the text as a whole as well as of the contents of individual chapters. As you look at Figure 5-1, on the following page, think about how many of these devices you already use.

### Question

Your next step is to examine the chapter headings and, on your own paper, write questions linked to those headings. These questions will focus your attention and increase your interest, helping you relate new ideas to what you already know and building your comprehension. You can take questions from the textbook or from your lecture notes, or come up with them on your own when you preview, based on what ideas you think are most important.

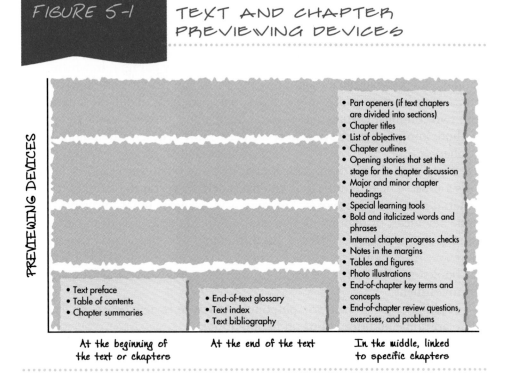

**FIGURE 5-1** TEXT AND CHAPTER PREVIEWING DEVICES

PREVIEWING DEVICES

- Part openers (if text chapters are divided into sections)
- Chapter titles
- List of objectives
- Chapter outlines
- Opening stories that set the stage for the chapter discussion
- Major and minor chapter headings
- Special learning tools
- Bold and italicized words and phrases
- Internal chapter progress checks
- Notes in the margins
- Tables and figures
- Photo illustrations
- End-of-chapter key terms and concepts
- End-of-chapter review questions, exercises, and problems

- Text preface
- Table of contents
- Chapter summaries

- End-of-text glossary
- Text index
- Text bibliography

At the beginning of the text or chapters

At the end of the text

In the middle, linked to specific chapters

| I. THE CONSUMER BUYING PROCESS | I. WHAT IS THE CONSUMER BUYING PROCESS? |
|---|---|
| A. Problem/Need Recognition | A. Why must consumers first recognize a problem or need before they buy a product? |
| B. Information Seeking | B. What is information seeking and who answers consumers questions? |
| C. Evaluation of Alternatives | C. How do consumers evaluate different products to narrow their choices? |
| D. Purchase Decision | D. Are purchasing decisions simple or complex? |
| E. Postpurchase Evaluations | E. What happens after the sale? |

Here is how this technique works. The column on the left contains primary- and secondary-level headings from a section of *Business*, an introductory text by Ricky W. Griffin and Ronald J. Ebert. The column on the right rephrases these headings in question form.

There is no "correct" set of questions. Given the same headings, you would create your own particular set of questions. The more useful kinds of questions are ones that engage the critical-thinking mind actions and processes found in Chapter 4.

## Read

Your questions give you a starting point for *reading,* the first *R* in PQ3R. Read the material with the purpose of answering each question you raised. Pay special attention to the first and last lines of every paragraph, which should tell you what the paragraph is about. As you read, record key words, phrases, and concepts in your notebook. Some students divide the notebook into two columns, writing questions on the left and answers on the right. This method, known as the Cornell note-taking system, is described in more detail in Chapter 6.

If you own the textbook, marking it up — in whatever ways you prefer — is a must. The notations that you make will help you to interact with the material and make sense of it. You may want to write notes in the margins, circle key ideas, or highlight key sections. Some people prefer to underline, although underlining adds more ink to the lines of text and may overwhelm your eye. Although writing in a textbook makes it difficult to sell it back to the bookstore, the increased depth of understanding you can gain is worth the investment.

Highlighting may help you pinpoint material to review before an exam. Here are some additional tips on highlighting:

Get in the habit of marking the text *after* you read the material.   If you do it while you are reading, you may wind up marking less important passages.

Highlight key terms and concepts.   Mark the examples that explain and support important ideas. You might try highlighting ideas in one color and examples in another.

Highlight figures and tables.   They are especially important if they summarize text concepts.

Avoid overmarking.   A phrase or two is enough in most paragraphs. Set off long passages with brackets rather than marking every line.

Write notes in the margins with a pen or pencil.   Comments like "main point" and "important definition" will help you find key sections later on.

Be careful not to mistake highlighting for learning.   You will not necessarily learn what you highlight unless you review it carefully. You may benefit from writing the important information you have highlighted into your lecture notes.

One final step in the reading phase is to divide your reading into digestible segments. Many students read from one topic heading to the next, then stop. Pace your reading so that you understand as you go. If you find you are losing the thread of the ideas you are reading, you may want to try smaller segments, or you may need to take a break and come back to it later.

## Recite

Once you finish reading a topic, stop and answer the questions you raised about it in the *Q* stage of PQ3R. You may decide to recite each answer aloud, silently speak the answers to yourself, tell the answers to another person as though you were teaching him or her, or write your ideas and answers in brief notes. Writing is often the most effective way to solidify what you have read. Use whatever techniques best suit your learning-style profile (see Chapter 2).

After you finish one section, move on to the next. Then repeat the question-read-recite cycle until you complete the entire chapter. If during this process you find yourself fumbling for thoughts, it means that you do not yet "own" the ideas. Reread the section that's giving you trouble until you master its contents. Understanding each section as you go is crucial because the material in one section often forms a foundation for the next.

## Review R

Review soon after you finish a chapter. Here are some techniques for reviewing.

- ➤ Skim and reread your notes. Then try summarizing them from memory.
- ➤ Answer the text's end-of-chapter review, discussion, and application questions.
- ➤ Quiz yourself, using the questions you raised in the Q stage. If you can't answer one of your own or one of the text's questions, go back and scan the material for answers.
- ➤ Review and summarize in writing the sections and phrases you have highlighted.
- ➤ Create a chapter outline in standard outline form or think-link form.
- ➤ Reread the preface, headings, tables, and summary.
- ➤ Recite important concepts to yourself, or record important information on a cassette tape and play it on your car's tape deck or your Walkman.
- ➤ Make flashcards that have an idea or word on one side and examples, a definition, or other related information on the other. Test yourself.
- ➤ Think critically: Break ideas down into examples, consider similar or different concepts, recall important terms, evaluate ideas, and explore causes and effects.
- ➤ Make think links that show how important concepts relate to one another.

Remember that you can ask your instructor if you need help clarifying your reading material. Your instructor is an important resource. Pinpoint the material you want to discuss, schedule a meeting with him or her during office hours, and come prepared with a list of questions. You may also want to ask what materials to focus on when you study for tests.

If possible, you should review both alone and with study groups. Reviewing in as many different ways as possible increases the likelihood of retention. Figure 5-2 shows some techniques that will help a study group maximize its time and efforts.

Repeating the review process renews and solidifies your knowledge. That is why it is important to set up regular review sessions — for example, once a week. As you review, remember that refreshing your knowledge is easier and faster than learning it the first time.

As you can see in Table 5-2 on p. 126, using PQ3R is part of being an active reader. Active reading involves the specific activities that help you retain what you learn.

## HOW CAN YOU READ CRITICALLY?

Your textbooks will often contain features that highlight important ideas and help you determine questions to ask while reading. As you advance in your education, however, many reading assignments will not be so clearly marked, especially if they are primary sources. You will need critical-reading skills in order to select the important ideas, identify examples that support them, and ask questions about the text without the aid of any special features or tools.

Critical reading enables you to consider reading material carefully, developing a thorough understanding of it through evaluation and analysis. A critical reader is able to discern what in a piece of reading material is true or useful, such as when using material as a source for an essay. A critical reader can also compare one piece of material to another and evaluate which makes more sense, which proves its thesis more successfully, or which is more useful for the reader's purpose.

Critical reading is reading that transcends taking in and regurgitating material. You can read critically by using PQ3R to get a basic idea of the material, asking questions based on the critical-thinking mind actions, shifting your perspective, and seeking understanding.

### Use PQ3R to "Taste" Reading Material

Sylvan Barnet and Hugo Bedau, authors of *Critical Thinking, Reading, and Writing—A Brief Guide to Argument*, suggest that the active reading of PQ3R will help you form an initial idea of what a piece of reading material is all about. Through previewing, skimming for ideas and examples, highlighting and writing comments and questions in the margins, and reviewing, you can develop a basic understanding of its central ideas and contents.[5]

Summarizing, part of the review process in PQ3R, is one of the best ways to develop an understanding of a piece of reading material. To construct a summary, focus on the central ideas of the piece and the main

**Summary,**
A concise restatement of the material, in your own words, that covers the main points.

**FIGURE 5-2    STUDY GROUP TECHNIQUES**

**Benefits**

**Increased motivation.** Because others will see your work and preparation, you may become more motivated.

**Solidifying knowledge.** When you discuss concepts or teach them to others, you reinforce what you know and how to think.

**Sharing each other's knowledge.** Each student has a unique body of knowledge, and students can learn from each other's specialties.

**Be careful about...**

**Group size.** Limiting the group to two to five people is usually best.

**Studying with friends.** Resist your temptation to socialize until you are done.

**Preparation.** Members should study on their own before the meeting, so that everyone can be a team player.

**Study Groups**

**Tips for Success**

**Choose a leader for each meeting.** Rotating the leadership helps all members take ownership of the group. Be flexible. If a leader has to miss class for any reason, choose another leader for that meeting.

**Set meeting goals.** At the start of each meeting, compile a list of questions you want to address.

**Adjust to different personalities.** Respect and communicate with members whom you would not necessarily choose as friends. The art of getting along will serve you well in the workplace, where you don't often choose your co-workers.

**Set a regular meeting schedule.** Try every week, every two weeks, or whatever the group can manage.

**Set general goals.** Determine what the group wants to accomplish over the course of a semester.

**Share the workload.** The most important factor is a willingness to work, not a particular level of knowledge.

examples that support those ideas. A summary does *not* contain any of your own ideas or your evaluation of the material. It simply condenses the material, making it easier for you to focus on the structure of the piece and its central ideas when you go back to read more critically. At that point, you can begin to evaluate the piece and introduce your own ideas. Using the mind actions will help you.

## TABLE 5-2   USE PQ3R TO BECOME AN ACTIVE READER

### ACTIVE READERS TEND TO . . .

| | |
|---|---|
| Divide material into manageable sections | Answer end-of-chapter questions and applications |
| Write questions | Create chapter outlines |
| Answer questions through focused note-taking | Create think links that map concepts in a logical way |
| Recite, verbally and in writing, the answers to questions | Make flashcards and study them |
| Highlight key concepts | Recite what they learned into a tape recorder and play the tape back |
| Focus on main ideas found in paragraphs, sections, and chapters | Rewrite and summarize notes and highlighted materials from memory |
| Recognize summary and support devices | Explain what they read to a family member or friend |
| Analyze tables, figures, and photos | Form a study group |

## Ask Questions Based on the Mind Actions

The essence of critical reading, as with critical thinking, is asking questions. Instead of simply accepting what you read, seek a more thorough understanding by questioning the material as you go along. Using the mind actions of the Thinktrix to formulate your questions will help you understand the material.

What parts of the material you focus on will depend on your purpose for reading. For example, if you are writing a paper on the causes of World War II, you might spend your time focusing on how certain causes fit your thesis. If you are comparing two pieces of writing that contain opposing arguments, you may focus on picking out their central ideas and evaluating how well the writers use examples to support these ideas.

You can question any of the following components of reading material:

➤ The central idea of the entire piece

➤ A particular idea or statement

➤ The examples that support an idea or statement

➤ The proof of a fact

➤ The definition of a concept

Following are some ways to critically question your reading material, based on the mind actions. Apply them to any component you want to question by substituting the component for the words "it" and "this."

| | |
|---|---|
| <u>Similarity:</u> | What does this remind me of, or how is it similar to something else I know? |
| <u>Difference:</u> | What different conclusions are possible? <br> How is this different from my experience? |
| <u>Cause and Effect:</u> | Why did this happen, or what caused this? <br> What are the effects or consequences of this? <br> What effect does the author want to have, or what is the purpose of this material? <br> What effects support a stated cause? |
| <u>Example to Idea:</u> | How would I classify this, or, what is the best idea to fit this example(s)? <br> How would I summarize this, or what are the key ideas? <br> What is the thesis or central idea? |
| <u>Idea to Example:</u> | What evidence supports this, or what examples fit this idea? |
| <u>Evaluation:</u> | How would I evaluate this? Is it valid or pertinent? <br> Does this example support my thesis or central idea? |

## Shift Your Perspective

Your understanding of perspective will help you understand that many reading materials are written from a particular perspective. Perspective often has a strong effect on how the material is presented. For example, if a recording artist and a music censorship advocate were to each write a piece about a controversial song created by that artist, their different perspectives would result in two very different pieces of writing.

To analyze perspective, ask questions like the following:

**What perspective is guiding this?** What are the underlying ideas that influence this material?

**Who wrote this, and what may be the author's perspective?** For example, a piece on a new drug written by an employee of the drug manufacturer may differ from a doctor's evaluation of the drug.

**What does the title of the material tell me about its perspective?** For example, a piece entitled "New Therapies for Diabetes" may be more informational, and "What's Wrong With Insulin Injections" may intend to be persuasive.

**How does the material's source affect its perspective?** For example, an article on health management organizations (HMOs) published in an HMO newsletter may be more favorable and one-sided than one published in *The New York Times*.

## Seek Understanding

Reading critically allows you to investigate what you read so that you can reach the highest possible level of understanding. Think of your reading process as an archaeological dig. The first step is to excavate a site and uncover the artifacts. In reading, that corresponds to your initial preview and reading of the material. As important as the excavation is, the process would be incomplete if you stopped there and just took home a bunch of items covered in dirt. The second half of the process is to investigate each item, evaluate what all of those items mean, and to derive new knowledge and ideas from what you discover. Critical reading allows you to complete that crucial second half of the process.

As you work through all of the different requirements of critical reading, remember that critical reading takes *time* and *focus*. Finding a time, place, and purpose for reading, covered earlier in the chapter, is crucial to successful critical reading. Give yourself a chance to gain as much as possible from what you read.

No matter where or how you prefer to study, your school's library (or libraries) can provide many useful services to help you make the most of classes, reading, studying, and assignments.

# WHAT DOES YOUR LIBRARY OFFER?

Your library can help you search for all kinds of information. First, learn about your library, its resources, and its layout. While some schools have only one library, other schools have a library network that includes one or more central libraries and smaller, specialized libraries that focus on specific academic areas. Take advantage of library tours, training sessions, and descriptive pamphlets. Spend time walking around the library on your own. If you still have questions, ask a librarian. A simple question can save hours of searching. The following sections will help you understand how your library operates.

### General Reference Works

*General reference works* give you an overview and lead you to more specific information. These works cover topics in a broad, nondetailed way. General reference guides are found in the front of most libraries and are often available on CD-ROM, a compact disk that contains millions of words and images. You access this information by inserting the disk into a specially designed computer. Among the works that fall into this category are:

➤ encyclopedias—for example, the multivolume *Encyclopedia Britannica*

*"With one day's reading a man may have the key in his hands."*

Ezra Pound

➤ almanacs—*The World Almanac and Book of Facts*

➤ dictionaries—*Webster's New World College Dictionary*

➤ biographical reference works—*Webster's Biographical Dictionary*

➤ bibliographies—*Books in Print*

## Specialized Reference Works

Look at *specialized reference works* to find more specific facts. Specialized reference works include encyclopedias and dictionaries that focus on a narrow field. The short summaries you will find there focus on critical ideas. Bibliographies that accompany the articles point you to the names and works of recognized experts. Examples of specialized references include the *International Encyclopedia of Film*, the *Encyclopedia of Computer Science and Technology*, and the *Dictionary of Education*.

## Library Book Catalog

Found near the front of the library, the *book catalog* lists every book the library owns. The listings usually appear in three separate categories: authors' names, book titles, and subjects. Not too long ago, most libraries stored their book catalog on index-sized cards in hundreds of small drawers. Today, many libraries have replaced these cards with computers. Using a terminal that has access to the library's computer records, you can search by specific author, title, and subject.

The computerized catalog in your college library is probably connected to the holdings of other college and university libraries. This gives you an on-line search capacity, which means that if you don't find the book you want in your local library, you can track it down in another library and request it through an interlibrary loan. *Interlibrary loan* is a system used by many colleges to allow students to borrow materials from a library other than the one at their school. Students request materials through their own library, where the materials are eventually delivered by the outside library. When you are in a rush, keep in mind that interlibrary loan may take a substantial amount of time.

## Periodical Indexes

*Periodicals* are magazines, journals, and newspapers which are published on a regular basis throughout the year. Examples include *Time, Business Week*, and *Science*. Many libraries display periodicals that are a year or two old and convert older copies to microfilm or microfiche (photocopies of materials reduced greatly in size and printed on film readable in a special reading machine—*microfilm* is a strip of film, and *microfiche* refers to individual leaves of film). Finding articles in publications involves a search of periodical indexes. The most widely used general index is the *Reader's Guide to Periodical Literature*, which is available on CD-ROM and in book form. The *Reader's Guide* indexes articles in more than 100 general-interest magazines and journals.

### Electronic Research

You will also find complete source material through a variety of electronic sources, including the Internet, on-line services, and CD-ROM. Here is a sampling of the kind of information you will find:

➤ complete articles from thousands of journals and magazines

➤ complete articles from newspapers around the world

➤ government data on topics as varied as agriculture, transportation, and labor

➤ business documents, including corporate annual reports

Your library is probably connected to the *Internet*, a worldwide computer network that links government, university, research, and business computers along the Information Superhighway. Tapping into the *World Wide Web*—a tool for searching the huge libraries of information stored on the Internet—gives you access to billions of written words and graphic images. The Internet is so vast that this book contains an Internet Research Appendix to help you explore it. After reading this Appendix, you will have many tools to aid you on your journeys along the Information Superhighway. If your college has its own Internet home page, start by spending some time browsing through it.

Although most libraries do not charge a fee to access the Internet, they may charge when you connect to commercial on-line services, including Nexis, CompuServe, and Prodigy. Ask your librarian about all fees and restrictions. Libraries also have electronic databases on CD-ROM. A database is a collection of data—or, in the case of most libraries, a list of related resources that all focus on one specific subject area—arranged so that you can search through it and retrieve specific items easily. For example, the DIALOG Information System includes hundreds of small databases in specialized areas. CD-ROM databases are generally smaller than on-line databases and are updated less frequently. However, there is never a user's fee.

# читать

This word may look completely unfamiliar to you, but anyone who can read the Russian language and alphabet will know that it means "read." People who read languages that use different kinds of characters, such as Russian, Japanese, or Greek, learn to process those characters as easily as you process the letters of your native alphabet. Your mind learns to process individually each letter or character you see. This ability enables you to move to the next level of understanding—making sense of those letters or characters when they are grouped to form words, phrases, and sentences.

Think of this concept when you read. Remember that your mind is an incredible tool, processing unmeasurable amounts of information so that you can understand the concepts on the page. Give it the best opportunity to succeed by reading as often as you can and by focusing on all of the elements that help you read to the best of your ability.

# Chapter 5: Applications

Name _____  Date _____

## Key Into Your Life: Opportunities to Apply What You Learn

### Exercise 1: Studying a Text Page

The following page is from the Groups and Organizations chapter in the sixth edition of John J. Macionis's *Sociology*, a Prentice Hall text.[6] Using what you learned in this chapter about study techniques, complete the questions on page 132:

## SOCIAL GROUPS

Virtually everyone moves through life with a sense of belonging; this is the experience of group life. A **social group** refers to *two or more people who identify and interact with one another*. Human beings continually come together to form couples, families, circles of friends, neighborhoods, churches, businesses, clubs, and numerous large organizations. Whatever the form, groups encompass people with shared experiences, loyalties, and interests. In short, while maintaining their individuality, the members of social groups also think of themselves as a special "we."

### Groups, Categories, and Crowds

People often use the term "group" imprecisely. We now distinguish the group from the similar concepts of category and crowd.

#### Category

A *category* refers to people who have some status in common. Women, single fathers, military recruits, homeowners, and Roman Catholics are all examples of categories.

Why are categories not considered groups? Simply because, while the individuals involved are aware that they are not the only ones to hold that particular status, the vast majority are strangers to one another.

#### Crowd

A *crowd* refers to a temporary cluster of individuals who may or may not interact at all. Students sitting together in a lecture hall do engage one another and share some common identity as college classmates; thus, such a crowd might be called a loosely formed group. By contrast, riders hurtling along on a subway train or bathers enjoying a summer day at the beach pay little attention to one another and amount to an anonymous aggregate of people. In general, then, crowds are too transitory and too impersonal to qualify as social groups.

The right circumstances, however, could turn a crowd into a group. People riding in a subway train that crashes under the city streets generally become keenly aware of their common plight and begin to help each other. Sometimes such extraordinary experiences become the basis for lasting relationships.

### Primary and Secondary Groups

Acquaintances commonly greet one another with a smile and the simple phrase "Hi! How are you?" The response is usually a well-scripted "Just fine, thanks. How about you?" This answer, of course, is often more formal than truthful. In most cases, providing a detailed account of how you are *really* doing would prompt the other person to beat a hasty and awkward exit.

Sociologists classify social groups by measuring them against two ideal types based on members' level of genuine personal concern. This variation is the key to distinguishing *primary* from *secondary* groups.

According to Charles Horton Cooley (1864–1929), who is introduced in the box, a **primary group** is *a small social group whose members share personal and enduring relationships*. Bound together by *primary relationships*, individuals in primary groups typically spend a great deal of time together, engage in a wide range of common activities, and feel that they know one another well. Although not without periodic conflict, members of primary groups display sincere concern for each other's welfare. The family is every society's most important primary group.

Cooley characterized these personal and tightly integrated groups as *primary* because they are among the first groups we experience in life. In addition, the family and early play groups also hold primary importance in the socialization process, shaping attitudes, behavior, and social identity.

*Source: Sociology*, 6/E by John J. Macionis, ©1997. Reprinted by permission of Prentice-Hall, Inc., Upper Saddle River, NJ.

1. Identify the headings on the page and the relationship among them. Which headings are primary-level headings; which are secondary; which are tertiary (third-level heads)? Which heading serves as an umbrella for the rest? _____

   _____

   _____

   _____

2. What do the headings tell you about the content of the page? _____

   _____

   _____

3. Identify the boldfaced and italicized terms. How do boldfaced terms differ from italicized terms?_____

   _____

   _____

4. After reading the chapter headings, write three study questions. List the questions below:

   _____

   _____

   _____

   _____

   _____

5. Using a marker pen, highlight key phrases and sentences. Write short marginal notes to help you review the material at a later point.

6. After reading this page, list four key concepts that you will need to study:

   a. _____

   b. _____

   c. _____

   d. _____

## Exercise 2: Focusing on Your Purpose for Reading

Read the following paragraphs on kinetic and potential energy and the first law of thermodynamics taken from *Life On Earth* by Teresa Audesirk and Gerald Audesirk[7]. When you have finished, answer the questions on pp. 134–135.

Among the fundamental characteristics of all living organisms is the ability to guide chemical reactions within their bodies along certain pathways. The chemical reactions serve many functions, depending on the nature of the organism: to synthesize the molecules that make up the organism's body, to reproduce, to move, even to think. Chemical reactions either require or release **energy**, which can be defined simply as *the capacity to do work*, including synthesizing molecules, moving things around, and generating heat and light. In this chapter we discuss the physical laws that govern energy flow in the universe, how energy flow in turn governs chemical reactions, and how the chemical reactions within living cells are controlled by the molecules of the cell itself. Chapters 7 and 8 focus on photosynthesis, the chief "port of entry" for energy into the biosphere, and glycolysis and cellular respiration, the most important sequences of chemical reactions that release energy.

## Energy and the Ability to Do Work

As you learned in Chapter 2, there are two types of energy: **kinetic energy** and **potential energy**. Both types of energy may exist in many different forms. Kinetic energy, or *energy of movement*, includes light (movement of photons), heat (movement of molecules), electricity (movement of electrically charged particles), and movement of large objects. Potential energy, or *stored energy*, includes chemical energy stored in the bonds that hold atoms together in molecules, electrical energy stored in a battery, and positional energy stored in a diver poised to spring (Fig. 4-1). Under the right conditions, kinetic energy can be transformed into potential energy, and vice versa. For example, the diver converted kinetic energy of movement into potential energy of position when she climbed the ladder up to the platform; when she jumps off, the potential energy will be converted back into kinetic energy.

To understand how energy flow governs interactions among pieces of matter, we need to know two things: (1) the quantity of available energy and (2) the usefulness of the energy. These are the subjects of the laws of thermodynamics, which we will now examine.

### The Laws of Thermodynamics Describe the Basic Properties of Energy

All interactions among pieces of matter are governed by the two **laws of thermodynamics**, physical principles that define the basic properties and behavior of energy. The laws of thermodynamics deal with "isolated systems," which are any parts of the universe that cannot exchange either matter or energy with any other parts. Probably no part of the universe is completely isolated from all possible exchange with every other part, but the concept of an isolated system is useful in thinking about energy flow.

### The First Law of Thermodynamics States That Energy Can Neither Be Created nor Destroyed

The **first law of thermodynamics** states that within any isolated system, energy can neither be created nor destroyed, although it can be changed in form (for example, from chemical energy to heat energy). In other words, within an isolated system *the total quantity of energy remains constant*. The first law is therefore often called the law of conservation of energy. To use a familiar example, let's see how the first law applies to driving your car (Fig. 4-2). We can consider that your car (with a full tank of gas), the road, and the surrounding air roughly constitute an isolated system. When you drive your car, you convert the potential chemical energy of gasoline into kinetic energy of movement and heat energy. The total amount of energy that was in the gasoline before it was burned is the same as the total amount of this kinetic energy and heat.

An important rule of energy conversions is this: Energy always flows "downhill," from places with a high concentration of energy to places with a low concentration of energy. This is the principle behind engines. As we described in Chapter 2, temperature is a measure of how fast molecules move. The burning gasoline in your car's engine consists of molecules moving at extremely high speeds: a high concentration of energy. The cooler air outside the engine consists of molecules moving at much lower speeds: a low concentration of energy. The molecules in the engine hit the piston harder than the air molecules outside the engine do, so the piston moves upward, driving the gears that move the car. Work is done. When the engine is turned off, it cools down as heat is transferred from the warm engine to its cooler surroundings. The molecules on both sides of the piston move at the same speed, so the piston stays still. No work is done.

a. *Reading for critical evaluation.* Evaluate the material by answering these questions:

Were the ideas clearly supported by examples? If you feel one or more were not supported, give an example.

_____

_____

_____

_____

Did the author make any assumptions that weren't examined? If so, name one or more.

_____

_____

Do you disagree with any part of the material? If so, which part, and why?

_____

_____

_____

Do you have any suggestions for how the material could have been presented more effectively?

_____

_____

_____

_____

b. *Reading for practical application.* Imagine you have to give a presentation on this material the next time the class meets. On a separate sheet of paper, create an outline or think link that maps out the key elements you would discuss.

c. *Reading for comprehension.* Answer the following questions to determine the level of your comprehension.

Name the two types of energy.

_____

_____

Which one "stores" energy?

_____

Can kinetic energy be turned into potential energy?

_____

What is the term that describes the basic properties and behaviors of energy?

_____

Mark the following statements as true (T) or false (F).

_____ Within any isolated system, energy can be neither created nor destroyed.

_____ Energy always flows downhill, from high concentration levels to low.

_____ All interactions among pieces of matter are governed by two laws of thermodynamics.

_____ Some parts of the universe are isolated from other parts.

## *KEY TO SELF-EXPRESSION: DISCOVERY THROUGH JOURNAL WRITING*

*To record your thoughts, use a separate journal or the lined pages at the end of the chapter.*

**Reading Challenges**   What is your most difficult challenge when reading assigned materials? A challenge might be a particular kind of reading material, a reading situation, or the achievement of a certain goal when reading. Considering the tools that this chapter presents, make a plan that addresses this challenge. What techniques might be able to help you most? How and when will you try them out? What positive effects do you anticipate they may have on you?

Name _____ Date _____

## Journal Entry

# NOTE-TAKING AND WRITING:

## Harnessing the Power of Words and Ideas

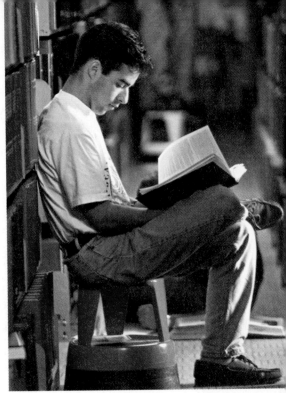

**W**ords, joined to form ideas, are tools that have enormous power. Whether you write an essay, a memo to a supervisor, or a love letter over e-mail, words allow you to take your ideas out of the realm of thought and give them a form that other people can read and consider. You can harness their power for your own. Set a goal for yourself: Strive continually to improve your knowledge of how to use words to construct understandable ideas.

This chapter will teach you the note-taking skills you need to record information successfully. It will show you how to express your written ideas completely and how good writing is linked to clear thinking. In class or at work, taking notes and writing well will help you stand out from the crowd.

In this chapter, you will explore answers to the following questions:

➤ How can note-taking help you?

➤ Which note-taking system should you use?

➤ How can you write faster when you take notes?

➤ Why does good writing matter?

➤ What are the elements of effective writing?

➤ What is the writing process?

# HOW DOES TAKING NOTES HELP YOU?

Notes help you learn when you are in class, doing research, or studying. Since it is virtually impossible to take notes on everything you hear or read, the act of note-taking encourages you to decide what is worth remembering. The positive effects of note-taking include:

➤ Your notes provide material that helps you study information and prepare for tests.

➤ When you take notes, you become an active, involved listener and learner.

➤ Notes help you think critically and organize ideas.

➤ The information you learn in class may not appear in any text; you will have no way to study it without writing it down.

➤ If it is difficult for you to process information while in class; having notes to read and make sense of later can help you learn.

➤ Note-taking is a skill for life that you will use on the job and in your personal life.

## Recording Information In Class

Your notes have two purposes: First, they should reflect what you heard in class, and second, they should be a resource for studying, writing, or comparing with your text material.

### Preparing to Take Class Notes

Taking good class notes depends on good preparation, including the following:

➤ If your instructor assigns reading on a lecture topic, you may choose to complete the reading before class so that the lecture becomes more of a review than an introduction.

➤ Use separate pieces of 8 1/2-by-11-inch paper for each class. If you use a three-ring binder, punch holes in papers your instructor hands out and insert them immediately following your notes for that day.

➤ Take a comfortable seat where you can easily see and hear, and be ready to write as soon as the instructor begins speaking.

➤ Choose a note-taking system that helps you handle the instructor's speaking style. While one instructor may deliver organized lectures at a normal speaking rate, another may jump from topic to topic or talk very quickly.

➤ Set up a support system with a student in each class. That way, when you are absent, you can get the notes you missed.

## What to Do During Class

Because no one has the time to write down everything he or she hears, the following strategies will help you choose and record what you feel is important, in a format that you can read and understand later.

➤ Date each page. When you take several pages of notes during a lecture, add an identifying letter or number to the date on each page: 11/27 A, 11/27 B, . . . or 11/27—1 of 3, 11/27—2 of 3.

➤ Add the specific topic of the lecture at the top of the page. For example:

  11/27A—<u>U.S. Immigration Policy After World War II</u>

➤ If your instructor jumps from topic to topic during a single class, try starting a new page for each new topic.

➤ Ask yourself critical-thinking questions as you listen: Do I need this information? Is the information important or is it just a digression? Is the information fact or opinion? If it is opinion, is it worth remembering? (Chapter 4 offers ideas about how to distinguish between fact and opinion.)

➤ Record whatever an instructor emphasizes (see Figure 6-1 for details).

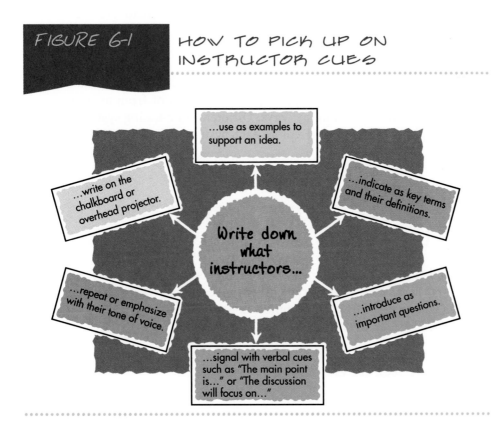

**FIGURE 6-1**   HOW TO PICK UP ON INSTRUCTOR CUES

Write down what instructors...

...use as examples to support an idea.

...write on the chalkboard or overhead projector.

...indicate as key terms and their definitions.

...repeat or emphasize with their tone of voice.

...introduce as important questions.

...signal with verbal cues such as "The main point is..." or "The discussion will focus on..."

> *"Omit needless words. . . .This requires not that the writer make all his sentences short, or that he avoid all detail and treat his subjects only in outline, but that every word tell."*
>
> William Strunk, Jr.
>
> (*Source:* William Strunk, Jr. and E.B. White. *The Elements of Style,* 3rd Edition. Copyright © 1979. All rights reserved. Reprinted by permission from Allyn & Bacon.)

➤ Continue to take notes during class discussions and question-and-answer periods. What your fellow students ask about may help you as well.

➤ Leave one or more blank spaces between points. This white space will help you review your notes, because information will appear in self-contained sections.

➤ Draw pictures and diagrams that help illustrate ideas.

➤ Indicate material that is especially important with a star, with underlining, with a highlighter pen, or by writing words in capital letters.

➤ If you cannot understand what the instructor is saying, leave a space and place a question mark in the margin. Then ask the instructor to explain it again after class or discuss it with a classmate. Fill in the blank when the idea is clear.

➤ Take notes until the instructor stops speaking. Students who stop writing a few minutes before the class is over can miss critical information.

➤ Make your notes as legible, organized, and complete as possible. Your notes are only useful if you can read and understand them.

### Make Notes a Valuable After-Class Reference

Class notes are a valuable study tool when you review them regularly. Try to begin your review within a day of the lecture. Read over the notes to learn the information, clarify abbreviations, fill in missing information, and underline or highlight key points. Try to review each week's notes at the end of that week. Think critically about the material, in writing, study group discussions, or quiet reflective thought. You might also try summarizing your notes, either as you review them or from memory.

You can take notes in many ways. Different note-taking systems suit different people and situations. Explore each system and choose what works for you.

## WHAT NOTE-TAKING SYSTEM SHOULD YOU USE?

You will benefit most from the system that feels most comfortable to you. As you consider each system, remember the learning-styles profile you compiled in Chapter 2. The most common note-taking systems include outlines, the Cornell system, and think links.

### Taking Notes in Outline Form

When a reading assignment or lecture seems well organized, you may choose to take notes in outline form. *Outlining* shows the relationships among ideas and their supporting examples through the use of line-by-line phrases set off by varying indentations.

Formal outlines indicate ideas and examples using Roman numerals, capital and lower-case letters, and numbers. When you are pressed for time, such as during class, you can use an informal system of consistent indenting and dashes instead. Formal outlines also require at least two headings on the same level—that is, if you have a II A you must also have a II B. Figure 6-2 on the following page shows an outline on civil rights legislation.

### Guided Notes

From time to time, an instructor may give you a guide, usually in the form of an outline, to help you take notes in the class. This outline may be on a page that you receive at the beginning of the class, on the board, or on an overhead projector.

Although *guided notes* help you follow the lecture and organize your thoughts during class, they do not replace your own notes. Because they are more of a basic outline of topics than a comprehensive coverage of information, they require that you fill in what they do not cover in detail. If you tune out in class because you think that the guided notes are all you need, you will most likely miss important information.

When you receive guided notes on paper, write directly on the paper if there is room. If not, use a separate sheet and write on it the outline categories that the guided notes suggest. If the guided notes are on the board or overhead, copy them down, leaving plenty of space in between for your own notes.

## Using the Cornell Note-Taking System

The *Cornell note-taking system*, also known as the T-note system, was developed more than 45 years ago by Walter Pauk at Cornell University.[1] The system is successful because it is simple—and because it works. It consists of three sections on ordinary note paper:

➤ *Section 1*, the largest section, is on the right. Record your notes here in informal outline form.

➤ *Section 2*, to the left of your notes, is the *cue column*. Leave it blank while you read or listen, then fill it in later as you review. You might fill it with comments that highlight main ideas, clarify meaning, suggest examples, or link ideas and examples. You can even draw diagrams.

➤ *Section 3*, at the bottom of the page, is the *summary area*, where you summarize the notes on the page. When you review, use this section to reinforce concepts and provide an overview.

FIGURE 6-2          SAMPLE FORMAL OUTLINE

Civil Rights Legislation: 1860–1968

I. Post-Civil War Era
   A. Fourteenth Amendment, 1868: equal protection of the law
      for all citizens
   B. Fifteenth Amendment, 1870: constitutional rights of citizens
      regardless of race, color, or previous servitude
II. Civil Rights Movement of the 1960s
   A. National Association for the Advancement of Colored People (NAACP)
      1. Established in 1910 by W.E.B. DuBois and others
      2. Legal Defense and Education fund fought school segregation
   B. Martin Luther King Jr., champion of nonviolent civil rights action
      1. Led bus boycott: 1955–1956
      2. Marched on Washington, D.C.: 1963
      3. Awarded NOBEL PEACE PRIZE: 1964
      4. Led voter registration drive in Selma, Alabama: 1965
   C. Civil Rights Act of 1964: prohibited discrimination in voting,
      education, employment, and public facilities
   D. Voting Rights Act of 1965: gave the government power to enforce
      desegregation
   E. Civil Rights Act of 1968: prohibited discrimination in the sale
      or rental of housing

When you use the Cornell system, create the note-taking structure before class begins. Picture an upside-down letter T and use Figure 6-3 as your guide. Make the cue column about 2 ½ inches wide and the summary area 2 inches tall. Figure 6-3 shows how a student used the Cornell system to take notes in an introduction-to-business course.

## Creating a Think Link

A *think link*, also known as a mind map, is a visual form of note-taking. When you draw a think link, you diagram ideas using shapes and lines that link ideas and supporting details and examples. The visual design makes the connections easy to see, and the use of shapes and pictures extends the material beyond just words. Many learners respond well to the power of visualization. You can use think links to brainstorm ideas for paper topics as well.

**Visualization,**
The interpretation of verbal ideas through the use of mental visual images.

FIGURE 6-3    NOTES TAKEN USING THE CORNELL SYSTEM

October 3, 199x, p.1

UNDERSTANDING EMPLOYEE MOTIVATION

Why do some workers have a better attitude toward their work than others?

Some managers view workers as lazy; others view them as motivated and productive.

Maslow's Hierarchy

self-actualization needs (challenging job)
esteem needs (job title)
Social needs (friends at work)
security needs (health plan)
physiological needs (pay)

Purpose of motivational theories
– To explain role of human relations in motivating employee performance
– Theories translate into how managers actually treat workers

2 specific theories
– Human resources model, developed by Douglas McGregor, shows that managers have radically different beliefs about motivation
  – Theory X holds that people are naturally irresponsible and uncooperative
  – Theory Y holds that people are naturally responsible and self-motivated
Maslow's Hierarchy of Needs says that people have needs in 5 different areas, which they attempt to satisfy in their work.
  – Physiological need: need for survival, including food and shelter
  – Security need: need for stability and protection
  – Social need: need for friendship and companionship
  – Esteem need: need for status and recognition
  – Self-actualization need: need for self-fulfillment
Needs at lower levels must be met before a person tries to satisfy needs at higher levels.
– Developed by psychologist Abraham Maslow

Two motivational theories try to explain worker motivation. The human resources model includes Theory X and Theory Y. Maslow's Hierarchy of Needs suggests that people have needs in 5 different areas: physiological, security, social, esteem, and self-actualization.

One way to create a think link is to start by circling your topic in the middle of a sheet of unlined paper. Next, draw a line from the circled topic and write the name of the first major idea at the end of that line. Circle the idea also. Then jot down specific facts related to the idea, linking them to the idea with lines. Continue the process, connecting thoughts to one another using circles, lines, and words.

A think link may be difficult to construct in class, especially if your instructor talks quickly. In this case, use another note-taking system during

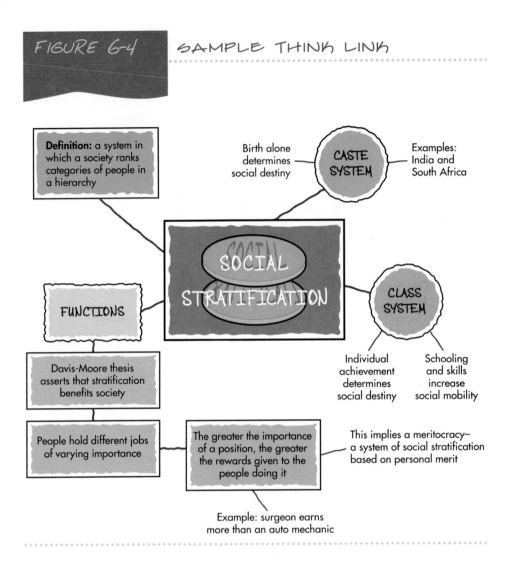

FIGURE 6-4    SAMPLE THINK LINK

**Definition:** a system in which a society ranks categories of people in a hierarchy

Birth alone determines social destiny

CASTE SYSTEM

Examples: India and South Africa

SOCIAL STRATIFICATION

FUNCTIONS

CLASS SYSTEM

Individual achievement determines social destiny

Schooling and skills increase social mobility

Davis-Moore thesis asserts that stratification benefits society

People hold different jobs of varying importance

The greater the importance of a position, the greater the rewards given to the people doing it

This implies a meritocracy— a system of social stratification based on personal merit

Example: surgeon earns more than an auto mechanic

class. Then make a think link as you review. Figure 6-4 shows a think link on a sociology concept called *social stratification*.

Once you choose a note-taking system, your success will depend on how well you use it. Personal shorthand will help you make the most of whatever system you choose.

## HOW CAN YOU WRITE FASTER WHEN TAKING NOTES?

When taking notes, many students feel they can't keep up with the instructor. Using some personal shorthand (not standard secretarial shorthand) can help to push the pen faster. *Shorthand* is writing that shortens words or replaces them with symbols. Because you are the only intended reader, you can misspell and abbreviate words in ways that only you understand.

The only danger with shorthand is that you might forget what your writing means. To avoid this problem, review your shorthand notes while your abbreviations and symbols are fresh in your mind. If there is any confusion, spell out words as you review.

Here are some suggestions that will help you master this important skill:

1. Use the following standard abbreviations in place of complete words:

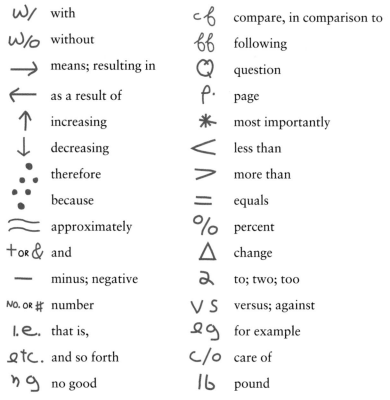

| | | | |
|---|---|---|---|
| w/ | with | c̸ | compare, in comparison to |
| w/o | without | ⨍⨍ | following |
| → | means; resulting in | ⟳ | question |
| ← | as a result of | p. | page |
| ↑ | increasing | ✳ | most importantly |
| ↓ | decreasing | < | less than |
| ∴ | therefore | > | more than |
| ∵ | because | = | equals |
| ≈ | approximately | % | percent |
| + or & | and | △ | change |
| — | minus; negative | 2 | to; two; too |
| NO. or # | number | vs | versus; against |
| i.e. | that is, | eg | for example |
| etc. | and so forth | c/o | care of |
| ng | no good | lb | pound |

2. Shorten words by removing vowels from the middle of words:

    prps  = purpose
    Crvtte = Corvette (as on a vanity license plate for a car)

3. Substitute word beginnings for entire words:

    assoc = associate; association
    info  = information

4. Form plurals by adding s:

    prblms = problems
    prntrs = printers

5. Make up your own symbols and use them consistently:

    b/4    = before
    2thake = toothache

6. Learn to rely on key phrases instead of complete sentences ("German—nouns capitalized" instead of "In the German language, all nouns are capitalized.")

While note-taking focuses on taking in ideas, writing focuses on expressing them. Next you will explore the roles that writing can play in your life.

# WHY DOES GOOD WRITING MATTER?

Good writing depends upon and reflects clear thinking. Therefore, a clear thought process is the best preparation for a well-written document, and a well-written document shows the reader a clear thought process. Good writing also depends on reading. The more you expose yourself to the work of other writers, the more you will develop your ability to express yourself well. Not only will you learn more words and ideas, but you will also learn about all the different ways a writer can put words together in order to express ideas. In addition, critical reading generates new ideas inside your mind, ideas you can use in your writing.

In school, almost any course you take will require you to write essays or papers in order to communicate your knowledge and thought process. In order to express yourself successfully in those essays and papers, you need good writing skills. Knowing how to write and express yourself is essential outside of school as well.

Instructors, supervisors, and other people who see your writing judge your thinking ability based on what you write and how you write it. Over the next few years you may write papers, essays, answers to essay test questions, job application letters, résumés, business proposals and reports, memos to co-workers, and letters to customers and suppliers. Good writing skills will help you achieve the goals you set out to accomplish with each writing task.

# WHAT ARE THE ELEMENTS OF EFFECTIVE WRITING?

Every writing situation is different, dependent upon three elements. Your goal is to understand each element before you begin to write:

> ➤ *Your purpose:* What do you want to accomplish with this particular piece of writing?
> ➤ *Your topic:* What is the subject about which you will write?
> ➤ *Your audience:* Who will read your writing?

Figure 6-5 shows how these elements are inter-dependent. As a triangle needs three points to be complete, a piece of writing needs these three elements.

## Writing Purpose

Writing without having set your purpose first is like driving without deciding where you want to arrive. You'll get somewhere, but chances are it won't be where you needed to go. Therefore, when you write, always define what you want to accomplish before you start.

There are many different purposes for writing. However, the two purposes you will most commonly use in classwork and on the job are to inform and to persuade.

FIGURE 6-5    THE THREE ELEMENTS OF WRITING

The purpose of *informative writing* is to present and explain ideas. A research paper on how hospitals use donated blood to save lives informs readers without trying to mold opinion. The writer presents facts in an unbiased way, without introducing a particular point of view. Most newspaper articles, except on the opinion and editorial pages, are examples of informative writing.

*Persuasive writing* has the purpose of convincing readers that your point of view is correct. Often, persuasive writing seeks to change the mind of the reader. For example, as a member of the student health committee, you write a newspaper column attempting to persuade readers to give blood. Examples of persuasive writing include newspaper editorials, business proposals, and books and magazine articles with a point of view.

Additional possible writing purposes include *entertaining* the reader and *narrating* (describing an image or event to the reader). Although most of your writing in school will inform or persuade, you may occasionally need to entertain or narrate as well. Sometimes purposes will even overlap—you might write an informative essay that entertains at the same time.

## Knowing Your Audience

In almost every case, a writer creates written material so that it can be read by others. The two partners in this process are the writer and the audience. Knowing who your audience is will help you communicate successfully.

### Key Questions About Your Audience

In school, your primary audience is your instructors. For many assignments, instructors will want you to assume that they are typical readers rather than informed instructors. Writing for typical readers usually means that you should be as complete as possible in your explanations.

At times you may write papers that intend to address informed instructors or a specific reading audience other than your instructors. In such cases, you may ask yourself some or all of the following questions, depending on which are relevant to your topic.

➤ What are my readers' ages, cultural backgrounds, interests, and experiences?

**Audience,**
The reader or readers of any piece of written material.

## How can I improve my writing?

### Erica Epstein, Ithaca College—Ithaca, New York, Education Major

I don't know if it was the school's fault or mine, but by the time I was in high school, I didn't do homework or reading. I just stopped paying attention. The classes were too boring. Fifteen weeks of the same topic was redundant. I think education should be interesting. The material should be tied in with something else so it has meaning. Instead, the teacher feeds you the information so you don't really have to put  much effort in. But now, even though I do all right, I have to work really hard to write a good paper. I think if I'd had a better start I wouldn't have to spend so much time rewriting my papers.

My teachers say the main problem is with my grammar. I tend to go from the past tense to the present tense in the wrong places. I just don't make proper sentences. I also have trouble organizing my material. I jump in and start writing. But I end up starting somewhere in the middle when I should be somewhere else. This is really frustrating. I had to take the writing class twice because I didn't get a high enough score the first time. I passed it this semester. I go to the writing center. They help me outline what I'm going to write. But I still end up rewriting my work before it's what I want. It's been really helpful but I know I still need to do more. What suggestions do you have?

### Tom Smith, University of Wyoming, Administration of Justice

First of all, just like you, I get help from the writing center at my school. They know a lot about what the different teachers expect of you, particularly the technical stuff like footnote and bibliography requirements. They also give great advice about phrasing and punctuation. I also ask several of my friends to edit my papers. Usually, they'll focus in  on the weaker points and then I can make the changes and strengthen my work. If your papers are sounding too chatty, this would probably be the best thing for you to do. They'll be able to show you where you've gotten off the point. I'm never bothered by their comments. In fact, I'm grateful because it helps my papers be more professional.

By the time three or four people have read my work, I'm usually pretty sure I've handled the problems. I also personally edit my papers about three or four times before I turn them in. I make sure I got my point across. I also try and look at my paper from an opposing perspective or different viewpoint. That way I can be sure my arguments are clear. Finally, if you don't have a reference book for writers, I suggest you go to your college bookstore and get one. And don't forget to use your spell-check and thesaurus. That way you'll be sure your spelling is correct and you can increase your vocabulary with every paper you write.

➤ What are their roles? Are they instructors, students, employers, customers?

➤ How much do they know about my topic? Are they experts in the field or beginners?

➤ Are they interested, or do I have to convince them to read what I write?

➤ Can I expect my audience to have an open or closed mind?

After you answer the questions about your audience, take what you have discovered into consideration as you write.

### Your Commitment to Your Audience

Your goal is to organize your ideas so that readers can follow them. Suppose, for example, you are writing an informative research paper for a non-expert audience on using on-line services to get a job. One way to accomplish your goal is to first explain what these services are and the kinds of help they offer, then describe each service in detail, and finally conclude with how these services will change job hunting in the twenty-first century.

Effective and successful writing involves following the steps of the *writing process*.

# WHAT IS THE WRITING PROCESS?

The writing process provides an opportunity for you to state and refine your thoughts until you have expressed yourself as clearly as possible. Critical thinking plays an important role every step of the way. The four main parts of the process are planning, drafting, revising, and editing.

## Planning

Planning gives you a chance to think about what to write and how to write it. Planning involves brainstorming for ideas, defining and narrowing your topic by using prewriting strategies, conducting research if necessary, writing a thesis statement, and writing a working outline. Although the steps in preparing to write are listed in sequence, in real life the steps overlap one another as you plan your document.

### Open Your Mind Through Brainstorming

Whether your instructor assigns a partially defined topic (novelist Toni Morrison) or a general category within which you make your own choice (women authors), you should brainstorm to develop ideas about what you want to write. Brainstorming is a creative technique that involves generating ideas about a subject without making judgments. You may want to look at the section on creativity in Chapter 4 for more details.

First, let your mind wander! Write down anything on the assigned subject that comes to mind, in no particular order. Then, organize that list into an outline or think link that helps you see the possibilities more clearly. To make the outline or think link, separate list items into general ideas or categories and sub-ideas or examples. Then associate the sub-ideas or examples with the ideas they support or fit. Figure 6-6 shows a portion of an outline that the student editor for this book, Michael B. Jackson, constructed from his brainstorming list. The assignment is a five-paragraph essay on a life-changing event. Here, only the subject that Michael eventually chose is shown broken down into different ideas.

### Narrow Your Topic Through Prewriting Strategies

When your brainstorming has generated some possibilities, you can narrow your topic. Focus on the sub-ideas and examples from your initial brainstorming session. Because they are relatively specific, they will be more likely to point you toward possible topics.

Choose one or more sub-ideas or examples that you like and explore them using prewriting strategies such as brainstorming, freewriting, and asking journalists' questions.[2]  Prewriting strategies will help you decide which of your possible topics you would most like to pursue.

**Prewriting strategies,** Techniques for generating ideas about a topic and finding out how much you already know before you start your research and writing.

FIGURE 6-6   PART OF A BRAINSTORMING OUTLINE

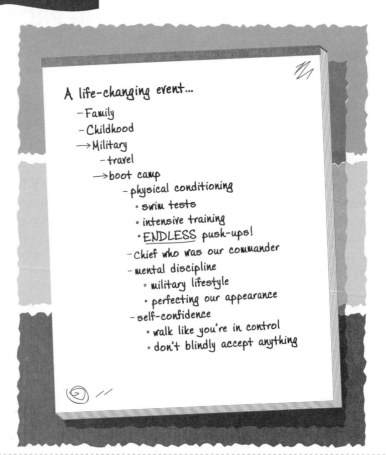

A life-changing event...
- Family
- Childhood
→ Military
    - travel
    → boot camp
        - physical conditioning
            ◦ swim tests
            ◦ intensive training
            ◦ ENDLESS push-ups!
        - Chief who was our commander
        - mental discipline
            ◦ military lifestyle
            ◦ perfecting our appearance
        - self-confidence
            ◦ walk like you're in control
            ◦ don't blindly accept anything

Brainstorming    The same process you used to generate ideas will also help you narrow your topic further. Generate thoughts about the possibility you have chosen and write them down. Then, organize them into categories, noticing any patterns that appear. See if any of the sub-ideas or examples seem as if they might make good topics.

Freewriting    Another stream-of-consciousness technique that encourages you to put down ideas on paper as they occur to you is called *freewriting*. When you freewrite, you write whatever comes to mind without censoring your ideas or worrying about grammar, spelling, punctuation, or organization. Freewriting helps you think creatively and gives you an opportunity to begin weaving in information that you know. Freewrite on the sub-ideas or examples you have created to see if you want to pursue any of them. Here is a sample of freewriting:

> Boot camp for the Coast Guard really changed my life. First of all, I really got in shape. We had to get up every morning at 5 A.M., eat breakfast, and go right into training. We had to do endless military-style push-ups — but we later found out that these have a purpose, to prepare us to hit the deck in the event of enemy fire. We had a lot of aquatic tests, once we were awakened at 3 A.M. to do one in full uniform! Boot camp also helped me to feel confident about myself and be disciplined. Chief Marzloff was the main person who made that happen. He was tough but there was always a reason. He got angry when I used to nod my head whenever he would speak to me, he said that made it seem like I was blindly accepting whatever he said, which was a weakness. From him I have learned to keep an eye on my body's movements when I communicate. I learned a lot more from him too.

Asking journalists' questions    When journalists start working on a story, they ask themselves Who? What? Where? When? Why? and How? You can use these *journalists' questions* to focus your thinking. Ask these questions about any sub-idea or example to discover what you may want to discuss. For example:

> *Who?*    Who was at boot camp? Who influenced me the most?
>
> *What?*    What about boot camp changed my life? What did we do?
>
> *When?*    When in my life did I go to boot camp, and for how long? When did we fulfill our duties?
>
> *Continued*

| | |
|---|---|
| *Where?* | Where was camp located? Where did we spend our day-to-day time? |
| *Why?* | Why did I decide to go there? Why was it such an important experience? |
| *How?* | How did we train in the camp? How were we treated? How did we achieve success? |

As you prewrite, don't forget to focus on the paper length, due date of your assignment, and any other requirements (such as topic area or purpose). These requirements influence your choice of a final topic. For example, if you had a month to write an informative 20-page paper on learning disabilities, you might choose to discuss the symptoms, diagnosis, effects, and treatment of Attention Deficit Disorder. If you were given a week to write a five-page persuasive essay, you might write about how elementary students with ADD need special training.

Prewriting will help you develop a topic broad enough to give you something with which to work but narrow enough to be manageable. Prewriting also helps you see what you know and what you don't know. If your assignment requires more than you already know, you may need to do research.

## Conduct Research

Much of the writing you do in college, such as when you must write a short essay for freshman composition or for an exam, will rely on what you already know about a subject. In these cases, prewriting strategies may generate all the ideas and information you need. In other writing situations, outside sources are necessary. Try doing your research in stages. In the first stage, look for a basic overview that can help you write a thesis statement. In the second stage, go into more depth in your research, tracking down information that will help you fill in the gaps and complete your thoughts.

## Write a Thesis Statement

Your work up until this point has prepared you to write a *thesis statement*, the central message you want to communicate. The thesis statement states your subject and point of view, reflects your writing purpose and audience, and acts as the organizing principle of your paper. It tells your readers what they should expect to read. Here is an example from Michael's paper:

| | |
|---|---|
| **Topic** | Coast Guard boot camp |
| **Purpose** | To inform and narrate |
| **Audience** | Instructor with unknown knowledge about the topic |
| **Thesis statement** | Chief Marzloff, our Basic Training Company Commander at the U.S. Coast Guard Basic Training Facility, shaped my life through physical conditioning, developing our self-confidence, and instilling strong mental discipline. |

A thesis statement is just as important in a short document, such as a letter, as it is in a long paper. For example, when you write a job application letter, a clear thesis statement will help you tell the recruiter why you deserve the job.

### Write a Working Outline

The final step in the preparation process involves writing a working outline. Use this outline as a loose guide instead of a finalized structure. As you draft your paper, your ideas and structure may change many times. Only through allowing changes and refinements to happen can you get closer and closer to what you really want to say. Some students prefer a more formal outline structure, while others like to use a think link. Choose whatever form suits you best.

### Create a Checklist

Use the checklist in Table 6-1 to make sure your preparation is complete. Under "Date Due," create your own writing schedule, giving each task an intended completion date. Work backwards from the date the assignment is due and estimate how long it will take to complete each step. Refer to Chapter 3 for time-management skills that will help you schedule your writing process.

## TABLE 6-1   PREPARATION CHECKLIST

| DATE DUE | TASK | IS IT COMPLETE? |
|---|---|---|
| | Brainstorm | |
| | Define and narrow | |
| | Use prewriting strategies | |
| | Conduct research if necessary | |
| | Write thesis statement | |
| | Write working outline | |
| | Complete research | |

As you develop your schedule, keep in mind that you'll probably move back and forth between tasks. You might find yourself doing two and even three things on the same day. Stick to the schedule as best you can, while balancing the other demands of your busy life, and check off your accomplishments on the list as you complete them.

# Drafting

Some people aim for perfection when they write a first draft. They want to get everything right—from word choice to tone to sentence structure to paragraph organization to spelling, punctuation, and grammar. Try to resist this tendency, because it may lead you to shut the door on ideas before you even know they are there.

A *first draft* involves putting ideas down on paper for the first time—but not the last! You may write many different versions of the assignment until you like what you see. Each version moves you closer to communicating exactly what you want to say in the way you want to say it. The process is like starting with a muddy pond and gradually clearing the mud away until your last version is a clear body of water, showing the rocks and the fish underneath the surface. Think of your first draft as a way of establishing the pond before you start clearing it up.

The elements of writing a first draft are freewriting, crafting an introduction, organizing the ideas in the body of the paper, formulating a conclusion, and citing sources.

## Freewriting Your Draft

If the introduction, body, and conclusion are the three parts of the sandwich, freewriting is the process of searching the refrigerator for the ingredients and laying them all out on the table. Take everything that you have developed in the planning stages and freewrite a very rough draft. Don't censor yourself. For now, don't consciously think about your introduction, conclusion, or structure within the paper body. Focus on getting your ideas out of the realm of thought and onto the paper, in whatever form they prefer to be at the moment.

When you have the beginnings of a paper in your hands, you can start to shape it into something with a more definite form. First, work on how you want to begin your paper.

## Writing an Introduction

The introduction tells your readers what the rest of the paper will contain. Including the thesis statement is essential. Here, for example, is a draft of an introduction for Michael's paper about the Coast Guard. The thesis statement is underlined at the end of the paragraph:

> Chief Marzloff took on the task of shaping the lives and careers of the youngest, newest members of the U.S. Coast Guard. During my eight weeks in training, he was my father, my instructor, my leader, and my worst enemy. He took his job very seriously and demanded that we do the same. <u>The Chief was instrumental in conditioning our bodies, developing our self-confidence, and instilling mental discipline within us.</u>

When you write an introduction, you might try to draw the reader in with an anecdote—a story that is directly related to the thesis. You can try other hooks, including a relevant quotation, dramatic statistics, and ques-

---

*"Clear a space for the writing voice. . . .you cannot will this to happen. It is a matter of persistence and faith and hard work. So you might as well just go ahead and get started."*

Anne Lamott

(*Source: Bird by Bird* by Anne Lamott, © 1994, Pantheon Books, a division of Random House, Inc.)

---

**Hooks,** Elements—including facts, quotes, statistics, questions, stories, or statements—that catch the reader's attention and encourage him or her to want to continue to read.

tions that encourage critical thinking. Whatever strategy you choose, be sure it is linked to your thesis statement. In addition, try to state your purpose without referring to its identity as a purpose. For example, in your introductory paragraph, state "Computer technology is infiltrating every aspect of business," instead of, "In this paper, my purpose is to prove that computer technology is infiltrating every aspect of business."

After you have an introduction that seems to set up the purpose of your paper, work on making sure the body fulfills that purpose.

## Creating the Body of a Paper

The body of the paper contains your central ideas and supporting evidence. *Evidence*—proof that informs or persuades—consists of the facts, statistics, examples, and expert opinions that you know or have gathered during research.

Look at the array of ideas and evidences within your draft in its current state. Think about how you might group certain items of evidence with the particular ideas they support. Then, when you see the groups that form, try to find a structure that helps you to organize them into a clear pattern. Here are some strategies to consider.

*Arrange ideas by time.* Describe events in order or in reverse order.

*Arrange ideas according to importance.* You can choose to start with the idea that carries the most weight and move to ideas with less value or influence. You can also move from the least important to the most important idea.

*Arrange ideas by problem and solution.* Start with a specific problem, then discuss one or more solutions.

## Writing the Conclusion

Your conclusion is a statement or paragraph that provides closure for your paper. Aim to summarize the information in the body of your paper, as well as to critically evaluate what is important about that information. Try one of the following devices:

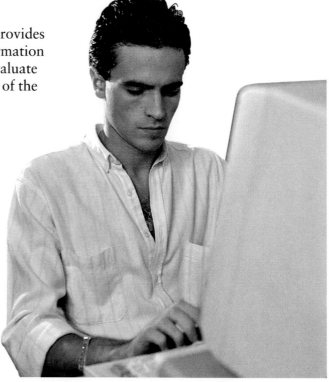

➤ a summary of main points (if material is longer than three pages)

➤ a story, a statistic, a quote, a question that makes the reader think

➤ a call to action

➤ a look to the future

As you work on your conclusion, try not to introduce new facts or restate what you feel you have proved ("I have successfully proven that violent cartoons are related to increased violence in children.") Let your ideas as they are presented in the body of the paper speak for themselves. Readers should feel that they have reached a natural point of completion.

### Crediting Authors and Sources

When you write a paper using any materials other than your own thoughts and recollections, the ideas you gathered in your research become part of your own writing. This does not mean that you can claim these ideas as your own or fail to attribute them to someone. You need to credit authors for their ideas and words in order to avoid plagiarism.

**Plagiarism,**
The act of using someone else's exact words, figures, unique approach, or specific reasoning without giving appropriate credit.

To prevent plagiarism, learn the difference between a quotation and a paraphrase. A *quotation* refers to a source's exact words, which are set off from the rest of the text by quotation marks. A *paraphrase* is a restatement of the quotation in your own words, using your own sentence structure. Restatement means to completely rewrite the idea, not just to remove or replace a few words. A paraphrase may not be acceptable if it is too close to the original.

Even an acceptable paraphrase requires a citation of the source of the ideas within it. Take care to credit any source that you quote, paraphrase, or use as evidence. To credit sources, write a footnote or endnote that describes the source. Use the format preferred by your instructor. Writing handbooks such as the *MLA Handbook* contain acceptable formats.

## Revising

When you *revise*, you critically evaluate the word choice, paragraph structure, and style of your first draft to see how it works. Any draft, no matter how good, can always be improved. Be thorough as you add, delete, replace, and reorganize words, sentences, and paragraphs. You may want to print out your draft and then spend time making notes and corrections on that hard copy before you make changes on a typewritten or computer printed version. Figure 6-7 on the next page shows a paragraph from Michael's first draft, with revision comments added.

In addition to revising on your own, some of your classes may include peer review (having students read each other's work and offer suggestions). A peer reviewer can tell you what comes across well and what may be confusing. Having a different perspective on your writing is extremely valuable. Even if you don't have an organized peer-review system, you may want to ask a classmate to review your work as a favor to you.

The elements of revision include being a critical writer, evaluating paragraph structure, and checking for clarity and conciseness.

### Being a Critical Writer

Critical thinking is as important in writing as it is in reading. Thinking critically when writing will help you move your papers beyond restating what you have researched and learned. Of course, your knowledge is an important part of your writing. What will make your writing even more important and unique, however, is how you use critical thinking to construct your own new ideas and knowledge from what you have learned.

The key to critical writing is asking the question, "So what?" For example, if you were writing a paper on nutrition, you might discuss a variety of good eating habits. Asking "So what?" could lead you into a discussion of *why* these habits are helpful, or, what positive effects they have. If you were

FIGURE 6-7

Of the changes that ~~happened to us,~~ the physical transformation is _[military recruits undergo]_

the ~~biggest.~~ _[most evident]_ ~~When we arrived at the training facility, it was January, cold~~ _[Too much.↗]_

~~and cloudy. At the time,~~ _[Maybe— upon my January arrival at the training facility,]_ I was a little thin, but I had been working out

and thought that I could physically do anything. Oh boy, was I wrong!

The Chief said to us right away: "Get down, maggots!" Upon this _[←— his trademark phrase]_

command, we all _[were]_ to drop to the ground and do _[endless]_ military-style push-ups.

Water survival tactics were also part of the training ~~that we had to complete.~~

_[unnecessary]_

Occasionally, my dreams of home were interrupted at 3 a.m. when we

had a surprise aquatic test. Although we ~~didn't feel too happy about~~ _[resented]_ this

sub-human treatment at the time, we learned to appreciate how the

conditioning was turning our bodies into fine-tuned machines.

_[mention how Chief was involved]_   _[say more about this (swimming in uniform incident?)]_

writing a paper on egg imagery in the novel _All the King's Men_ by Robert Penn Warren, you might list all the examples you noticed of that imagery. Then, asking "So what?" could lead you to evaluate why that imagery is so strong and what idea you think those examples convey.

As you revise, ask yourself questions that can help you think through ideas and examples, come up with your own original insights about the material, and be as complete and clear as possible. Use the mind actions to guide you. Here are some examples of questions you may ask:

**EX**  Are these examples clearly connected to the idea?

△ △  Are there any similar concepts or facts I know of that can add to how I support this?

What else can I recall that can help to support this idea?

In evaluating any event or situation, have I clearly indicated the causes and effects?

What new idea comes to mind when I think about these examples or facts?

How do I evaluate any effect/fact/situation? Is it good or bad, useful or not?

What different arguments might a reader think of that I should address here?

Finally, critical thinking can help you evaluate the content and form of your paper. As you start your revision, ask yourself the following questions.

> ➤ Will my audience understand my thesis and how I've supported it?
> ➤ Does the introduction prepare the reader and capture attention?
> ➤ Is the body of the paper organized effectively?
> ➤ Is each idea fully developed, explained, and supported by examples?
> ➤ Are my ideas connected to one another through logical transitions?
> ➤ Do I have a clear, concise, simple writing style?
> ➤ Does the paper fulfill the requirements of the assignment?
> ➤ Does the conclusion provide a natural ending to the paper?

## Check for Clarity and Conciseness

Aim to say what you want to say in the clearest, most efficient way possible. A few well-chosen words will do your ideas more justice than a flurry of language. Try to eliminate extra words and phrases. Rewrite wordy phrases in a more concise, conversational way. For example, you can write "if" instead of "in the event that," or "now" instead of "this point in time." "Capriciously, I sauntered forth to the entryway and pummeled the door that loomed so majestically before me," might become, "I skipped to the door and knocked loudly."

*"See revision as 'envisioning again.' If there are areas in your work where there is a blur or vagueness, you can simply see the picture again and add the details that will bring your work closer to your mind's picture."*

Natalie Goldberg

(*Source:* From *Writing Down the Bones* by Natalie Goldberg, © 1986. Reprinted by arrangement with Shambhala Publications, Inc., 300 Massachusetts Avenue, Boston, MA 02115)

# Editing

In contrast to the critical thinking of revising, *editing* involves correcting technical mistakes in spelling, grammar, punctuation, as well as checking style consistency for elements such as abbreviations and capitalizations. Editing comes last, after you are satisfied with your ideas, organization, and style of writing. If you use a computer, you might want to use the grammar-check and spellcheck functions to find mistakes. A spell-checker helps, but you still need to check your work on your own. While a spell-checker won't pick up the mistake in the following sentence, someone who is reading for sense will:

They are not hear on Tuesdays.

Look also for *sexist language*, which characterizes people based on their gender. Sexist language often involves the male pronoun *he* or *his*. For example "An executive often spends hours each day going through his electronic mail" implies that executives are always men. A simple change will eliminate the sexist language: "Executives often spend hours each day going through their electronic mail," or, "An executive often spends hours each day going through his or her electronic mail." Try to be sensitive to words that leave out or slight women. *Mail carrier* is preferable to *mailman; student* to *coed.*

*Proofreading* is the last stage of editing, occurring when you have a final version of your paper. Proofreading means reading every word and sentence in the final version to make sure they are accurate. Look for technical mistakes, run-on sentences, and sentence fragments. Look for incorrect word usage and references that aren't clear.

Teamwork can be a big help as you edit and proofread, because another pair of eyes may see errors that you didn't notice on your own. If possible, have someone look over your work. Ask for feedback on what is clear and what is confusing. Then ask the reader to edit and proofread for errors.

## A Final Checklist

You are now ready to complete your revising and editing checklist. All the tasks listed in Table 6-2 should be complete when you submit your final paper.

Your final paper reflects all the hard work you put in during the writing process. Figure 6-8 shows the final version of Michael's paper.

## TABLE 6-2   REVISING AND EDITING CHECKLIST

| DATE DUE | TASK | IS IT COMPLETE? |
|---|---|---|
| | Check the body of the paper for clear thinking and adequate support of ideas | |
| | Finalize introduction and conclusion | |
| | Check word spelling and usage | |
| | Check grammar | |
| | Check paragraph structure | |
| | Make sure language is familiar and concise | |
| | Check punctuation | |
| | Check capitalization | |
| | Check transitions | |
| | Eliminate sexist language | |

FIGURE 6-8

March 19, 1997
Michael B. Jackson

### BOYS TO MEN

His stature was one of confidence, often misinterpreted by others as cockiness. His small frame was lean and agile, yet stiff and upright, as though every move were a calculated formula. For the longest eight weeks of my life, he was my father, my instructor, my leader, and my worst enemy. His name is Chief Marzloff, and he had the task of shaping the lives and careers of the youngest, newest members of the U.S. Coast Guard. As our Basic Training Company Commander, he took his job very seriously and demanded that we do the same. Within a limited time span, he conditioned our bodies, developed our self-confidence, and instilled within us a strong mental discipline.

Of the changes that recruits in military basic training undergo, the physical transformation is the most immediately evident. Upon my January arrival at the training facility, I was a little thin, but I had been working out and thought that I could physically do anything. Oh boy, was I wrong! The Chief wasted no time in introducing me to one of his trademark phrases: "Get down, maggots!" Upon this command, we were all to drop to the ground and produce endless counts of military-style push-ups. Later, we found out that exercise prepared us for hitting the deck in the event of enemy fire. Water survival tactics were also part of the training. Occasionally, my dreams of home were interrupted at about 3 a.m. when our company was selected for a surprise aquatic test. I recall one such test that required us to swim laps around the perimeter of a pool while in full uniform. I felt like a salmon swimming upstream, fueled only by natural instinct. Although we resented this sub-human treatment at the time, we learned to appreciate how the strict guidance of the Chief was turning our bodies into fine-tuned machines.

Beyond physical ability, Chief Marzloff also played an integral role in the development of our self-confidence. He would often declare in his raspy voice, "Look me in the eyes when you speak to me! Show me that you believe what you're saying!" He taught us that anything less was an expression of disrespect. Furthermore, he appeared to attack a personal habit of my own. It seemed that whenever he would speak to me individually, I would nervously nod my head in response. I was trying to demonstrate that I understood, but to him, I was blindly accepting anything that he said. He would roar, "That is a sign of weakness!" Needless to say, I am now conscious of all bodily motions when communicating with others. The Chief also reinforced self-confidence through his own example. He walked with his square chin up and chest out, like the proud parent of a new-born baby. He always gave the appearance that he had something to do, and that he was in complete control. Collectively, all of the methods that the Chief used were successful in developing our self-confidence.

Perhaps the Chief's greatest contribution was the mental discipline that he instilled in his recruits. He taught us that physical ability and self-confidence were nothing without the mental discipline required to obtain any worthwhile goal. For us, this discipline began with adapting to the military lifestyle. Our day began promptly at 0500 hours, early enough to awaken the oversleeping roosters. By 0515 hours, we had to have showered, shaved, and perfectly donned our uniforms. At that point, we were marched to the galley for chow, where we learned to take only what is necessary, rather than indulging. Before each meal, the Chief would warn, "Get what you want, but you will eat all that you get!" After making good on his threat a few times, we all got the point. Throughout our stay, the chief repeatedly stressed the significance of self-discipline. He would calmly utter, "Give a little now, get a lot later." I guess that meant different things to all of us. For me, it was a simple phrase that would later become my personal philosophy on life. The Chief went to great lengths to ensure that everyone under his direction possessed the mental discipline required to be successful in boot camp or in any of life's challenges.

Chief Marzloff was a remarkable role model and a positive influence on many lives. I never saw him smile, but it was evident that he genuinely cared a great deal about his job and all the lives that he touched. This man single-handedly conditioned our bodies, developed our self-confidence, and instilled a strong mental discipline that remains in me to this day. I have not seen the Chief since March 28, 1992, graduation day. Over the years, however, I have incorporated many of his ideals into my life. Above all, he taught us the true meaning of the U.S. Coast Guard slogan, "Semper Peratus" (Always Ready).

# Suà

*Suà* is a Shoshone Indian word, derived from the Uto-Aztecna language, meaning "think." While much of the Native American tradition in the Americas focuses on oral communication, written languages have allowed Native American perspectives and ideas to be understood by readers outside the Native American culture. The writings of Leslie Marmon Silko, J. Scott Momaday, and Sherman Alexis have expressed important insights that all readers can consider.

Think of *suà*, and of how thinking can be communicated to others through writing, every time you begin to write. The power of writing allows you to express your own insights so that others can read them and perhaps benefit from knowing them. Explore your thoughts, sharpen your ideas, and remember the incredible power of the written word.

# Chapter 6: Applications

Name _____ Date _____

 *Key Into Your Life: Opportunities to Apply What You Learn*

### Exercise 1: Evaluate Your Notes

Choose one particular class period from the last two weeks. Have a classmate photocopy his or her notes from that class period for you. Then evaluate your notes by comparing them with your classmate's. Think about:

➤ Do your notes make sense?
➤ How is your handwriting?
➤ Do the notes cover everything that was brought up in class?
➤ Are there examples to back up ideas?
➤ What note-taking system is used?
➤ Will these notes help you study?

Write your evaluation here _____

_____

_____

_____

_____

_____

What ideas or techniques from your classmate's notes do you plan to use in the future? _____

_____

_____

### Exercise 2: Class vs. Reading

Pick a class for which you have a regular textbook. Choose a set of class notes on a subject that is also covered in that textbook. Read the textbook section that corresponds to the subject of your class notes, taking notes as you go. Compare your reading notes to the notes you took in class.

Did you use a different system with the textbook, or the same as in class? Why? _____

_____

_____

_____

      Which notes can you understand better? Why do you think that's true?

_____

_____

_____

_____

      What did you learn from your reading notes that you want to bring to your class note-taking strategy?_____

_____

_____

## Exercise 3: Prewriting

Choose a topic you are interested in and know something about—for example, college sports, handling stress in a stressful world, our culture's emphasis on beauty and youth, or child rearing. Narrow your topic, then use the following prewriting strategies to discover what you already know about the topic and what you would need to learn if you had to write an essay about the subject for one of your classes. (If necessary, continue this prewriting exercise on a separate sheet of paper.)

    Brainstorm your ideas: _____

_____

_____

_____

_____

_____

Freewrite: _____

_____

_____

_____

_____

_____

_____

_____

_____

Ask journalists' questions: _____

_____

_____

_____

_____

_____

_____

## Exercise 4:  Writing a Thesis Statement

Write two thesis statements for each of the following topics. The first statement should try to inform the reader, while the second should try to persuade. In each case, writing a thesis statement will require that you narrow the topic:

➤ *The rising cost of a college education*
  Thesis with an informative purpose _____

  _____

  _____

  Thesis with a persuasive purpose _____

  _____

  _____

➤ *Taking care of your body and mind*
  Thesis with an informative purpose _____

  _____

  _____

Thesis with a persuasive purpose _____

_____

_____

➤ *Career choice*
Thesis with an informative purpose _____

_____

_____

Thesis with a persuasive purpose _____

_____

_____

## KEY TO SELF-EXPRESSION: DISCOVERY THROUGH JOURNAL WRITING

*To record your thoughts, use a separate journal or the lined pages at the end of the chapter.*

**Your Relationship With Words**    Some people love to work with words—writing them, reading them, speaking them—while others would rather do anything else. Do you enjoy writing in school, or does writing intimidate you? Do you write anything outside of school? Discuss how you feel about writing.

Name _____ Date _____

Journal Entry

Prentice Hall

Name _____ Date _____

## Journal Entry

Prentice Hall

# LISTENING, MEMORY, AND TEST TAKING:

## Taking In, Retaining, and Demonstrating Knowledge

College exposes you daily to facts, opinions, and ideas. It is up to you to take in, retain, and demonstrate knowledge of what you learn, for use in or out of school. You can accomplish these goals through active listening, focused use of your memory skills, and thorough preparation for taking tests.

Listening is one of the primary ways of taking in information. Memory skills can help you retain what you've listened to so that you can recall it for a paper, a discussion, or a test. After you've listened and remembered, test taking is your key to demonstrating what you have learned to your instructor or others. In this chapter, you will learn strategies to improve your ability to take in, remember and show knowledge of what you have learned.

In this chapter, you will explore answers to the following questions:

➤ How can you become a better listener?

➤ How does memory work?

➤ How can you improve your memory?

➤ How can tape recorders help you listen, remember, and study?

➤ How can preparation help improve test scores?

➤ What strategies can help you succeed on tests?

➤ How can you learn from test mistakes?

# HOW CAN YOU BECOME A BETTER LISTENER?

The act of hearing isn't quite the same as the act of listening. While *hearing* refers to sensing spoken messages from their source, *listening* involves a complex process of communication. Successful listening results in the speaker's intended message reaching the listener. In school, and at home, poor listening results in communication breakdowns and mistakes, and skilled listening promotes progress and success.

Ralph G. Nichols, a pioneer in listening research, studied 200 students at the University of Minnesota over a nine-month period. His findings, summarized in Table 7-1, demonstrate that effective listening depends as much on a positive attitude as on specific skills.[1]

Listening is a teachable—and learnable—skill. Improving your learning skills involves managing listening challenges and becoming an active listener. Although becoming a better listener will help in every class, it is especially important in subject areas that are difficult for you.

## Manage Listening Challenges

Classic studies have shown that immediately after listening, students are likely to recall only half of what was said. This is partly due to particular listening challenges, including divided attention and distractions, the tendency to shut out the message, the inclination to rush to judgment, and partial hearing loss or learning disabilities.[2] To help create a positive listening environment, in both your mind and your surroundings, explore how to manage these challenges.

### Divided Attention and Distractions

Internal and external distractions often divide your attention. *Internal distractions* include anything from hunger to headache to personal worries. Something the speaker says may also trigger a recollection that may cause your mind to drift. In contrast, *external distractions* include noises (whispering, honking horns, screaming sirens) and even excessive heat or cold. It can be hard to listen in an overheated room that is putting you to sleep.

Your goal is to reduce distractions and focus on what you're hearing. Sitting where you can see and hear clearly will help you listen well. Dress comfortably and try not to go to class hungry or thirsty.

### Shutting Out the Message

Instead of paying attention to everything the speaker says, many students fall into

| TABLE 7-1 | WHAT HELPS AND HINDERS LISTENING |
|---|---|
| **LISTENING IS HELPED BY ...** | **LISTENING IS HINDERED BY ...** |
| ...making a conscious decision to work at listening; viewing difficult material as a listening challenge. | ...caring little about the listening process; tuning out difficult material. |
| ...fighting distractions through intense concentration. | ...refusing to listen at the first distraction. |
| ...continuing to listen when a subject is difficult or dry, in the hope that one might learn something interesting. | ...giving up as soon as one loses interest. |
| ...withholding judgment until hearing everything. | ...becoming preoccupied with a response as soon as a speaker makes a controversial statement. |
| ...focusing on the speaker's theme by recognizing organizational patterns, transitional language, and summary statements. | ...getting sidetracked by unimportant details. |
| ...adapting note taking style to the unique style and organization of the speaker. | ...always taking notes in outline form, even when a speaker is poorly organized, leading to frustration. |
| ...pushing past negative emotional responses and forcing oneself to continue to listen. | ...letting an initial emotional response shut off continued listening. |
| ...using excess thinking time to evaluate, summarize, and question what one just heard and anticipating what will come next. | ...thinking about other things and, as a result, missing much of the message. |

the trap of focusing on specific points and shutting out the rest of the message. Creating a positive listening environment includes accepting responsibility for listening. While the instructor communicates information to you, he or she cannot force you to listen. You are responsible for taking in that information. Instructors often cover material from outside the textbook during class and then test on that material. If you work to take in the whole message in class, you will be able to read over your notes later and think critically about what is most important.

## The Rush to Judgment

People tend to stop listening when they hear something they don't like. If you rush to judge what you've heard, your focus turns to your personal reaction rather than the content of the speaker's message. Judgments also involve reactions to the speakers themselves. If you do not like your instructors or if you have preconceived notions about their ideas or cultural background, you may decide that their words have little value.

Work to recognize and control your judgments. Being aware of what you tend to judge will help you avoid putting up a barrier against incoming messages that clash with your opinions or feelings. Try to see education as a continuing search for evidence, regardless of whether it supports or negates your point of view.

### Partial Hearing Loss and Learning Disabilities

Good listening techniques don't solve every listening problem. Students who have a partial hearing loss have a physical explanation for why listening is difficult. If you have some level of hearing loss, seek out special services that can help you listen in class. You may require special equipment or might benefit from tutoring. You may be able to arrange to meet with your instructor outside of class to clarify your notes.

Other disabilities, such as Attention Deficit Disorder (ADD) or a problem with processing heard language, can cause difficulties with both focusing on and understanding that which is heard. People with such disabilities have varied ability to compensate for and overcome them. If you have a disability, don't blame yourself for having trouble listening. Your counseling center, student health center, advisor, and instructors should be able to give you particular assistance in working through your challenges.

## HOW DOES MEMORY WORK?

You need an effective memory in order to use the knowledge you take in throughout your life. Human memory works like a computer. Both have essentially the same purpose: to encode, store, and retrieve information.

During the *encoding stage*, information is changed into usable form. On a computer, this occurs when keyboard entries are transformed into electronic symbols and stored on a disk. In the brain, sensory information becomes impulses that the central nervous system reads and codes. You are encoding, for example, when you study a list of chemistry formulas.

During the *storage stage* information is held in memory (the mind's version of a computer hard drive) for later use. In this example, after you complete your studying of the formulas, your mind stores them until you need to use them.

During the *retrieval stage*, memories are recovered from storage by recall, just as a saved computer program is called up by name and used again. In this example, your mind would retrieve the chemistry formulas when you had to take a test or solve a problem.

Memories are stored in three different storage banks. The first, called *sensory memory*, is an exact copy of what you see and hear, and lasts for a second or less. Certain information is then selected from sensory memory and moves into *short-term memory*, a temporary information storehouse that lasts no more than 10 to 20 seconds. You are consciously aware of material in your short-term memory. While unimportant information is quickly dumped, important information is transferred to *long-term memory*—the mind's more permanent storehouse.

Having information in long-term memory does not mean that you will be able to recall it when needed. Particular techniques can help you improve your recall.

# HOW CAN YOU IMPROVE YOUR MEMORY?

Your accounting instructor is giving a test tomorrow on the use of book-keeping programs. You feel confident, since you spent hours last week memorizing the material. Unfortunately, by the time you take the test, you may remember very little. That's because most forgetting occurs within minutes after memorization.

In a classic study conducted in 1885, researcher Herman Ebbinghaus memorized a list of meaningless three-letter words such as CEF and LAZ. Within one short hour he measured that he had forgotten more than 50 percent of what he learned. After two days, he knew fewer than 30 percent. Although his recall of the syllables remained fairly stable after that, the experiment shows how fragile memory can be, even when you take the time and energy to memorize information.[3]

People who have superior memories may have an inborn talent for remembering. More often, though, they have mastered techniques for improving recall. Remember that techniques aren't a cure-all for memory difficulties, especially for those who may have disabilities such as ADD. If you have a disability, the following memory techniques may help you but may not be enough. Seek specific assistance if you consistently have trouble remembering.

**THE FAR SIDE** By GARY LARSON

"Mr. Osborne, may I be excused? My brain is full."

*Source:* The Far Side © 1986 Far Works, Inc. Used by permission of Universal Press Syndicate. All rights reserved.

## Memory Improvement Strategies

As a student, your job is to understand, learn, and remember information, from general concepts to specific details. The following suggestions will help improve your recall.

### Develop a Will to Remember

Why can you remember the lyrics to dozens of popular songs but not the functions of the pancreas? Perhaps this is because you want to remember them, you connect them with a visual image, or you have an emotional tie to them. To achieve the same results at school or on the job, tell yourself that what you are learning is important and that you need to remember it. Saying these words out loud can help you begin the active, positive process of memory improvement.

## Understand What You Memorize

Make sure that everything you want to remember makes sense. Something that has meaning is easier to recall than something that is gibberish. This basic principle applies to everything you study—from biology and astronomy to history and English literature.

## Recite, Rehearse, and Write

When you *recite* material, you repeat it aloud in order to remember it. Reciting helps you retrieve information as you learn it and is a crucial step in studying (see Chapter 5). *Rehearsing* is similar to reciting, but is done in silence, in your mind. It involves the process of repeating, summarizing, and associating information with other information. *Writing* is rehearsing on paper. The act of writing solidifies the information in your memory.

## Separate Main Points From Unimportant Details

If you use critical-thinking skills to select and focus on the most important information, you can avoid overloading your mind with extra clutter. To focus on key points, highlight only the most important information in your texts and write notes in the margins about central ideas. When you review your lecture notes, highlight or rewrite the most important information to remember.

## Study During Short but Frequent Sessions

Research shows that you can improve your chances of remembering material if you learn it more than once. To get the most out of your study sessions, spread them over time. A pattern of short sessions followed by brief periods of rest is more effective than continual studying with little or no rest. Even though you may feel as though you accomplish a lot by studying for an hour without a break, you'll probably remember more from three 20-minute sessions. Try sandwiching study time into breaks in your schedule, such as when you have time between classes.

## Separate Material Into Manageable Sections

When material is short and easy to understand, studying it start to finish may work. For longer material, you may benefit from dividing it into logical sections, mastering each section, putting all the sections together, and then testing your memory of all the material. Actors take this approach when learning the lines of a play, and it can work just as well for students.

## Use Visual Aids

Any kind of visual representation of study material can help you remember. You may want to convert material into a think link or outline. Write material in any visual shape that helps you recall it and link it to other information.

Flashcards are a great visual memory tool. They give you short, repeated review sessions that provide immediate feedback. Make them from 3-by-5-inch index cards. Use the front of the card to write a word, idea, or phrase

**FIGURE 7-2**  FLASH CARDS HELP YOU MEMORIZE IMPORTANT FACTS

**CARD 1**

THEORY

FRONT

—DEFINITION: Explanation for a phenomenon based on careful and precise observations

—Part of the scientific method

—Leads to hypotheses

BACK

**CARD 2**

HYPOTHESIS

FRONT

—Prediction about future behavior that is derived from observations and theories

—Methods for testing hypotheses: case studies, naturalistic observations, and experiments

BACK

you want to remember. Use the back side for a definition, explanation, and other key facts. Figure 7-2 shows two flashcards for studying psychology.

Here are some additional suggestions for making the most of your flash cards:

➤ *Use the cards as a self-test.* Divide the cards into two piles: the material you know and the material you are learning. You may want to use rubber bands to separate the piles.

➤ *Carry the cards with you and review them frequently.* You'll learn the most if you start using cards early in the course, well ahead of exam time.

➤ *Shuffle the cards and learn information in various orders.* This will help avoid putting too much focus on some information and not enough on others.

➤ *Test yourself in both directions.* First, look at the terms or ideas and provide definitions or explanations. Then turn the cards over and reverse the process.

# Mnemonic Devices

Certain show business performers entertain their audiences by remembering the names of 100 strangers or flawlessly repeating 30 ten-digit phone numbers. These performers probably have superior memories, but genetics alone can't produce these results. They also rely on memory techniques, known as mnemonic devices (pronounced neh MAHN ick) to help them.

Mnemonic devices work by connecting information you are trying to learn with simpler information or information that is familiar. Instead of learning new facts by rote (repetitive practice), associations give you a hook on which to hang these facts and retrieve them. Mnemonic devices make information familiar and meaningful through unusual, unforgettable mental associations and visual pictures.

Here's an example to prove the power of mnemonics. Suppose you want to remember the names of the first six presidents of the United States. The first letters of their last names—Washington, Adams, Jefferson, Madison, Monroe, and Adams—together read W A J M M A. To remember them, you might add an "e" after the "J" and create a short nonsense word, "wajemma." To remember their first names—George, John, Thomas, James, James, and John—you might set the names to the tune of "Happy Birthday" or any musical tune that you know.

Visual images and acronyms are a few of the more widely used kinds of mnemonic devices. Apply them to your own memory challenges.

## Create Visual Images and Associations

Visual images are easier to remember than images that rely on words alone. In fact, communication through visual images goes back to the prehistoric era, when people made drawings that still exist on cave walls. It's no accident that the phrase "a picture is worth a thousand words" is so familiar. The best mental pictures often involve colors, three-dimensional images, action scenes, and disproportionate, funny, or ridiculous images.

Especially for visual learners, turning information into mental pictures helps improve memory. To remember that the Spanish artist Picasso painted "The Three Women," you might imagine the women in a circle dancing to a Spanish song with a pig and a donkey (pig-asso). Don't reject outlandish images—as long as they help you.

## Create Acronyms

Another helpful association method involves the use of the acronym. The acronym "Roy G. Biv" often helps students remember the colors of the spectrum. Roy G. Biv stands for **R**ed, **O**range, **Y**ellow, **G**reen, **B**lue, **I**ndigo, **V**iolet. In history, you can remember the big-three Allies during World War II—Britain, America, and Russia—with the acronym BAR.

When you can't create a name like Roy G. Biv, create an acronym from an entire sentence, in which the first letter of each word in the sentence stands for the first letter of each memorized term. When science students want to remember the list of planets in order of their distance from the sun, they learn the sentence: <u>M</u>y <u>v</u>ery <u>e</u>legant <u>m</u>other just <u>s</u>erved <u>u</u>s <u>n</u>ine <u>p</u>ickles. (Mercury, Venus, Earth, Mars, Jupiter, Saturn, Uranus, Neptune, and Pluto.)

---

**Mnemonic devices,** Memory techniques that involve associating new information with information you already know.

> "The true art of memory is the art of attention."
> Samuel Johnson

**Acronym,** A word formed from the first letters of a series of words, created in order to help you remember the series.

Improving your memory requires energy, time, and work. In school, it also helps to master PQ3R, the textbook study technique that was introduced in Chapter 5. By going through the steps in PQ3R and using the specific memory techniques described in this chapter, you will be able to learn more in less time—and remember what you learn long after exams are over.

# HOW CAN TAPE RECORDERS HELP YOU LISTEN, REMEMBER, AND STUDY?

The selective use of a tape recorder can provide helpful backup to your listening and memory skills and to your study materials. It's important, though, not to let tape recording substitute for active participation. Not all students like to use tape recorders, but if you choose to do so, here are some guidelines and a discussion of potential effects.

## Guidelines for Using Tape Recorders

**Ask the instructor whether he or she permits tape recorders in class.**    Some instructors don't mind, while others don't allow students to use them.

**Use a small, portable tape recorder.**    Sit near the front for the best possible recording.

**Participate actively in class.**    Take notes just as you would if the tape recorder were not there.

**Use tape recorders to make study tapes.**    Questions on tape can be like audio flashcards. One way to do it is to record study questions, leaving 10–15 seconds between questions for you to answer out loud. Recording the correct answer after the pause will give you immediate feedback. For example, part of a recording for a writing class might say, "The three elements of effective writing are . . . (10–15 seconds) . . . topic, audience, and purpose."

## Potential Positive Effects of Using Tape Recorders

➤ You can listen to an important portion of the lecture over and over again.

➤ You can supplement or clarify sections of the lecture that confused you or that you missed.

➤ Tape recordings can provide additional study materials to listen to when you exercise or drive in your car.

➤ Tape recordings can help study groups reconcile conflicting notes.

➤ If you miss class, you might be able to have a friend record the lecture for you.

Potential Negative Effects of Using Tape Recorders

➤ You may tend to listen less in class.

➤ You may take fewer notes, figuring that you will rely on your tape.

➤ It may be time-consuming. When you attend a lecture in order to record it and then listen to the entire recording, you have taken twice as much time out of your schedule.

➤ If your tape recorder malfunctions or the recording is hard to hear, you may end up with very little study material, especially if your notes are sparse.

Think critically about whether using a tape recorder is a good idea for you. If you choose to try it, let the tape recorder be an additional resource for you instead of a replacement for your active participation and skills. Tape-recorded lectures and study tapes are just one study resource you can use in preparation for the tests that will often come your way.

# HOW CAN PREPARATION HELP IMPROVE TEST SCORES?

Many people don't look forward to taking tests. If you are one of those people, try thinking of exams as preparation for life. When you volunteer, get a job, or work on your family budget, you'll have to apply what you know. This is exactly what you do when you take a test.

Like a runner who prepares for a marathon by exercising, eating right, taking practice runs, and getting enough sleep, you can take steps to master your exams. Your first step is to study until you know the material that will be on the test. Your next step is to use the following strategies to become a successful test taker: Identify test type, use specific study skills, prepare physically, and conquer test anxiety.

## Identify Test Type and Material Covered

Before you begin studying, try to determine the type of test and what it will cover:

➤ Will it be a short-answer test with true/false and multiple-choice questions, an essay test, or a combination?

➤ Will the test cover everything you studied since the semester began or will it be limited to a narrow topic?

➤ Will the test be limited to what you learned in class and in the text or will it also cover outside readings?

Your instructors may answer these questions for you. Even though they may not tell you the specific questions that will be on the test, they might let you know what blocks of information will be covered and the question format. Some instructors may even drop hints throughout the semester about possible test questions. While some comments are direct ("I might ask a question on the subject of _____ on your next exam"), other clues are subtle. For example, when instructors repeat an idea or when they express personal interest in a topic ("One of my favorite theories is . . . "), they are letting you know that the material may be on the test.

Here are a few other strategies for predicting what may be on a test:

**Use PQ3R to identify important ideas and facts.**    Often, the questions you write and ask yourself when you read assigned materials may be part of the test. In addition, any textbook study questions are good candidates for test material.

**If you know people who took the instructor's course before, ask them about class tests.**    Try to find out how difficult the tests are and whether the test focuses more on assigned readings or class notes. Ask about instructor preferences. If you learn that the instructor pays close attention to detail such as facts or grammar, plan your work accordingly.

**Examine old tests if instructors make them available in class or on reserve in the library.**    If you can't get copies of old tests, use clues from the class to predict test questions. After taking the first exam in the course, you will have a lot more information about what to expect in the future.

## Use Specific Study Skills

Certain study skills are especially useful for test taking. They include choosing study materials, setting a study schedule, critical thinking, and taking a pretest.

### Choose Study Materials

Once you have identified as much as you can about the subject matter of the test, choose the materials that contain the information you need to study. You can save yourself time by making sure that you aren't studying anything you don't need to. Go through your notes, your texts, any primary source materials that were assigned, and any handouts from your instructor. Set aside any materials you don't need so they don't take up your valuable time.

### Set a Study Schedule

Use your time-management skills to set a schedule that will help you feel as prepared as you can be. Consider all the relevant factors—the materials you need to study, how many days or weeks until the test date, and how much time you can study each day. If you establish your schedule ahead of time and write it in your date book, you will be much more likely to follow it.

Schedules will vary widely according to situation. For example, if you have only three days before the test and no other obligations during that time, you might set two 2-hour study sessions for yourself during each day. On the other hand, if you have two weeks before a test date, classes during the day, and work three nights a week, you might spread out your study sessions over the nights you have off work during those two weeks.

### Prepare Through Critical Thinking

Using the techniques from Chapter 4, approach your test preparation critically, working to understand rather than just to pass the test by repeating facts. As you study, try to connect ideas to examples, analyze causes and effects, establish truth, and look at issues from different perspectives. Although it takes work, critical thinking will promote a greater understanding of the subject and probably a higher grade on the exam. Using critical thinking is especially important for essay tests. Prepare by identifying potential essay questions and writing your responses.

### Take a Pretest

Use questions from the ends of textbook chapters to create your own pretest. Choose questions that are likely to be covered on the test, then answer them under testlike conditions—in quiet, with no books or notes to help you, and with a clock telling you when to quit. Try to duplicate the conditions of the actual test. If your course doesn't have an assigned text, develop questions from your notes and from assigned outside readings.

## Prepare Physically

When taking a test, you often need to work efficiently under time pressure. If your body is tired or under stress, you will probably not think as clearly or perform as well. If you can, avoid pulling an all-nighter. Get some sleep so that you can wake up rested and alert. If you are one of the many who press the snooze button in their sleep, try setting two alarm clocks and placing them across the room from your bed. That way you'll be more likely to get to your test on time.

Eating right is also important. Sugar-laden snacks will bring your energy up only to send it crashing back down much too soon. Similarly, too much caffeine can add to your tension and make it difficult to focus. Eating nothing will leave you drained, but too much food can make you want to take a nap. The best advice is to eat a light, well-balanced meal before a test. When time is short, grab a quick-energy snack such as a banana, some orange juice, or a granola bar.

## Conquer Test Anxiety

A certain amount of stress can be a good thing. Your body is on alert, and your energy motivates you to do your best. For many students, however, the time before and during an exam brings a feeling of near-panic known as *test anxiety*. Described as a bad case of nerves that makes it hard to think or remember, test anxiety can make your life miserable and affect how you do on tests. When anxiety blocks performance, here are some suggestions:

**Prepare so you'll feel in control.**  The more you know about what to expect on the exam, the better you'll feel. Find out what material will be covered, the format of the questions, the length of the exam, and the percentage of points assigned to each question.

## How can I prepare for exams?

### Jeff Felardeau, Selkirk College—Nelson, B.C., Adult Basic Education

I've been out of school for quite a long time, so when I returned and had to memorize material for exams, I just wasn't prepared. The labor work I was doing didn't require me to use my memorization skills. I had the most difficulty memorizing for classes like biology and any of the sciences where you have to memorize a lot of facts. I'd work hard by repeating the information over and over in my mind, but I'd only be able to recall it for a short time afterwards—long-term learning wasn't there. Whenever I'd prepare for an exam, I'd find myself in a "cram" mode because I didn't remember any of the material from class. It was like learning the material all over again.

I took a class called College Success which gave me some good study tips. They taught me things like mind-mapping, listening skills, and note-taking styles. They also taught me to use word associations and visualization to help remember the material. It's helped me improve a lot but still, I get stuck in old habits and patterns and forget to apply the methods that that will really help me improve. I know that if I don't change these old study patterns and habits, I'll hit the wall sooner or later. I can't keep using methods that served me in the past but are no longer effective for where I am today. What do you suggest?

### Miriam Kapner, New England Conservatory, Boston, MA., Junior in Oboe Performance

Even though you have a good understanding of what it takes to prepare for an exam, the key is to remain disciplined. If your mind is wandering in class and you find you're staring out the window looking at those clouds, remember that you have control of your mind. By staying focused in class you will

not have to study so much when exam time rolls around. Although we all fall victim to daydreaming, try and gain control of your mind by thinking of your goals or by using simple mind tricks. Even if the class has a very dry teacher, there are ways to keep focused. One day a friend and I sat down and figured out exactly how much each class was costing us. When we realized the amount of money we were spending for that hour, it was a real eye-opener. If I'm really having a hard time, then I make sure I ask at least two questions per class. This forces me to pay attention.

In order to memorize, you need to be able to find some order. It helps if you have a reference point to begin with and then look for certain patterns or categories. I also use mnemonic devices to help me remember. In fact, I can still remember the ones I learned in elementary school: General Electric Lights Never Dim for the first five books of the Bible and of course, Every Good Boy Does Fine for the lines in the treble clef. But mainly, whatever steps you take to improve your preparation for exams, remember that you are in control of your mind—not the other way around.

Put the test in perspective.    No matter how important it may seem, a test is only a small part of your educational experience and an even smaller part of your life. Your test grade does not reflect the kind of person you are or your ability to succeed in life.

Make a study plan.    Divide the plan into a series of small tasks. As you finish each one, you'll feel a sense of accomplishment and control.

Practice relaxation.    When you feel test anxiety coming on, take some deep breaths, close your eyes, and visualize positive mental images related to the test, like getting a good grade and finishing confidently with time to spare.

### Test Anxiety and the Returning Adult Student

If you're returning to school after a layoff of five, ten, or even twenty years, you may wonder if you can compete with younger students or if your mind is still able to learn new material. To counteract these feelings of inadequacy, focus on how your life experiences have given you skills you can use. For example, managing work and a family requires strong time management, planning, and communication skills that can help you plan your study time, juggle school responsibilities, and interact with students and instructors.

In addition, your life experiences give you examples with which you can understand ideas in your courses. For example, your relationship experiences may help you understand concepts in a psychology course; managing your finances may help you understand economics or accounting practices; and work experience may give you a context for what you learn in a business management course. If you let yourself feel positive about your knowledge and skills, you may improve your ability to achieve your goals.

# WHAT STRATEGIES CAN HELP YOU SUCCEED ON TESTS?

Even though every test is different, there are general strategies that will help you handle almost all tests, including short-answer and essay exams.

## Write Down Key Facts

Before you even look at the test, write down any key information—including formulas, rules, and definitions—that you studied recently or even right before you entered the test room. Use the back of the question sheet or a piece of scrap paper for your notes (make sure it is clear to your instructor that this scrap paper didn't come into the test room already filled in!). Recording this information right at the start will make forgetting less likely.

## Begin With an Overview of the Exam

Even though exam time is precious, spend a few minutes at the start of the test to get a sense of the kinds of questions you'll be answering, what kind of thinking they require, the number of questions in each section, and the point value of each section. Use this information to schedule the time you spend on each section. For example, if a two-hour test is divided into two sections of equal point value—an essay section with four questions and a short-answer section with sixty questions—you can spend an hour on the essays (fifteen minutes per question) and an hour on the short-answer section (one minute per question).

As you make your calculations, think about the level of difficulty of each section. If you think you can handle the short-answer questions in less than an hour and that you'll need more time with the essays, rebudget your time in a way that works for you.

## Know the Ground Rules

A few basic rules apply to any test. Following them will give you the advantage.

**Read test directions.**   While a test made up of 100 true/false questions and one essay may look straightforward, the directions may tell you to answer eighty, or that the essay is a optional bonus. Some questions or sections may be weighted more heavily than others. Try circling or underlining key words and numbers that remind you of the directions.

**Begin with the parts or questions that seem easiest to you.**   Starting with what you know best can boost your confidence and help you save time to spend on the harder parts.

**Watch the clock.**   Keep track of how much time is left and how you are progressing. You may want to plan your time on a scrap piece of paper, especially if you have one or more essays to write. Wear a watch or bring a small clock with you to the test room. A wall clock may be broken, or there may be no clock at all! Also, take your time. Rushing is almost always a mistake, even if you feel you've done well. Stay till the end so you can refine and check your work.

**Master the art of intelligent guessing.**   When you are unsure of an answer, you can leave it blank or you can guess. In most cases, guessing will benefit you. First eliminate all the answers you know—or believe—are wrong. Try to narrow your choices to two possible answers; then, choose the one that makes more sense to you. When you recheck your work, decide if you would make the same guesses again, making sure there isn't a qualifier or fact that you hadn't noticed before.

**Qualifier,**
A word, such as *always*, *never*, or *often*, that changes the meaning of another word or word group.

**Follow directions on machine-scored tests.**   Machine-scored tests require that you use a special pencil to fill in a small box on a computerized answer sheet. Use the right pencil (usually a  number 2) and mark your answer in the correct space. Neatness counts on these tests, because the computer can misread stray pencil marks or partially erased answers. Periodically, check the answer number against the question number to make sure they match. One question skipped can cause every answer following it to be marked incorrect.

## Use Critical Thinking To Avoid Errors

When the pressure of a test makes you nervous, critical thinking can help you work through each question thoroughly and avoid errors. Following are some critical-thinking strategies to use during a test.

**Recall facts, procedures, rules, and formulas.** You base your answers on the information you recall. Think carefully to make sure you recall it accurately.

**Think about similarities.** If you don't know how to attack a question or problem, consider any similar questions or problems that you have worked on in class or while studying.

**Notice differences.** Especially with objective questions, items that seem different from what you have studied may indicate answers you can eliminate.

**Think through causes and effects.** For a numerical problem, think through how you plan to solve it and see if the answer—the effect of your plan—makes sense. For an essay question that asks you to analyze a condition or situation, consider both what caused it and what effects it has.

**Find the best idea to match the example or examples given.** For a numerical problem, decide what formula (idea) best applies to the example or examples (the data of the problem). For an essay question, decide what idea applies to, or links, the examples given.

**Support ideas with examples.** When you put forth an idea in an answer to an essay question, be sure to back up your idea with an adequate number of examples that fit.

**Evaluate each test question.** In your initial approach to any question, evaluate what kinds of thinking will best help you solve it. For example, essay questions often require cause-and-effect and idea-to-example thinking, while objective questions often benefit from thinking through similarities and differences.

The general strategies you have just explored also can help you address specific types of test questions.

## Master Different Types of Test Questions

Although the goal of all test questions is to discover how much you know about a subject, every question type has its own way of asking what you know. Objective questions, such as multiple choice or true/false, test your ability to recall, compare, and contrast information and to choose the right answer from among several choices. Subjective questions, usually essay questions, demand the same information recall but ask that you analyze the mind actions and thinking processes required, then organize, draft, and

**Objective questions,** Short-answer questions that test your ability to recall, compare, and contrast information and to choose the right answer from a limited number of choices.

refine a written response. The following guidelines will help you choose the best answers to both types of questions.

## Multiple-Choice Questions

Multiple-choice questions are the most popular type on standardized tests. The following strategies can help you answer these questions:

**Read the directions carefully.** While most test items ask for a single correct answer, some give you the option of marking several choices that are correct.

**First read each question thoroughly.** Then look at the choices and try to answer the question.

**Underline key words and phrases in the question.** If the question is complicated, try to break it down into small sections that are easy to understand.

**Pay special attention to qualifiers such as *only, except*, etc.** For example, negative words in a question can confuse your understanding of what the question asks ("Which of the following is *not . . .*").

**If you don't know the answer, eliminate those answers that you know or suspect are wrong.** Your goal is to narrow down your choices. Here are some questions to ask:

> ➤ Is the choice accurate in its own terms? If there's an error in the choice—for example, a term that is incorrectly defined—the answer is wrong.

> ➤ Is the choice relevant? An answer may be accurate, but it may not relate to the essence of the question.

> ➤ Are there any qualifiers, such as *always, never, all, none*, or *every*? Qualifiers make it easy to find an exception that makes a choice incorrect. For example, the statement that "children *always* begin talking before the age of two" can be eliminated as an answer to the question, "When do children generally start to talk?"

> ➤ Do the choices give you any clues? Does a puzzling word remind you of a word you know? If you don't know a word, does any part of the word (prefix, suffix, or root) seem familiar to you?

**Look for patterns that may lead to the right answer, then use intelligent guessing.** Test-taking experts have found patterns in multiple-choice questions that may help you get a better grade. Here is their advice:

> ➤ Consider the possibility that a choice that is more *general* than the others is the right answer.

> ➤ Look for a choice that has a middle value in a range (the range can be from small to large, from old to recent). This choice may be the right answer.

**Subjective questions.** Essay questions that require you to express your answer in terms of your own personal knowledge and perspective.

"*A little knowledge that acts is worth infinitely more than much knowledge that is idle.*"

Kahlil Gibran

➤ Look for two choices with similar meanings. One of these answers is probably correct.

**Make sure you read every word of every answer.** Instructors have been known to include answers that are right except for a single word.

**When questions are keyed to a long reading passage, read the questions first.** This will help you focus on the information you need to answer the questions.

Here are some examples of the kinds of multiple-choice questions you might encounter in an Introduction to Psychology course[4] (the correct answer follows each question):

---

1. Arnold is at the company party and has had too much to drink. He releases all of his pent-up aggression by yelling at his boss, who promptly fires him. Arnold normally would not have yelled at his boss, but after drinking heavily he yelled because_____.

   a. parties are places where employees are supposed to be able to "loosen up"

   b. alcohol is a stimulant

   c. alcohol makes people less concerned with the negative consequences of their behavior

   d. alcohol inhibits brain centers that control the perception of loudness

   *(The correct answer is C)*

2. Which of the following has not been shown to be a probable cause of or influence in the development of alcoholism in our society?

   a. intelligence          c. personality

   b. culture               d. genetic vulnerability

   *(The correct answer is A)*

---

## True/False Questions

True/false questions test your knowledge of facts and concepts. Read them carefully to evaluate what they truly say. Try to take these questions at face value without searching for hidden meaning. If you're truly stumped, guess (unless you're penalized for wrong answers).

Look for qualifiers in true/false questions—such as *all, only, always, because, generally, usually*, and *sometimes*—that can turn a statement that would otherwise be true into one that is false, or vice versa. For example, "The grammar rule, 'I before E except after C,' is *always* true" is *false*, whereas "The grammar rule, 'I before E except after C,' is *usually* true," is *true*. The qualifier makes the difference. Here are some examples of the kinds of true/false questions you might encounter in an Introduction to Psychology course.

Are the following questions true or false?

1. Alcohol use is always related to increases in hostility, aggression, violence, and abusive behavior. (False)
2. Marijuana is harmless. (False)
3. Simply expecting a drug to produce an effect is often enough to produce the effect. (True)

## Essay Questions

An essay question allows you to use writing to demonstrate your knowledge and express your views on a topic. Start by reading the questions and deciding which to tackle (sometimes there's a choice). Then focus on what each question is asking, the mind actions you will have to use, and the writing directions. Read the question carefully and do everything you are asked to do. Some essay questions may contain more than one part.

Watch for certain action verbs that can help you figure out what to do. Figure 7-3 on the next page, explains some words commonly used in essay questions. Underline these words as you read any essay question and use them as a guide.

Next, budget your time and begin to plan. Create an informal outline or think link to map your ideas and indicate examples you plan to cite to support those ideas. Avoid spending too much time on introductions or flowery prose. Start with a thesis idea or statement that states in a broad way what your essay will say (see Chapter 6 for a discussion of thesis statements). As you continue to write your first paragraph, introduce the essay's points, which may be sub-ideas, causes and effects, or examples. Wrap it up with a concise conclusion.

Use clear, simple language in your essay. Support your ideas with examples, and look back at your outline to make sure you are covering everything. Try to write legibly. If your instructor can't read your ideas, it doesn't matter how good they are. If your handwriting is messy, try printing, skipping every other line, or writing on only one side of the paper.

Do your best to save time to reread and revise your essay after you finish getting your ideas down on paper. Look for ideas you left out and sentences that might confuse the reader. Check for mistakes in grammar, spelling, punctuation, and usage. No matter what subject you are writing about, having a command of these factors will make your work all the more complete and impressive.

Here are some examples of essay questions you might encounter in your Introduction to Psychology course. In each case, notice the action verbs from Figure 7-3.

1. Summarize the theories and research on the causes and effects of daydreaming. Discuss the possible uses for daydreaming in a healthy individual.
2. Describe the physical and psychological effects of alcohol and the problems associated with its use.

*FIGURE 7-3*   COMMON ACTION VERBS ON ESSAY TESTS

**Analyze**—Break into parts and discuss each part separately.

**Compare**—Explain similarities and differences.

**Contrast**—Distinguish between items being compared by focusing on differences.

**Criticize**—Evaluate the positive and negative effects of what is being discussed.

**Define**—State the essential quality or meaning. Give the common idea.

**Describe**—Visualize and give information that paints a complete picture.

**Discuss**—Examine in a complete and detailed way, usually by connecting ideas to examples.

**Enumerate/List/Identify**—Recall and specify items in the form of a list.

**Explain**—Make the meaning of something clear, often by making analogies or giving examples.

**Evaluate**—Give your opinion about the value or worth of something, usually by weighing positive and negative effects, and justify your conclusion.

**ILLUSTRATE**—Supply examples.

**Interpret**—Explain your personal view of facts and ideas and how they relate to one another.

**OUTLINE**—Organize and present the sub-ideas or main examples of an idea.

**PROVE**—Use evidence and argument to show that something is true, usually by showing cause and effect or giving examples that fit the idea to be proven.

**Review**—Provide an overview of ideas and establish their merits and features.

**State**—Explain clearly, simply, and concisely, being sure that each word gives the image you want.

**SUMMARIZE**—Give the important ideas in brief.

**Trace**—Present a history of the way something developed, often by showing cause and effect.

## HOW CAN YOU LEARN FROM TEST MISTAKES?

The purpose of a test is to see how much you know, not merely to achieve a grade. The knowledge that comes from attending class and studying should allow you to correctly answer test questions. Knowledge also comes when you learn from your mistakes. If you don't learn from what you get wrong on a test, you are likely to repeat the same mistake again on another test and in life. Learn from test mistakes just as you learn from mistakes in your personal and business life.

Try to identify patterns in your mistakes by looking for:

➤ *careless errors*—In your rush to complete the exam, did you misread the question or directions, blacken the wrong box, skip a question, or use illegible handwriting?

➤ *conceptual or factual errors*—Did you misunderstand a concept or never learn it in the first place? Did you fail to master certain facts? Did you skip part of the assigned text or miss important classes in which ideas were covered?

You may want to rework the questions you got wrong. Based on the feedback from your instructor, try rewriting an essay, recalculating a math problem, or redoing the questions that follow a reading selection. As frustrating as they are, remember that mistakes show that you are human, and they can help you learn. If you see patterns of careless errors, promise yourself that next time you'll try to budget enough time to double-check your work. If you pick up conceptual and factual errors, rededicate yourself to better preparation.

When you fail a test, don't throw it away. First, take comfort in the fact that a lot of students have been in your shoes and that you are likely to improve your performance. Then recommit to the process by reviewing and analyzing your errors. Be sure you understand why you failed. You may want to ask for an explanation from your instructor. Finally, develop a plan to really learn the material if you didn't understand it in the first place.

In Sanskrit, the written language of India and other Hindu countries, the characters above read *sem ma yeng chik*, meaning, "do not be distracted." This advice can refer to focus for a task or job at hand, the concentration required to critically think and talk through a problem, or the mental discipline of meditation.

Think of this concept as you strive to improve your listening and memory techniques. Focus on the task, the person, or the idea at hand. Try not to be distracted by other thoughts, other people's notions of what you should be doing, or any negative messages. Be present in the moment to truly hear and remember what is happening around you. Do not be distracted.

# Chapter 7: Applications

Name _____          Date _____

 Key Into Your Life: Opportunities to Apply What You Learn

## Exercise 1: Optimum Listening Conditions

➤ Describe a recent classroom situation in which you had an easy time listening to the instructor:

Where are you? _____

What is the instructor discussing? _____

Is it a straight lecture or is there give-and-take between instructor and students? _____

_____

What is your state of mind? (List factors that might affect your ability to listen.) _____

_____

_____

_____

Are there any external barriers to communication? If yes, what are they, and how do they affect your concentration? _____

_____

_____

➤ Now describe a situation where you have found it more difficult to listen.

Where are you? _____

What is the instructor discussing? _____

Is it a straight lecture or is there give-and-take between instructor and students? _____

_____

What is your state of mind? (List factors that might affect your ability to listen.) _____

_____

_____

_____

Are there any external barriers to communication? If yes, what are they, and how do they affect your concentration? _____

_____

_____

➤ Examine the two situations. Based on your descriptions, name three conditions that are crucial for you to listen effectively.

1. _____

2. _____

3. _____

What steps can you take to recreate these conditions in more difficult situations like the second one you described? _____

_____

_____

## Exercise 2: Create a Mnemonic Device

Look back at all the memory principles examined in this chapter. Using what you learned about mnemonic devices, create a mnemonic that allows you to remember these memory principles quickly. You can create a mental picture or an acronym. If you are using a mental picture, describe it here; if you are using an acronym, write it and then indicate what each letter stands for.

_____

_____

_____

_____

Think of other situations in which you used a mnemonic device to remember something. What was the device? How effective was it in helping you remember the information?

_____

_____

_____

_____

_____

### Exercise 3: Learning From Your Mistakes

For this exercise, use an exam on which you made one or more mistakes.

➤ Why do you think you answered the question(s) incorrectly? _____

_____

_____

➤ Did any qualifying terms, such as *always, sometimes, never, often, occasionally, only, no* and *not,* make the question(s) more difficult or confusing? What steps could you have taken to clarify the meaning?

_____

_____

_____

➤ Did you try to guess the correct answer? If so, why do you think you made the wrong choice?_____

_____

_____

_____

➤ Did you feel rushed? If you had had more time, do you think you would have gotten the right answer(s)? What could you have done to budget your time more effectively?

_____

_____

_____

➤ If an essay question was a problem, what do you think went wrong? What will you do differently the next time you face an essay question on a test?

_____

_____

_____

_____

_____

## KEY TO SELF EXPRESSION: DISCOVERY THROUGH JOURNAL WRITING

*To record your thoughts, use a separate journal or the lined page at the end of the chapter.*

Talk about how you feel about tests and how you generally perform when you take them.

As you walk into a room for a test, does your heart race or your mind go blank? Do you feel apprehensive? Does your performance on tests accurately reflect what you know or do your tests scores fall short of your knowledge? If there is a gap between your knowledge and your scores, why do you think this gap exists? What can you do to work through any test anxiety you have?

Name _____ Date _____

## Journal Entry

# RELATING TO OTHERS:
## Appreciating Your Diverse World

The greater part of your waking life involves interaction with people—family and friends, peers, fellow students, co-workers, instructors, and many more. When you put energy into your relationships and open the lines of communication, you can receive much in return. Having a strong network of relationships can help you grow and progress toward your goals.

This chapter will explore the issues of diversity that can hinder or help how you perceive others and relate to them. You will also explore communication styles, personal relationships, and the roles you can play in groups and on teams. Finally, you will read about various kinds of conflict and criticism, examining how to handle them so they benefit you instead of setting you back.

In this chapter, you will explore answers to the following questions:

➤ How can you understand and accept others?

➤ How can you express yourself effectively?

➤ How do your personal relationships define you?

➤ How can you handle conflict and criticism?

➤ What role do you play in groups?

# HOW CAN YOU UNDERSTAND AND ACCEPT OTHERS?

Human interaction is an essential element of life. In a diverse world, many people are different from what you are familiar with and perceive as "normal." In this section you will explore diversity in your world, the positive effects of accepting diversity, and how to overcome barriers to understanding. The first requirements for dealing with differences are an open mind and a willingness to learn.

## Diversity in Your World

For centuries, travel to different countries was seen as part of a complete education. Edith Wharton, a nineteenth-century author, wrote a story called "False Dawn" in which a character named Mr. Raycie recommends travel to his son: "A young man, in my opinion, before setting up for himself, must see the world; form his taste; fortify his judgment. He must study the most famous monuments, examine the organization of foreign societies, and the habits and customs of those older civilizations . . . I believe he will be able to learn much."[1] When cultures were so separated, learning about differences was best accomplished through travel.

Today, although traveling is still a valuable way to learn, different places and people often come to you. More and more, diversity is part of your community, on your television, on your Internet browser, at your school, in your workplace, and in your family. It used to be that most people lived in societies with others who seemed very similar to them. Now, differences are often woven into everyday life.

You may encounter examples of diversity like these:

➤ Communities with people from different stages of life

➤ Co-workers who represent a variety of ethnic origins

➤ Classmates who speak a number of different languages

➤ Social situations featuring people from various cultures, religions, and sexual orientations

➤ Individuals who marry a person or adopt a child from a different racial or religious background

➤ Diverse restaurants, services, and businesses in the community

➤ Neighborhoods with immigrants from a variety of social-class backgrounds

➤ Different lifestyles as reflected in books, magazines and newspapers, television, movies, music, the Internet, and other forms of popular culture

➤ People in the workplace who have a variety of disabilities—some more obvious than others

Each person has a choice about how to relate to others—or *whether* to relate to them. No one can force you to interact with any other person, or

**Diversity,**
The variety that occurs in every aspect of humanity, involving both visible and invisible characteristics.

to adopt a particular attitude as being "right." Considering two important responsibilities may help you sort through your options.

*Your responsibility to yourself* lies in being true to yourself, in taking time to think through your reactions to other people. When you evaluate your thoughts, try to also consider their source: Have you heard these ideas from other people or organizations or the media? Do you agree with them, or does a different approach feel better to you? Through critical thinking you can arrive at decisions about which you feel comfortable and confident.

*Your responsibility to others* lies in treating people with tolerance and respect. No one will like everyone he or she meets, but acknowledging that others deserve respect and have a right to their opinions will build bridges of communication. The more people accept one another, the more all kinds of relationships will be able to thrive.

## The Positive Effects of Diversity

More than just "a nice thing to do," accepting diversity has very real benefits to people in all kinds of relationships. Acceptance and respect form the basis for any successful interaction. As more situations bring diverse people into relationships, communication will become more and more dependent upon acceptance and mutual understanding.

Consider how positive relationships with diverse people may contribute to success. Relationships among family, friends, and neighbors affect personal life. Relationships among students, instructors, and other school personnel affect student life. Relationships among co-workers, supervisors, and customers/clients affect work life. Understanding and communication in these relationships can bring positive effects such as satisfying relationships, achievement, and progress. Failure to understand and communicate well can have negative effects.

For example, examine the potential effects of reactions to diversity in the following situations. Although each of these situations focuses on the reaction of only one person, it's important to note that both parties need to work together to establish mutual trust and openness.

**A male Hispanic employee has a female African-American supervisor.** If the employee believes negative stereotypes about women or African-American people and resists taking directions from the supervisor, he may lose his job or be viewed as a liability. On the other hand, if the employee can respect the supervisor's authority and consider any different methods or ideas she has, their relationship is more likely to become supportive and productive. He may then be more likely to feel comfortable, perform well, and move up at work.

**A learning-disabled student has an Asian instructor.** If the student assumes that Asian people are superior and intimidating, letting that opinion lead her to resist the advice and directions her instructor gives her, she may do poorly in the class or drop the course. On the other hand, if the student stays open to what the instructor has to offer, the instructor may feel

> "Minds are like parachutes. They only function when they are open."
> Sir James Dewar

respected and may be more encouraging. The student may then be more likely to pay attention in class, work hard, and advance in her education.

**A Caucasian man has a sister who adopts a biracial child.** If the man cuts off contact with his sister because he fears racial differences and doesn't approve of racial mixing, he may deny himself her support and create a rift in the family. On the other hand, if the man can accept the new family member and respect his sister's choice, she may feel more supported and continue to support him in turn. The situation may help to build a close and rewarding family relationship.

Accepting others isn't always easy, and it's common to let perceptions about people block your ability to communicate. Following are some barriers that can hinder your ability to accept and understand others, and suggestions for how to overcome them.

## Barriers to Understanding

You deserve to feel positive about who you are, where you come from, what you believe, and the others with whom you identify. However, problems arise when people use the power of group identity to put others down or cut themselves off from others. Table 8-1 shows how an open-minded approach can differ from an approach that is characterized by barriers.

Stereotypes, prejudice, discrimination, and fear of differences all can form barriers to communication.

### Stereotypes

As you learned in Chapter 4, an assumption is an idea that you accept without looking for proof. A stereotype occurs when an assumption is made about a person or group of people, based on one or more characteristics. You may have heard stereotypical assumptions such as these: "Women are too emotional for business." "African-Americans can run fast and sing well." "Hispanics are Catholic and have tons of kids." "White people are cold and power-hungry." "Gay people sleep around." "Learning-disabled people can't hold down jobs." "Older people can't learn new things." Stereotypes are as common as they are destructive.

Why might people stereotype? Here are a few reasons:

**People seek patterns and logic.** Trying to make sense of a complex world is part of human nature. People often try to find order by using the labels and categories that stereotypes provide.

**Stereotyping is quick and easy.** Making an assumption about a person from observing an external characteristic is easier than working to know a person as a unique individual. Labeling a group of people based on a characteristic they seem to have in common takes less time and energy than exploring the differences and unique qualities within the group.

**Movies, magazines, and other media encourage stereotyping.** The more people see stereotypical images—the unintelligent blonde, the funny overweight person, the evil white businessman—the easier it is to believe that such stereotypes are universal.

> **Stereotype,**
> A standardized mental picture that represents an oversimplified opinion or uncritical judgment.

## TABLE 8-1   A CLOSED-MINDED APPROACH VS. AN OPEN-MINDED APPROACH

| YOUR ROLE | SITUATION | CLOSED-MINDED APPROACH | OPEN-MINDED APPROACH |
|---|---|---|---|
| Team member on the job | A co-worker from from India observes a Hindu religious ritual at lunchtime. | You stare at the religious ritual, thinking it weird. You feel that this co-worker should just blend in and act like everyone else. | Your observe the ritual, respecting how the person expresses religious beliefs. You look up Hindu religion in your spare time to learn more. |
| Fellow student | For an assignment, you are paired up with a student old enough to be your mother. | You figure that the student will be closed off to the modern world. You think that she might also act like a parent and preach to you about how to do the assignment. | You avoid thinking that this student will act like your parents and get to know her as an individual. You stay open to what you can learn from her experiences and knowledge. |
| Friend | You are invited to dinner at a friend's house for the first time. When he introduces you to his partner, you realize that he is gay. | You are turned off by the idea of two men in a relationship and by gay culture in general. You are uncomfortable and make an excuse to leave early. You avoid your friend from then on. | You have dinner with your friend and his partner. You learn that they have a committed, supportive relationship. You take the opportunity to learn more about who they are and what their lives are like. |
| Employee | Your new boss is Japanese-American, hired from a competing company. | You assume that your new boss is very hard-working, expecting unrealistic things things from you and your co-workers. You assume she doesn't take time to socialize. | Your rein in your assumptions, knowing they are based on stereotypes, and approach your new boss with an open mind. |

The ease of stereotypes comes at a high price. First and foremost, stereotypes can perpetuate harmful generalizations and falsehoods about others. These false ideas can promote discrimination. For example, if an employer believes that Vietnamese people cannot speak English well, he might not even bother to interview them. Secondly, stereotypes also communicate the message that you don't care about or respect others enough to discover who they really are. This may encourage others to stereotype you in return. Others may not give you a chance if they feel that you haven't given them a chance.

**Addressing stereotypes.**   Recall from the critical-thinking material in Chapter 4 the questions you can ask about an assumption in order to examine its validity. Apply these questions to stereotypes:

1. In what cases is this stereotype true, if ever? In what cases is it not true?

2. Has stereotyping others benefited me? Has it hurt me? In what ways?

3. If someone taught me this stereotype, why? Did that person think it over or just accept it?

4. What harm could be done by always accepting this stereotype as true?

Using these steps, think through the stereotypes you assume are true. When you hear someone else use a stereotype and you know some information that disproves it, volunteer that information. Encourage others to think through stereotypes and to reject them if they don't hold up under examination.

Give others the benefit of the doubt. Thinking beyond stereotypes is an important step toward more open lines of communication.

## Prejudice

**Prejudice,**
A preconceived judgment or opinion, formed without just grounds or sufficient knowledge.

Prejudice occurs when people "prejudge," meaning that they make a judgment before they have sufficient knowledge upon which to base that judgment. People often form prejudiced opinions on the basis of a particular characteristic—gender, race, culture, abilities, sexual orientation, religion, and so on. You may be familiar with the labels for particular kinds of prejudice, such as *racism* (prejudice based on race) or *ageism* (prejudice based on age). Any group can be subjected to prejudice, although certain groups have more often been on the receiving end of such closed-minded attitudes. Prejudice can lead people to disrespect, harass, and put down others. In some cases, prejudice may lead to unrealistic expectations of others that aren't necessarily negative, such as if someone were to judge all Jewish people as excelling in business.

Prejudice can have one or more causes. Some common causes include the following.

**People experience the world through the lens of their own particular identity.** You grow up in a particular culture and family and learn their attitudes. When you encounter different ideas and ways of life, you may react by categorizing them. You may also react with ethnocentrism—the idea that your group is better than anyone else's.

**When people get hurt, they may dislike or blame anyone who seems similar to the person who hurt them.** Judging others based on a bad experience is human, especially when a particular characteristic raises strong emotions.

**Jealousy and fear of personal failure can lead a person to want to put others down.** When people are feeling insecure about their own abilities, they might find it easier to devalue the abilities of others rather than to take risks and try harder themselves.

The many faces of prejudice often show on college campuses. A student may not want to work with an in-class group that contains people of another race. Campus clubs may tend to limit their membership to a particular group and exclude others. Religious groups may devalue the beliefs of other religions. Groups that gather based on a common characteristic might be harassed by others. Women or men may find that instructors or fellow students judge their abilities and attitudes based on their gender. All of these attitudes severely block attempts at mutual understanding.

Addressing prejudice.    Being critical of people who are different cuts you off from all kinds of perspectives and people that can enhance the quality of your life. Critical thinking is your key to changing prejudicial attitudes. For example, suppose you find yourself thinking that a certain student in your class isn't the type of person you want to get to know. Ask yourself: Where did I get this attitude? Am I accepting someone else's judgment? Am I making judgments based on how this person looks or speaks or behaves? How does having this attitude affect me or others? If you see that your attitude needs to change, have the courage to activate that change by considering the person with an open, accepting mind.

Another tactic, and often an extremely difficult one, is to confront people you know when they display a prejudiced attitude. It can be hard to stand up to someone and risk a relationship or, if the person is your employer, even a job. On the other hand, your silence may imply that you agree. Evaluate the situation and decide what choice is most suitable and is true to your values. Ask yourself if you can associate with a person if he or she thinks or behaves in a way that you do not respect.

You have a range of choices when deciding whether to reveal your feelings about someone's behavior. You can decide not to address it at all. You may drop a humorous hint and hope that you make your point. You may make a small comment to "test the waters" and see how the person reacts, hoping that later you can have a more complete discussion about it. Whatever you do, express your opinion respectfully. Perhaps the other person will take that chance to rethink the attitude; perhaps he or she will not. Either way, you have taken an important stand.

## Discrimination

Discrimination occurs when people deny others opportunities because of their perceived differences. Prejudice often accompanies discrimination. Discrimination can mean being denied jobs or advancement, equal educational opportunities, equal housing opportunities, services, or access to events, people, rights, privileges, or commodities.

Discrimination happens in all kinds of situations, revolving around gender, language, race, culture, and other factors. A 32-year-old married woman may not win a job because the interviewer assumes that she will become pregnant. A Russian person may be fired from a restaurant job because his English is heavily accented. Sheryl McCarthy, an African-American columnist for *New York Newsday*, sees it on the street. "Nothing is quite so basic and clear as having a cab go right past your furiously waving body and pick up the white person next to you," she says in her book, *Why Are the Heroes Always White?*[2] "Sometimes you can debate whether racism was the motivating factor in an act; here there is no doubt whatsoever." Even so-called majority populations may now experience the power of discrimination. For example, a qualified white man may be passed up for a promotion in favor of a female or minority employee.

The disabled are often targets of discrimination because people may believe that they are depressed and incapacitated. John Hockenberry, a wheelchair-using paraplegic who travels the world in his work as an award-winning journalist, challenges the idea that disabled people lead lives of unproductive misery. "My body may have been capable of less, but virtually all of what it could do was suddenly charged with meaning. This feeling was the hardest to translate to the outside, where people wanted to believe that I must have to paint things in this way to keep from killing myself," he says in his memoir *Moving Violations*.[3]

Obesity can invite discrimination as well. People who are overweight may have trouble winning jobs or moving up at work. Even shopping for clothing can present limited options. Only recently have certain name-brand designers begun to create clothing in women's sizes above 12, and many designers still discriminate.

Addressing discrimination.     U.S. federal law states that it is unlawful for you to be denied an education, work or the chance to apply for work, housing, or basic rights based on your race, creed, color, age, gender, national or ethnic origin, religion, marital status, potential or actual pregnancy, or potential or actual illness or disability (unless the illness or disability prevents you from performing required tasks, and unless accommodations for the disability are not possible). Unfortunately, the law is frequently broken, with the result that incidents go unnoticed. Many times people don't report incidents, fearing trouble from those they accuse. Sometimes people don't even notice their attitudes seeping through, such as in an interview situation.

First and foremost, be responsible for your own behavior. Never knowingly participate in or encourage discrimination. When you act on prejudicial attitudes by discriminating against someone, the barrier to communication this discrimination causes hurts you as well as anyone else involved. A person who feels denied and shut out may be likely to do the same to you, and may even encourage others to do so.

Second, if you witness a discriminatory act or feel that you have been discriminated against, decide whether you want to approach an authority about it. You may want to begin by talking to the person who can most directly affect the situation—an instructor, your supervisor, a housing authority. Don't assume that people know when they hurt or offend someone. For example, if you have a disability and you find that accommodations haven't been made for you at school, speak up. Meet with an advisor to discuss your needs for transport, equipment, or a particular schedule.

If you don't find satisfaction and change at that level, try the next level of authority (an administrator, your supervisor's boss, a government official). If that doesn't produce results, you can take legal action, although legal struggles can take a lot of time and drain a great deal of money out of your pocket. At each decision stage, weigh all the positive and negative effects and evaluate whether the action is feasible for you. Although keeping quiet may not bring change, you may not be able to act right away. In the long run, if you are able to stand up for what you believe, your actions may be worthwhile.

# REAL WORLD PERSPECTIVE

## How can I adjust to diversity?

### Carrie Nelson, University of Guadalajara—Centro de Estudios para Extranjeros

Once I made the decision to study Spanish, the idea of studying abroad in a Spanish-speaking country was simultaneous. I have always been fascinated with learning about other cultures and being introduced to new ideas. Once I started filling out forms for the school in Mexico and buying my plane ticket, however, I began to question my decision. I wondered if I could really handle this big of a change in my life. But in my heart I knew that I had made the right decision.

Now that I am actually studying in Guadalajara, Mexico, I cannot imagine how I could have been nervous. This is one of the best decisions I have ever made, although I have had to adjust to living here. In some aspects the Mexican and American cultures are very similar but in other regards they can be very different. For example, in the U.S. the customer is considered the most important person and expects to be served very quickly. In Mexico the customer is important but the way of life is much more relaxed. Therefore if a clerk gets a personal phone call they will most likely talk to that person whether there is a customer waiting or not.

Every day I experience something new or begin to better understand the differences in our cultures. By learning about other people, I am learning more about myself and the beauty and complexity of people. Still, I would like to deepen my relationship with the people of Guadalajara. I realize I am just scratching the surface of this experience. Do you have any suggestions?

### Tan Pham, Gonzaga University—Spokane, Washington

In 1981, I escaped from Vietnam after having tried unsuccessfully 13 different times. Like your experience in Guadalajara, I found being in a new country both wonderfully enriching and overwhelming at the same time.

When I first arrived in the U.S., I was amazed at the way the people value time. In Vietnam, as in Guadalajara, things are much slower. But here, time is seen as money. I learned it was very important to arrive at my appointments at the exact time they were scheduled. I was also amazed at the technology: the computers and the transportation.

When you visit another country there is so much to learn. My recommendation is that you stay open to the experience. Let go of your past and fully embrace the new life you have accepted. Remember not to isolate yourself. Talk to the people. Avoid socializing just with people from your own country. Try to immerse yourself fully in the new culture. Also, ask for help. Most people are very sincere in their desire to help you. Each land has unique opportunities. Take advantage of them as you explore your new world.

### Fear of Differences

It's human instinct to fear the unknown. Many people stop long before they actually explore anything unfamiliar. They allow their fear to prevent them from finding out anything about what's outside their known world. As cozy as that world can be, it also can be limiting, cutting off communication from people who could enrich that world in many different ways.

The fear of differences has many effects. A young person who fears the elderly may avoid visiting a grandparent in a nursing home. A person of one religion might reject friendships with those of other religions out of a fear of different religious beliefs. Someone in a relationship may fear the commitment of marriage. A person might turn down an offer to buy a house in a neighborhood that is populated with people from a different ethnic group. In each case, the person may deny him or herself a chance to learn a new perspective, communicate with new individuals, and grow from new experiences.

**Address fear of differences.**    Diversity doesn't mean that you have to feel comfortable with everyone or agree with what everyone else believes. The fear of differences, though, can keep you from discovering anything outside your own world. Challenge yourself by looking for opportunities to expose yourself to differences. Today's world increasingly presents such opportunities. You can choose a study partner in class who has a different ethnic background. You can expand your knowledge with books or magazines. You can visit a museum or part of town that introduces a culture new to you. You can attend an unfamiliar religious service with a friend. Gradually broaden your horizons and consider new ideas.

If you think others are uncomfortable with differences, encourage them to work through their discomfort. Explain the difference so that it doesn't seem so mysterious. Offer to help them learn more in a setting that isn't threatening. Bring your message of the positive effects of diversity to others.

> "I have a dream that one day on the red hills of Georgia the sons of former slaves and the sons of former slave owners will be able to sit down together at the table of brotherhood."
>
> Martin Luther King, Jr.

## Accepting and Dealing with Differences

Successful interaction with the people around you benefits everyone. The success of that exchange depends upon your ability to accept differences. How open can you be? Your choices range from rejecting all differences to freely celebrating them, with a range of possibilities in between. Ask yourself important questions about what course of action you want to take. Realize that the opinions of family, friends, the media, and any group with which you identify may sometimes lead you into perspectives and actions that you haven't thought through completely. Do your best to sort through outside opinions and make a choice that feels right.

At the forefront of the list of ways to deal with differences is mutual respect. Respect for yourself and others is essential. Admitting that other people's cultures, behaviors, races, religions, appearances, and ideas deserve as much respect as your own promotes communication and learning.

What else can you do to accept and deal with differences?

**Avoid judgments based on external characteristics.** These include skin color, weight, facial features, or gender.

**Cultivate relationships with people of different cultures, races, perspectives, and ages.** Find out how other people live and think, and see what you can learn from them.

**Educate yourself and others.** "We can empower ourselves to end racism through massive education," say Tamara Trotter and Joycelyn Allen in *Talking Justice: 602 Ways to Build and Promote Racial Harmony*.[4] "Take advantage of books and people to teach you about other cultures. Empowerment comes through education. If you remain ignorant and blind to the critical issues of race and humanity, you will have no power to influence positive change." Read about other cultures and people.

**Be sensitive to the particular needs of others at school and on the job.** Think critically about their situations. Try to put yourself in their place by asking yourself questions about what you would feel and do if you were in a similar situation.

**Work to listen to people whose perspectives clash with or challenge your own.** Acknowledge that everyone has a right to his or her opinion, whether or not you agree with it.

**Look for common ground**—parenting, classes, personal challenges, interests.

**Help other people, no matter how different they may be.** Sheryl McCarthy writes about an African-American man who, in the midst of the 1992 Los Angeles riots, saw a man being beaten and helped him to safety. "When asked why he risked grievous harm to save an Asian man he didn't even know, Williams said, 'Because if I'm not there to help someone else, when the mob comes for me, will there be someone there to save me?'"[5] Continue the cycle of kindness.

**Explore your own background, beliefs, and identity.** Share what you learn with others.

**Cultivate your own personal diversity.** You may be one of the growing population of people who have two, three, or ten different cultures in your background. Perhaps your father is Native American and Filipino and Scottish, and your mother is Creole (French, Spanish, and African-American). Respect and explore your heritage. Even if you identify only with one group or culture, there are many different sides of you.

**Take responsibility for making changes instead of pointing the finger at someone else.** Avoid blaming problems in your life on certain groups of people.

Learn from the atrocities of history like slavery and the Holocaust. Cherish the level of freedom you have and seek continual improvement at home and elsewhere in the world.

Teach your children about other cultures.   Impress upon them the importance of appreciating differences while accepting that all people have equal rights.

Recognize that people everywhere have the same basic needs.   Everyone loves, thinks, hurts, hopes, fears, and plans. People are united through their essential humanity.

Expressing your ideas clearly and interpreting what others believe are crucial keys to communicating within a diverse world. The following section examines how you can communicate most effectively with the people around you.

# HOW CAN YOU EXPRESS YOURSELF EFFECTIVELY?

The only way for people to know each other's needs is to communicate as clearly and directly as possible. Successful communication promotes successful school, work, and personal relationships. Exploring communication styles, addressing communication problems, and using specific success strategies will help you express yourself effectively.

## Adjusting to Communication Styles

Communication is an exchange between two or more people. The speaker's goal is for the listener (or listeners) to receive the message exactly as the speaker intended. Different people, however, have different styles of communicating. Problems arise when one person has trouble "translating" a message that comes from someone who uses a different style. There are at least four communication styles into which people tend to fit: the Intuitor, the Senser, the Thinker, and the Feeler. Of course, people may shift around or possess characteristics from more than one category, but for most people one or two styles are dominant. Recognizing specific styles in others will help you communicate more clearly.[6]

### The Styles

The following are characteristics of each communication style.

A person using the *Intuitor* style is interested in ideas more than details, often moves from one concept or generalization to another without referring to examples, values insight and revelations, talks about having a vision, looks toward the future, and can be oriented toward the spiritual.

A person showing the style of *Senser* prefers details or concrete examples to ideas and generalizations, is often interested in the parts rather than the whole, prefers the here-and-now to the past or future, is suspicious of sudden insights or revelations, and feels that "seeing is believing."

A person using the *Thinker* style prefers to analyze situations, likes to solve problems logically, sees ideas and examples as useful if they help to figure something out, and becomes impatient with emotions or personal stories unless they have a practical purpose.

A person showing the style of *Feeler* is concerned with ideas and examples that relate to people, often reacts emotionally, is concerned with values and their effects on people and other living things, doesn't like "cold logic" or too much detail.

You can benefit from shifting from style to style according to the situation, particularly when trying to communicate with someone who prefers a style different from yours. Shifting, however, is not always easy or possible. The most important task is to try to understand the different styles and to help others understand yours. In general, no one style is any better than another. Each has its own positive effects that enhance communication and negative effects that can hinder it, depending on the situation.

## Identifying Your Styles

These four styles are derived from the Myers-Briggs Type Indicator (MBTI). Because the learning style assessments are also in part derived from the MBTI, you will notice similarities between those assessments and these communication styles. Table 8-2 shows how some learning styles may correspond loosely to the communication styles. Not all individual learning styles within the assessments are mentioned, and the styles that are noted may correspond with different styles in different situations, but these matchups depict the most common associations. Finding where your learning styles fit may help you to determine your dominant communication style or styles.

## TABLE 8-2 LEARNING STYLES AND COMMUNICATION STYLES

| COMMUNICATION STYLE | LEARNING STYLES INVENTORY | PATHWAYS TO LEARNING (MULTIPLE INTELLIGENCES) | PERSONALITY SPECTRUM |
|---|---|---|---|
| **INTUITOR** | Theoretical, Holistic | Intrapersonal | Adventurer |
| **SENSER** | Factual | Bodily-Kinesthetic | Organizer |
| **THINKER** | Linear | Logical-Mathematical | Thinker |
| **FEELER** | Reflective | Interpersonal | Giver |

### Adjusting to the Listener's Style

When you are the speaker, you will benefit from an understanding of both your own style and the styles of your listeners. It doesn't matter how clear you think you are being if the person you are speaking to can't "translate" your message by understanding your style. Try to take your listener's style into consideration when you communicate.

Following is an example of how adjusting to the listener can aid communication.

**An intuitor-dominant instructor to a senser-dominant student:** "Your writing isn't clear." The student's reply: "What do you mean?"

➤ *Without adjustment:* If the intuitor doesn't take note of the senser's need for detail and examples, he or she may continue with a string of big-picture ideas that might further confuse and turn off the senser. "You need to elaborate more. Try writing with your vision in mind. You're not considering your audience."

➤ *With adjustment:* If the intuitor shifts toward a focus on detail and away from his or her natural focus on ideas, the senser may begin to understand, and the lines of communication can open. "You introduced your central idea at the beginning but then didn't really support it until the fourth paragraph. You need to connect each paragraph's idea to the central idea. Also, not using a lot of examples for support makes it seem as though you are writing to a very experienced audience."

### Adjusting to the Communicator's Style

As a facet of communication, listening is just as important as speaking. When you are the listener, try to stay aware of the communication style of the person who is speaking to you. Observe how that style satisfies, or doesn't satisfy, what a person of your particular style prefers to hear. Work to understand the speaker in the context of his or her style and translate the message into one that makes sense to you.

Following is an example of how adjusting to the communicator can boost understanding.

**A feeler-dominant employee to a thinker-dominant supervisor:** "I'm really upset about how you've talked down to me. I don't think you've been fair. I haven't been able to concentrate since our discussion and it's hurting my performance."

➤ *Without adjustment.* If the thinker becomes annoyed with the feeler's focus on emotions, he or she may ignore them, putting up an even stronger barrier between the two people. "There's no reason to be upset. I told you clearly and specifically what needs to be done. There's nothing else to discuss."

➤ *With adjustment.* If the thinker considers that emotions are dominant in the feeler's perspective, he or she could respond to those emotions in a way that still searches for the explanations and logic the thinker understands best: "Let's talk about how you feel. Please explain to me what has caused you to become upset, and we'll discuss how we can improve the situation."

## Overcoming Communication Problems

Communication problems may occur when information is not clearly presented, or when those who receive information filter it through their own perspectives and interpret it in different ways. A few of the most common communication problems follow, along with strategies to help you combat them.

### Problem: Unclear or incomplete explanation
### Solution: Support ideas with examples

When you clarify a general idea with supporting examples that illustrate how it works and what effects it causes, you will help your receiver understand what you mean and therefore have a better chance to hold his or her attention.

For example, if you tell a friend to take a certain class, that friend might not take you seriously until you explain why. If you then communicate the positive effects of taking that class (progress toward a major, an excellent instructor, friendly study sessions), you may get your message across. The same principle applies to your attitude toward this course. If others communicate to you specific examples of how your work in the course will benefit your education, career, and personal life, you may be more likely to apply yourself.

Work situations benefit from explanation as well. As a supervisor, if you assign a task without explanation, you might get a delayed response or find mistakes in your employee's work. If, however, you explain the possible positive effects of the task, you'll have better results.

### Problem: Attacking the receiver
### Solution: Send "I" messages

When a conflict arises, often the first instinct is to pinpoint what someone else did wrong. "You didn't lock the door!" "You never called last night!" "You left me out!" Making an accusation, especially without proof, puts the other person on the defensive and shuts down the lines of communication.

Using "I" messages will help you communicate your own needs rather than focusing on what you think someone else did wrong or should do differently. "I felt uneasy when I came to work and the door was unlocked." "I became worried about you when I didn't hear from you last night." "I felt disappointed when I realized that I couldn't join the party." "I" statements soften the conflict by highlighting the *effects* that the other person's actions have had on you, rather than the person or the actions themselves. When you focus on your own response and needs, your receiver may feel more free to respond, perhaps offering help and even acknowledging mistakes.

If you often feel dissatisfied and tense after an exchange, you may benefit from focusing more on your own needs when you communicate. Translate your anger into an "I" statement before speaking. Ask the other person, "Can we decide together how to improve this situation? Here's how I feel about what has happened." Using "I" statements will bring better results.

## Problem: Passive or aggressive communication styles

## Solution: Become assertive

**Assertive,**

Able to declare and affirm one's own opinions while respecting the rights of others to do the same.

Among the three major communication styles—aggressive, passive, assertive—the one that conveys a message in the clearest, most productive way is the assertive style. The other two, while commonly used, throw the communication out of balance. An aggressive communicator often denies the receiver a chance to respond, while a passive communicator may have trouble getting the message out. Assertive behavior strikes a balance between aggression and passivity. If you can be an assertive communicator, you will be more likely to get your message across while assuring that others have a chance to speak as well. Table 8-3 compares some characteristics of each kind of communicator.

*Aggressive* communicators focus primarily on their own needs. They can become angry and impatient when those needs are not immediately satisfied. In order to become more assertive, aggressive communicators might try to take time to think before speaking, avoid ordering people around, use "I" statements, and focus on listening to what the other person has to say.

*Passive* communicators deny themselves the power that aggressive people grab. They focus almost exclusively on the needs of others instead of on their own needs, experiencing frustration and tension that remains unexpressed. In order to become more assertive, passive communicators might try to acknowledge anger or hurt more often, speak up when they feel strongly about something, realize that they have a right to make requests, and know that their ideas and feelings are as important as anyone else's.

*Source:* ©Nina Paley

## TABLE 8-3 AGGRESSIVE, PASSIVE, AND ASSERTIVE STYLES

| AGGRESSIVE | PASSIVE | ASSERTIVE |
| --- | --- | --- |
| Loud, heated arguing | Concealing one's own feelings | Expressing feelings without being nasty or overbearing |
| Physically violent encounters | Denying one's own anger | Acknowledging emotions but staying open to discussion |
| Blaming, name-calling, and verbal insults | Feeling that one has no right to express anger | Expressing self and giving others the chance to express themselves equally |
| Walking out of arguments before they are resolved | Avoiding arguments | Using "I" statements to defuse arguments |
| Being demanding: "Do this" | Being noncommittal: "You don't have to do this unless you really want to . . . " | Asking and giving reasons: "I would appreciate it if you would do this, and here's why . . . " |

## Communication Success Strategies

These additional strategies can help improve your communication.

Think before you speak.    Spoken too soon, ideas can come out sounding nothing like you intended them to. Taking time to think, or even rehearsing mentally, can help you choose the best combination of words. Think it through and get it right the first time.

Don't withhold your message for too long.    One danger of holding back is that a problem or negative feeling may become worse. Speaking promptly has two benefits: (1) you solve the problem sooner, and (2) you are more likely to focus on the problem at hand than to spill over into other issues.

Communicate in a variety of ways, and be sensitive to cultural differences. Remember that words, gestures, and tones mean different things to different people.

Be clear, precise, and to the point.    Say exactly what you need to say. Link your ideas to clear examples, avoiding any extra information that can distract.

Communication is extremely important for building and maintaining personal relationships. Explore the role those relationships play in who you are.

# HOW DO YOUR PERSONAL RELATIONSHIPS DEFINE YOU?

The relationships you have with friends, family members, and significant others often take center stage. Jobs and schooling can come and go, but you rely on the people with whom you share your life.

In addition to being part of your life, the people around you help to define who you are. Since birth, you have learned by taking in information from verbal and nonverbal language. The chain of learning stretches back through time, each link formed by an exchange of information between people. Those with whom you live, play, study, and work are primary sources of ideas, beliefs, and ways of living. You grow and change as you have new experiences, evaluate them, and decide what to learn from them.

These influential relationships can affect other areas of your life. You have probably experienced conflict that caused you to be unable to sleep, eat, or get any work done. On the other hand, a successful relationship can have positive effects on your life, increasing your success at work or at school. Following are some strategies for improving your personal relationships.

## Relationship Strategies

If you can feel good about your personal relationships, other areas of your life will benefit. Here are some suggestions.

**Make personal relationships a high priority.**    Nurture the ones you have and be open to developing new ones. Life is meant to be shared. In some marriage ceremonies, the bride and groom share a cup of wine that symbolizes life. One of the reasons for this tradition is to double the sweetness of life by tasting it together, and to cut the bitterness in half by sharing it. Any personal relationship can benefit from the experience of this kind of sharing.

**Invest time.**    You devote time to education, work, and the other priorities in your life. Relationships need the same investment. They are like plants in a garden, needing nourishment to grow and thrive. Your attention provides that nourishment. In addition, spending time with people you like can relieve everyday stress and strain. When you make time for others, everyone benefits.

**Spend time with people you respect and admire.**    Life is too short to hang out with people who bring you down, encourage you to participate in activities you don't approve of, or behave in ways that upset you. Develop relationships with people whom you respect, whose choices you admire, and who inspire you to be all that you can be. This doesn't mean that you have to agree with everything that others do. For example, you may disagree with a friend who lets his child watch a lot of TV. However, you may severely disapprove of someone who disciplines a child violently, and you may choose to end your association with that person.

**Work through tensions.**    Negative feelings can multiply when left unspoken. Unexpressed feelings about other issues may cause you to become disproportionately angry over a small issue. A small annoyance over dishes in the sink can turn into a gigantic fight about everything under the sun. Get to the root of the problem. Discuss it, deal with it, and move on.

**Refuse to tolerate violence.** It isn't easy to face the problem of violence or to leave a violent relationship. People may tolerate violence out of a belief that it will end, a desire to keep their families together, a self-esteem so low that they believe they deserve what they get, or a fear that trying to leave may lead to greater violence. No level of violence is acceptable. Someone who behaves violently toward you cannot possibly have your best interests at heart. If you find that you are either an aggressor or a victim, do your best to get help.

**Show appreciation.** In this fast-moving world, people don't thank each other often enough. If you think of something positive, say it. Thank someone for a service, express your affection with a smile. A little positive reinforcement goes a long way toward nurturing a relationship.

**If you want a friend, be a friend.** The Golden Rule, "Do unto others as you would have them do unto you," never goes out of style. If you treat a friend with the kind of loyalty and support that you appreciate yourself, you are more likely to receive the same in return.

**Take risks.** It can be frightening to reveal your deepest dreams and frustrations, to devote yourself to a friend, or to fall in love. You can choose not to reveal yourself or give yourself to a friendship at all. However, giving is what feeds a relationship, bringing satisfaction and growth. If you take the plunge, you risk disappointment and heartbreak, but you stand to gain the incredible benefits of companionship, which for most people outweigh the risks.

**Keep personal problems in their place.** Solve personal problems with the people directly involved and no one else. If at all possible, try not to bring your emotions into class or work. Doing so may hurt your performance while doing nothing to help your problem. If you are overwhelmed by a personal problem, try to address it before you go to class or work. If it's impossible to address it at that time, at least make a plan that you can carry out later. Making some step toward resolving the problem will help you concentrate on other things.

**If it doesn't work out, find ways to cope.** Everyone experiences strain and breakups in intimate relationships, friendships, and family ties. Be kind to yourself and use coping strategies that help you move on. Some people need lots of time alone; others need to spend time with their friends and family. Some seek more formal counseling. Some people throw their energy into a project, a job, a class, a new workout regimen, or anything else that will take their mind off what hurts. Some just need to cry it out and be miserable for a while. Some write in a journal or write letters to the person that they never mail. Do what's right for you, and believe that sooner or later you can emerge from the experience stronger and with new perspective.

Now and again, your personal relationships will experience conflict. Following are ideas for how to deal with conflict and criticism in a productive and positive way.

# HOW CAN YOU HANDLE CONFLICT AND CRITICISM?

Conflict and criticism, as unpleasant as they can often be, are natural elements in the dynamic of getting along with others. It's normal to want to avoid people or situations that cause distress. However, if you can face your fears and think through them critically, you can gain valuable insight into human nature—your own and that of others. You may be able to make important changes in your life based on what you learn.

## Conflict Strategies

Conflicts both large and small arise when there is a clash of ideas or interests. You may have small conflicts with a housemate over food left out overnight, a door left unlocked, or a bill that needs paying. On the other end of the spectrum, you might encounter major conflicts with your partner about finances, with an instructor about a failing grade, or with a person who treats you unfairly because of your race, gender, age, or ethnic origin.

Conflict can create anger and frustration, shutting down communication. The two most destructive tendencies are to avoid the conflict altogether (a passive tactic) or to let it escalate into a blowout fight (an aggressive tendency). Avoidance doesn't make the problem go away—in fact, it will probably worsen. If you tend to be passive, assert yourself by acknowledging and expressing your feelings as soon as you can put them into words. On the other hand, a shouting match gives no one an opportunity or desire to listen. If you tend to be aggressive, give yourself time to cool down before you address a conflict. Try to express what you feel without letting your emotions explode.

If calmly and intelligently handled, conflict can shed light on new ideas and help to strengthen bonds between those involved. The primary keys to conflict resolution are calm communication and critical-thinking skills. Think through any conflict using what you know about problem solving.

Identify and analyze the problem.   Determine the severity of the problem by looking at its effects on everyone involved. Then, find and analyze the causes of the problem.

Brainstorm possible solutions.   Consider as many angles as you can, without judgment. Explore what ideas you can come up with from what you or others have done in a similar situation.

Explore each solution.   Evaluate the positive and negative effects of each solution. Why might each work, or not work, or work partially? What would take into account everyone's needs? What would cause the least stress? Make sure everyone has a chance to express an opinion.

Choose, carry out, and evaluate the solution you decide is best.    When you have implemented your choice, evaluate its effects. Decide whether you feel it was a good choice.

One more hint: Use "I" statements. Focus on the effects the problem has had on you rather than focusing on someone who caused it. Show that you are taking responsibility for your role in the exchange.

## Dealing With Criticism and Feedback

No one gets everything right all the time. People use constructive criticism and feedback to communicate what went wrong and to suggest improvements. Consider any criticism carefully.  If you always interpret criticism as a threat, you will close yourself off from learning. Even if you eventually decide that you disagree, you can still learn from exploring the possibility. Know that you are strong enough to embrace criticism and become a better person because of it.

Criticism can be either constructive or unconstructive. Criticism is considered *constructive* when it is offered supportively and contains useful suggestions for improvement. On the other hand, *unconstructive* criticism focuses on what went wrong, doesn't offer alternatives or help, and is often delivered in a negative or harsh manner. Whereas constructive criticism can promote a sense of hope for improvement in the future, unconstructive criticism can create tension, bad feelings, and defensiveness.

Any criticism can be offered constructively or unconstructively. Consider a case where someone has continually been late to work. A supervisor can offer criticism in either of these ways:

**Feedback,**
Evaluative or corrective information about an action or process.

**Constructive,**
Promoting improvement or development.

> *Constructive:* The supervisor talks privately with the employee. "I've noticed that you have been late to work a lot. Other people have had to do some of your work. Is there a problem that is keeping you from being on time? Is it something that I or someone else can help you with?"

> *Unconstructive:* The supervisor watches the employee slip into work late. The supervisor says, in front of other employees, "Nice to see you could make it. If you can't start getting here on time, I might look for someone else who can."

If you can learn to give constructive criticism and deal with whatever criticism comes your way from others, you will improve your relationships and your productivity. When offered constructively and carefully considered, criticism can bring about important changes.

### Giving Constructive Criticism

When you offer criticism, use the following steps to communicate clearly and effectively:

*"Do not use a hatchet to remove a fly from your friend's forehead."*

Chinese proverb

1. *Criticize the behavior rather than the person.* In addition, make sure the behavior you intend to criticize is changeable. Chronic lateness can be changed; a physical inability to perform a task cannot.

2. *Define specifically the behavior you want to change.* Try not to drag any side issues into the conversation.

3. *Balance criticism with positive words.* Alternate critical comments with praise in other areas.

4. *Stay calm and be brief.* Avoid threats, ultimatums, or accusations. Use "I" messages; choose positive, nonthreatening words, so the person knows that your intentions are positive.

5. *Explain the effects caused by the behavior that warrants the criticism.* Help the person understand why a change needs to happen, and talk about options in detail. Compare and contrast the effects of the current behavior with the effects of a potential change.

6. *Offer help in changing the behavior.* Lead by example.

### Receiving Criticism

When you find yourself on the receiving end of criticism, use these coping techniques:

1. *Listen to the criticism before you speak up.* Resist the desire to defend yourself until you've heard all the details. Decide if the criticism is offered in a constructive or unconstructive manner.

2. *Think the criticism through critically.* Evaluate it carefully. While some criticism may come from a desire to help, other comments may have less honorable origins. People often criticize others out of jealousy, anger, frustration, or displaced feelings. In cases like those, it is best (though not always easy) to let the criticism wash right over you.

3. *If it is unconstructive, you may not want to respond at that moment.* Unconstructive criticism can inspire anger that might be destructive to express. Wait until you cool down and think about the criticism to see if there is anything important hiding under how it was presented. Then, tell the person that you see the value of the criticism, but also communicate to him or her how the delivery of the criticism made you feel. If he or she is willing to talk in a more constructive manner, continue with the following steps below. If not, your best bet may be to consider the case closed and move on.

4. *If it is constructive, ask for suggestions of how to change the criticized behavior.* You could ask, "How would you handle this if you were in my place?"

5. *Before the conversation ends, summarize the criticism and your response to it.* Repeat it back to the person who offered it. Make sure both of you understand the situation in the same way.

6. *If you feel that the criticism is valid, plan a specific strategy for correcting the behavior.* Think over what you might learn from changing your behavior. If you don't agree with the criticism even after the whole conversation, explain your behavior from your point of view.

Remember that the most important feedback you will receive in school is from your instructors, and the most important on-the-job feedback will come from your supervisors, more experienced peers, and occasionally clients. Making a special effort to take in this feedback and consider it carefully will help you learn many important lessons. Even when the criticism is not warranted, the way you respond is important. Furthermore, knowing how to handle conflict and criticism will help you define your role and communicate with others when you work in groups.

# WHAT ROLE DO YOU PLAY IN GROUPS?

Group interaction is an important part of your educational, personal, and working life. With a team project at work or a cooperative learning exercise in school, for example, being able to work well together is necessary in order to accomplish a goal.

The two major roles in the group experience are those of *participant* and *leader*. Any group needs both in order to function successfully. Become aware of the role you tend to play when relating to others. Try different roles to help you decide where you can be most effective. The following strategies (from *Contemporary Business Communication*, by Louis E. Boone, David L. Kurtz, and Judy R. Block) are linked to either participating or leading.[7]

## Being an Effective Participant

Some people are happiest when participating in group activities that someone else leads and designs. They don't feel comfortable in a position of control or having the power to set the tone for the group as a whole. They trust others to make those decisions, preferring to help things run smoothly by taking on an assigned role in the project and seeing it through. Participators need to remember that they are "part owners" of the process. Each team member has a responsibility for, and a stake in, the outcome. The following strategies will help a participant to be effective.

### Participation Strategies

Get involved.    If a decision you don't like is made by a group of which you are a member, and you stayed uninvolved in the decision, you have no one to blame but yourself for not speaking up. Put some energy into your participation and let people know your views. You are as important a team member as anyone else, and your views are likewise valuable.

**Be organized.** When you participate with the group as a whole, or with any of the team members, stay focused and organized. The more organized your ideas are, the more people will listen, take them into consideration, and be willing to try them.

**Be willing to discuss.** Everyone has an equal right to express his or her ideas. Even as you enthusiastically present your opinions, be willing to consider those of others. Keep an open mind and think critically about other ideas before you assume they won't work. If a discussion heats up, take a break or let a more neutral group member mediate.

**Keep your word.** Make a difference by doing what you say you're going to do. Let people know what you have accomplished. If you bring little or nothing to the process, your team may feel as if you weigh them down.

**Focus on ideas, not people.** One of the easiest ways to start an argument is for participants to attack group members themselves instead of discussing their ideas. Separate the person from the idea, and keep the idea in focus.

**Play fairly.** Give everyone a chance to participate. Be respectful of other people's ideas. Don't dominate the discussion or try to control or manipulate others.

## Being an Effective Leader

Some people prefer to initiate the action, make decisions, and control how things proceed. They have ideas they want to put into practice and enjoy explaining them to others. They are comfortable giving direction to people and guiding group outcomes. Leaders often have a big-picture perspective; it allows them to see how all of the different aspects of a group project can come together. In any group setting the following strategies will help a leader succeed.

### Leadership Strategies

**Define and limit projects.** One of the biggest ways to waste time and energy is to assume that a group will know its purpose and will limit tasks on its own. A group needs a leader who can define the purpose of the gathering and limit tasks so the group doesn't take on too much. Some common purposes are giving/exchanging information, brainstorming, making a decision, delegating tasks, or collaborating on a project.

**Map out who will perform which tasks.** A group functions best when everyone has a particular contribution to make. You don't often choose who you work with—in school, at work, or in your family—but you can help different personalities work together by exploring who can do what best. Give people specific responsibilities and trust that they will do their jobs.

**Set the agenda.** The leader is responsible for establishing and communicating the goal of the project and how it will proceed. Without a plan, it's easy to get off track. Having a written agenda to which group members can refer is helpful. A good leader invites advice from others when determining group direction.

**Focus progress.**   Even when everyone knows the plan, it's still natural to wander off the topic. The leader should try to rein in the discussion when necessary, doing his or her best to keep everyone to the topic at hand. When challenges arise midstream, the leader may need to help the team change direction.

**Set the tone.**   Different group members bring different attitudes and mental states to a gathering. Setting a positive tone helps to bring the group together and motivate people to peak performance. When a leader values diversity in ideas and backgrounds and sets a tone of fairness, respect, and encouragement, group members may feel more comfortable contributing their ideas.

**Evaluate results.**   The leader should determine whether the team is accomplishing its goals. If the team is not moving ahead, the leader needs to make changes and decisions.

If you don't believe you fit into the traditional definition of a leader, remember that there are other ways to lead that don't involve taking charge of a group. You can lead others by setting an honorable example in your actions, choices, or words. You can lead by putting forth an idea that takes a group in a new direction. You can lead by being the kind of person whom others would like to be.

It takes the equal participation of all group members to achieve a goal. Whatever role works best for you, know that your contribution is essential. You may even play different roles with different groups, such as if you were a participator at school and a leader in a self-help group. Finally, stay aware of group dynamics; they can shift quickly and move you into a new position you may or may not like. If you don't feel comfortable, speak up. The happier each group member is, the more effectively the group as a whole will function.

# Kente

The African word *kente* means "that which will not tear under any condition." *Kente* cloth is worn by men and women in African countries such as Ghana, Ivory Coast, and Togo. There are many brightly colored patterns of *kente*, each beautiful, unique, and special.

Think of how this concept applies to being human. Like the cloth, all people are unique, with brilliant and subdued aspects. Despite any mistreatment or misunderstanding by the people you encounter in your life, you need to work to remain strong so that you don't tear and give way to disrespectful behavior. This strength can help you to endure, stand up against any injustice, and fight peacefully but relentlessly for the rights of all people.

# Chapter 8: Applications

Name _____   Date _____

 Key Into Your Life: Opportunities to Apply What You Learn

### Exercise 1: Diversity Discovery

Express your own personal diversity. Describe yourself in response to the following questions.

What ethnic background(s) do you have?

_____

_____

_____

Name one or more facts about you that someone wouldn't know from simply looking at you.

_____

_____

_____

Name two values or beliefs that govern how you live, what you pursue, and/or with whom you associate.

_____

_____

_____

What other characteristics or choices define your uniqueness?

_____

_____

_____

Now, join with a partner in your class. Try to choose someone you don't know well. Your goal is to communicate what you have written to your partner, and for your partner to communicate to you in the same way. Spend ten minutes talking together and take notes on what the other person says. At the end of that period, join together as a class. Each person will describe his or her partner to the class.

What did you learn about your partner that surprised you? _____

_____

_____

_____

What did you learn that went against any assumptions you may have made about that person based on his or her appearance, background, or behavior?_____

_____

_____

_____

Has this exercise changed the way you see this person or other people? Why or why not?_____

_____

_____

## Exercise 2: Your Communication Style

Look back at the four styles on pp. 206–207: Intuitor, Thinker, Feeler, and Senser. Which describes you the best? Rank the four styles, listing first the one that fits most, and listing last the one that fits least.

1. _____

2. _____

3. _____

4. _____

Of the two styles that best fit you, which one has more positive effects on your ability to communicate? What are those effects?

_____

_____

Which style has more negative effects? What are they?

_____

_____

To determine whether you are primarily passive, aggressive, or assertive, read the following sentences and circle the ones that sound like something you would say to a peer.

1. Get me the keys.
2. Would you mind if I stepped out just for a second?
3. Don't slam the door.
4. I'd appreciate it if you would have this done by two o'clock.
5. I think maybe it needs a little work just at the end, but I'm not sure.
6. Please take this back to the library.
7. You will have a good time if you join us.
8. Your loss.
9. I don't know, if you think so. I'll try it.
10. Let me know what you want me to do.
11. Turn it this way and see what happens.
12. We'll try both our ideas and see what works best.
13. I want it on my desk by the end of the day.
14. Just do what I told you.
15. If this isn't how you wanted it to look, I can change it. Just tell me and I'll do it.

Aggressive communicators would be likely to use sentences 1, 3, 8, 13, and 14.

Passive communicators would probably opt for sentences 2, 5, 9, 10, and 15.

Assertive communicators would probably choose sentences 4, 6, 7, 11, and 12.

In which category did you choose the most sentences? _____

If you scored as an assertive communicator, you are on the right track. If you scored in the aggressive or passive categories, analyze your style. What are the effects? Give an example in your own life of the effects of your style.

_____

_____

Turn back to p. 210 to review suggestions for aggressive or passive communicators. What can you do to improve your skills?

_____

_____

## Exercise 3: Problem Solving Close to Home

Divide into small groups of two to five. Assign one group member to take notes. Discuss the following questions, one by one:

1. What are the three largest problems my school faces with regard to how people get along with and accept others?
2. What could my school do to deal with the three problems listed above?
3. What can each individual student do to deal with the three problems listed above? (Talk about what you specifically feel that you can do.)

When you are finished, gather as a class. Each group should share their responses with the class. Observe the variety of problems and solutions. Notice whether more than one group came up with one or more of the same problems. You may want to assign one person in the class to gather all of the responses together. That person, together with your instructor, could put these responses into an organized document that you can share with the upper-level administrators at your school.

## KEY TO SELF-EXPRESSION: DISCOVERY THROUGH JOURNAL WRITING

*To record your thoughts, use a separate journal or the lined page at the end of the chapter.*

New Perspective[8]   Imagine that you have no choice but to change either your gender (male/female) or your racial/ethnic/religious group. Which would you change, and why? What do you anticipate would be the positive and negative effects of the change—in your social life, in your family life, on the job, at school? How would what you know and experience before the change affect how you would behave after the change?

## Journal Entry

# MANAGING CAREER AND MONEY:

## Reality Resources

Many people either love their jobs but don't make much money, or dislike their jobs but are paid well. Still other people have neither job satisfaction nor a good paycheck to show for their work. The most ideal career interests and challenges you *and* pays you enough to live comfortably.

Career exploration, job-hunting strategy, and money management can work together to help you find that ideal career. In this chapter, you will first look at career exploration and how to balance work and school. Then you will explore how to bring in money with financial aid and how to manage the money you have. Managing your resources and investigating career options can help you develop skills and insights that will serve you throughout your life.

In this chapter, you will explore answers to the following questions:

➤ How can you plan your career?

➤ How can you juggle work and school?

➤ What should you know about financial aid?

➤ How can strategic planning help you manage money?

➤ How can you create a budget that works?

# HOW CAN YOU PLAN YOUR CAREER?

College is an ideal time to investigate careers, because so many different resources are available to you. Students are in all different stages of thought when it comes to careers. You may not have thought too much about it yet. You may have already had a career for years and are looking for a change. You may have been set on a particular career but are now having second thoughts. Regardless of your starting point, now is the time to make progress.

Even outside this particular chapter, everything you read and work on in this book is geared toward workplace success. As you work on the exercises, you think critically, become a team player, hone writing skills, and develop long-term planning, all of which prepare you to thrive in any career.

## Define a Career Path

Aiming for a job in a particular career area requires planning the steps that can get you there. Whether these steps take months or years, they help you focus your energies on your goal. Defining a career path involves investigating yourself, exploring potential careers, and building knowledge and experience.

### Investigate Yourself

When you explore your learning style in Chapter 2, evaluate your ideal note-taking system in Chapter 6, or look at how you relate to others in Chapter 8, you build self-knowledge. Gather everything that you know about yourself, from this class or from any of your other life experiences, and investigate. What do you know or do best? Out of jobs you've had, what did you like and not like to do? How would you describe your personality? And finally, what kinds of careers make the best use of everything you are?

Don't feel as though you should automatically know what you want to do. Most students who have not been in the workplace don't know what career they want to pursue. Students who have been working often return to school to explore other careers that they might prefer. More and more, people are changing careers many times in their lives instead of sticking with one choice. This discovery is a lifelong process.

The potential for change applies to majors as well. If you declare a major and decide later that you don't like it, feel glad that you were able to discover that fact about yourself.

### Explore Potential Careers

Career possibilities extend far beyond what you can imagine. Brainstorm about career areas. Ask instructors, relatives, and fellow students about careers that they have or know about. Check your library for books on careers or biographies of people who worked in fields that interest you. Explore careers you discover through reading the newspaper, novels, or nonfiction. If a character in your favorite movie has a job you think you'd like, see what you can find out about it.

## TABLE 9-1 CRITICAL THINKING QUESTIONS FOR CAREER INVESTIGATION

| | |
|---|---|
| What can I do in this area that I like/am good at? | Do I respect the company and/or the industry? |
| What are the educational requirements (certificates or degrees, courses)? | Do companies in this industry generally accommodate special needs (child care, sick days, flex time, or working at home)? |
| What skills are necessary? | Do I need to belong to a union? |
| What wage or salary is normal for an entry-level position, and what benefits can I expect? | Are there opportunities in this industry within a reasonable distance from where I live? |
| What kinds of personalities are best suited to this kind of work? | What other expectations are there beyond the regular workday (travel, overtime, etc.)? |
| What are the prospects for moving up to higher-level positions? | Do I prefer a service or manufacturing industry? |

Your school's career center is an important resource in your investigation. The career center may offer job listings, occupation lists, assessments of skills and personality types, questionnaires to help you pinpoint career areas that may suit you, informational material about different career areas, and material about various companies. The people who work at the center can help you sort through the material.

Use your critical-thinking skills to broaden your question-asking beyond just what tasks you perform for any given job. Many other factors will be important to you. Look at Table 9-1 for some of the kinds of questions you might ask as you talk to people or investigate materials.

Within every career field, a wide array of job possibilities exists that you might not see right away. For example, the medical world involves more than just doctors and nurses. Emergency medical technicians respond to emergencies, administrators run hospitals, researchers test new drugs, lab technicians administer specific procedures such as X-rays, pharmacists administer prescriptions, retirement community employees work with the elderly, and more.

Within each job, there is also a variety of tasks and skills that often go beyond what you know. You may know that an instructor teaches, but you may not see that instructors also often write, research, study, create course outlines, create strategy with other instructors, give presentations, and counsel. Push past your first impression of any career and explore what else it entails. Expand your choices as much as you can using thorough investigation and an open mind.

### Build Knowledge and Experience

Having knowledge and experience specific to the career area you want to pursue will be valuable on the job hunt. Courses, internships, jobs, and volunteering are four great ways to build both.

Courses.   When you narrow your career exploration to a couple of areas that interest you, look through your school course catalog and take a course or two in those fields. How you react to these courses will give you important clues as to how you feel about the area in general. Be careful to evaluate your experience based on how you feel about the subject matter and not other factors. Think critically. If you didn't like a course, what was the cause: an instructor you didn't like, a time of day when you tend to lose energy, or truly a lack of interest in the material?

In addition, interview an instructor who teaches a subject related to a career field that interests you. Find out what courses you have to take to major in the field, what jobs are available in the field, what credentials (degrees and/or training) you need for particular jobs, and so on.

**Internship,**
A temporary work program in which a student can gain supervised practical experience in a particular professional field.

Internships.   An internship may or may not offer pay. While this may be a financial drawback, the experience you can gather and contacts you can make may be worth the work. Many internships take place during the summer, but some part-time internships are also available during the school year. Companies that offer internships are looking for people who will work hard in exchange for experience you can't get in the classroom.

Absorb all the knowledge you can while working as an intern. If you discover a career worth pursuing, you'll have the internship experience behind you when you go job hunting. Internships are one of the best ways to show a prospective employer some "real world" experience and initiative.

Jobs.   No matter what you do for money while you are in college, whether it is in your area of interest or not, you may discover career opportunities that appeal to you. Someone who takes a third-shift legal proofreading job to make extra cash might discover an interest in the law. Someone who answers phones for a newspaper company might be drawn into journalism. Stay aware of the possibilities around you.

Volunteering.   Offering your services in the community or at your school can introduce you to career areas and increase your experience. Some schools have programs that can help you find opportunities to work as an aid on campus or volunteer off campus. Recently, certain schools have even begun listing volunteer activities on student transcripts. Find out what services your school offers. Volunteer activities are important to note on your résumé. Many employers seek candidates who have shown commitment through volunteering.

## Map Out Your Strategy

After you've gathered enough information to narrow your career goals, plan strategically to achieve them. Make a career time line that illustrates the steps toward your goal, as shown in Figure 9-1. Mark years and half-year points (and months for the first year), and write in the steps where you think they should take place. If your plan is five years long, indicate what you plan to do by the fourth, third, and second years, and then the first year, including

FIGURE 9-1    CAREER TIME LINE

```
1 month  ─┐★  Enter community college on
3 months ─┤      part-time schedule
6 months ─┤  Meet with advisor to discuss desired
         │      major and required courses

1 year   ─┤

         ─┤  Declare major in secondary education

2 years  ─┤  Switch to full-time class schedule

         ─┤

3 years  ─┤  Graduate with associate's degree

         ─┤  Transfer to 4-year college

4 years  ─┤  Work part-time as classroom aid

         ─┤

5 years  ─┤  Student teaching

         ─┤  Graduate with bachelor's degree
         │      and teaching certificate
6 years  ─★  Have a job teaching high school
```

a six-month goal and a one-month goal for that first year. Set goals that establish who you will talk to, what courses you will take, what skills you will work on, what jobs or internships you will investigate, and any other research you need to do. Your path may change, of course—use your time line as a guide rather than as a rigid plan.

The road to a truly satisfying career can be long. Although changing careers used to be a risky and rare practice, now people commonly have as many as five careers over the course of their lives, and this number may continue to rise. Seek support as you work toward your goals. Confide in supportive people, talk positively to yourself, and read inspiring books. Two helpful books are *What Color Is Your Parachute?*, by Richard Nelson Bolles, and *Zen and the Art of Making a Living: A Practical Guide to Creative Career Design*, by Laurence G. Boldt.

## Seek Mentors

**Mentor,**
A person of knowledge or authority who becomes a trusted counselor or guide.

You may go to many different people for career advice, but if you are lucky, you may find among them a true mentor. A mentor takes a special interest in helping you to reach your goals. People often seek a mentor who has excelled in a career area or specific skill in which they also wish to excel. You may also be drawn to a person who, no matter what their skills or specialty, has ideas and makes choices that you admire and want to emulate.

Because it requires depth and devotion on both sides, a mentoring relationship often evolves from a special personal relationship. A relative, instructor, friend, supervisor, or anyone else whom you admire and respect may become your mentor. Think about whom you go to when you are confused, troubled, need guidance, or seek support. Also, consider who may know a lot about a skill or career area you want to pursue. Some schools have faculty or peer mentoring programs to help match students with people who can help them. Check your student handbook or ask your advisor if this is offered at your school.

Mentoring relationships demand time and energy on both sides. A mentor can give you a private audience for questions and problems, advice tailored to your needs, a wealth of experience, support, guidance, and trust. A mentor cares about you deeply enough to be devoted to your success and growth, taking pleasure in your development. You owe it to your mentor to be open to his or her ideas and to respectfully take his or her advice into consideration. You and your mentor can learn from each other, receive positive energy from your relationship, and grow and develop together.

## Know What Employers Want

Certain basic skills will make you an excellent job candidate no matter what career you decide to pursue. Employers look for particular skills and qualities that signify an efficient and effective employee. You can continue to develop these skills as you work in current and future jobs—and you will, if you always strive to improve.

**Communication skills.** Being able to listen well and express yourself in writing and speaking is a key to workplace success. Much can be accomplished through efficient, open communication. Being able to adjust to different communication styles is an important factor.

**Problem solving.** Any job will present problems that need to be solved. An employee who knows how to assess any situation and apply the problem-solving process to it will stand out.

**Decision making.** Decisions large and small are made in every workplace every day. Knowing how to think through and make decisions will help you in any job.

**Teamwork.** It is a rare workplace that has only one employee, and even then, that person will interact with different kinds of people on the phone or through a computer. The importance of being able to work well with others cannot be overemphasized. If there is a weak link in any team, the whole company suffers.

**Intercultural communication.** The workplace is becoming increasingly diverse. The more you can work well with people different from yourself and open your mind to their points of view, the more valuable an employee you will be.

**Leadership.** The ability to influence others in a positive way will earn you respect and keep you in line for promotions. Taking the lead will often command attention.

**Creativity.** When you can see the big picture as well as the details and can let your mind come up with unexpected new concepts and plans, you will bring valuable suggestions to your workplace.

**Commitment.** You will encounter many difficult situations at work. The ability to continue to work hard through such situations is extremely important. In addition, if you introduce a new and creative idea, you can gain support for it through having a strong commitment to it yourself.

**Values and integrity.** Your personal values and integrity will help guide everything you do. In your actions and decisions, consider what you value and what you believe is right.

> *"Whatever you think you can do or believe you can do, believe it. Action has magic, grace, and power in it."*
>
> Johann Wolfgang von Goethe

These skills appear throughout this book, and they are as much a part of your school success as they are of your work success. The more you develop them now, the more employable and promotable you will prove yourself to be. You may already use them on the job if you are a student who works.

Many students need to work and take classes at the same time in order to fund the education that they hope will move them into better careers. While you may not necessarily work in a career area that interests you, you can hold a job that helps you pay the bills and still make the most of your school time.

## HOW CAN YOU JUGGLE WORK AND SCHOOL?

What you are studying today can prepare you to find a job, when you graduate, that suits your abilities and brings in enough money to support your needs and lifestyle choices. In the meantime, though, you can make work a part of your student life in order to make money, explore a career, and/or increase your future employability through contacts or résumé building.

As the cost of education continues to rise, more and more students are working and taking classes at the same time. In the school year 1992–93, 79 percent of undergraduates worked while in school. Most student workers 23 years of age or under worked part-time jobs (37.8 percent). Of students over the age of 23, a majority worked full-time jobs (nearly 55 percent).[1] Figure 9-2 shows working statistics for both community-college and four-year-college students.

Being an employed student isn't for everyone. Adding a job to the list of demands on your time and energy may create problems if it sharply reduces study time or family time. However, many people want to work and many need to work in order to pay for school. Ask yourself important questions about why or why not to work. Weigh the potential positive and negative effects of working. From those answers you can make a choice that you feel benefits you most.

## Effects of Working While in School

Working while in school has many different positive and negative effects, depending on the situation. Evaluate any job opportunity by looking at these effects. Following are some that might come into play.

### Potential Positive Effects

Money earned.    A job can provide crucial income to pay for rent, transportation, food, and important bills. It may even help you put some savings away in order to create a financial cushion.

General and career-specific experience.    Important learning comes from hands-on work. Your education "in the trenches" can complement your

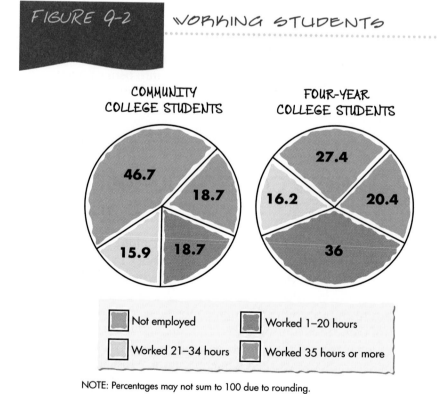

FIGURE 9-2    WORKING STUDENTS

COMMUNITY COLLEGE STUDENTS

46.7
18.7
15.9
18.7

FOUR-YEAR COLLEGE STUDENTS

27.4
16.2
20.4
36

- Not employed
- Worked 1–20 hours
- Worked 21–34 hours
- Worked 35 hours or more

NOTE: Percentages may not sum to 100 due to rounding.

*Source:* U.S. Department of Education, National Center for Education Statistics, 1992–93 National Postsecondary Student Aid Study (NPSAS:93), Undergraduate Data Analysis System.

classroom experience. Even if you don't work in your chosen field, you can improve universal skills such as teamwork and communication.

Being able to keep a job you currently hold.   If you leave a job temporarily, your company might not be able to hold your position open until you come back. New mothers who want to take a longer maternity leave than company policy permits may run into this problem. Consider adjusting your responsibilities or hours while still holding down your job.

Keeping busy.   Work can provide a stimulating break from studying. In fact, working up to 15 hours a week may actually enhance academic performance, because working students often manage their time more efficiently and may gain confidence from their successes in the workplace. Working on campus may help you manage your time and connect to your school experience.

### Potential Negative Effects

Time commitment.   Whereas a nonworking student splits time between academic and personal life, a working student must add a third, time-consuming factor. More responsibilities and less time to fulfill them demands more efficient time management. Many schools recommend that students not work more than twenty hours a week while taking a full course load.

Adjusting priorities.   The priority level of your job may vary. For a student who depends on the income, work may take priority over study time. Evaluate priorities carefully. Realize that you may have to reduce social activities, exercise at home, cut back on nonacademic activities, or lighten your course load in order to maintain a job and still get studying done. Your job is important, but if you are also committed to school, earning a good GPA may be just as crucial.

Shifting gears.   Unless your job meshes with your classroom curriculum, it may take some effort to shift gears mentally as you move back and forth between academia and the workplace. Each environment has its own set of people, responsibilities, joys, and problems. Establish mental boundaries that can help you shake off academic stress while at work, and vice versa.

   If you consider the positive and negative effects and decide that working will benefit you, you should establish what you need in a job.

## Establishing Your Needs

Think about what you need in a job before you begin your job hunt. Table 9-2 on p. 235 shows factors you may want to consider. Evaluate any potential job in terms of these needs.

## Sources of Job Information

Many different routes can lead to satisfying jobs. Use your school's career planning and placement office, networking skills, classified ads, employment agencies, and on-line services to help you explore.

### Your School's Career Planning and Placement Offices

Generally, the career planning and placement office deals with post-graduation job placements, while the student employment office, along with the financial aid office, has more information about working while in school. At either location you might find general workplace information, listings of job opportunities, sign-ups for interviews, and contact information for companies. The career office may hold frequent informational sessions on different topics. Your school may also sponsor job or career fairs that give you a chance to explore job opportunities.

Many students, because they don't seek job information until they're about to graduate, miss out on much of what the career office can do. Don't wait until the last minute. Start exploring your school's career office early in your university life. The people and resources there can help you at every stage of your career and job exploration process.

### Networking

**Networking,**

The exchange of information and/or services among individuals, groups, or institutions.

Networking is one of the most important job-hunting strategies. With each person you get to know, you build your network and tap into someone else's. Imagine a giant think link connecting you to a web of people just a couple of phone calls away. Of course, not everyone with whom you network will come through for you. Keep in contact with as many people as possible in the hope that someone will. You never know who that person might be.

**Contact,**

A person who serves as a carrier or source of information.

With whom can you network? Friends and family members may know of jobs or other people who can help you. At your school, instructors, administrators, or counselors may give you job or contact information. People at school employment or career offices can help you locate work. Some schools even have opportunities for students to interact with alumni. Look to your present and past work experience for more leads. Employers or co-workers may know someone who needs new employees. A former employer might even hire you back with similar or adjusted hours, if you left on good terms.

The contacts with whom you network aren't just sources of job opportunities. They are people with whom you can develop lasting, valuable relationships. They may be willing to talk to you about how to get established, the challenges on the job, what they do each day, how much you can expect to make, or any other questions you have similar to those in Table 9-1. Thank your contacts for their help and don't forget them. Networking is a two-way street. Even as you receive help, be ready to extend yourself to others who may need help and advice from you.

### Classified Ads

Some of the best job listings are in daily or periodic newspapers. Most papers print help-wanted sections in each issue, organized according to career field categories. At the beginning of most help-wanted sections you

## TABLE 9-2  WHAT YOU MAY NEED IN A JOB

| NEED | DESCRIPTION |
|------|-------------|
| **SALARY/WAGE LEVEL** | Consider how much money you need to make month by month and yearly. You may need to make a certain amount for the year as a whole, but you may need to earn more of that total amount during the months when you are paying tuition. Consider also the amount that justifies taking the time to work. If a job pays well but takes extra hours that should go toward studying or classes, it might not be worth it. Take time to compare the positive effects with the negative effects of any job's pay structure. |
| **TIME OF DAY** | When you can work depends on your school schedule. For example, if you take classes Monday, Tuesday, and Thursday during the day, you could look for a job with weekend or evening hours. If you attend evening classes, a daytime job could work fine. |
| **HOURS PER WEEK (PART-TIME VS. FULL-TIME)** | If you take classes part time, you may choose to work a full-time job. If you are a full-time student, it may be best to work part time. Balance your priorities so that you can accomplish your schoolwork and still make the money you need. |
| **DUTIES PERFORMED** | If you want hands-on experience in your chosen field, narrow your search to jobs that can provide it. On the other hand, if a regular paycheck is your priority, you might not care as much about what you do. Consider if there is anything you absolutely hate to do. Working somewhere and/or doing something that makes you miserable may not be worth any amount of money. |
| **LOCATION** | Weigh the effects of how long it takes to get to a job against what you are getting out of it, and decide whether it is worth your while. A job at or near your school may give unparalleled convenience. When you know you can get to work quickly, you can schedule your day more tightly and get more done. |
| **FLEXIBILITY** | Even if your classes are at regular times, you might have other projects and meetings at various times. Do you need a job that offers flexibility, allowing you to shift your working time when you have to attend to an academic or family responsibility that takes priority? Choose according to the flexibility you require. |
| **AFFILIATION WITH SCHOOL OR FINANCIAL AID PROGRAM** | Some financial aid packages, especially if they involve funds from your school, can require you to take work at the school or a federal organization. In that case you would have to choose among the opportunities offered. |
| **ACCOMMODATION OF SPECIAL NEEDS** | If you have a hearing or vision impairment, reduced mobility, children for whom you need day care, or other special needs, you may want to find an employer who can and will accommodate them. |

will find an index that tells you the categories and on what pages they begin in the listings. Individual ads describe the kind of position available and will give a telephone number or post office box for you to contact. Some ads will include additional information such as job requirements, a contact person, and the salary or wages offered.

You can run your own classified ads if you have a skill you want to advertise. Many college students make extra cash by doing specific tasks for campus employees or other students, such as typing, editing, cleaning, tutoring, or baby sitting. You may want to advertise your particular job skills in your school or local paper.

### On-Line Services

The Internet is growing as a source of job listings. Through it you can access job search databases such as the Career Placement Registry and U. S. Employment Opportunities. Web sites such as CareerPath.com and CareerMosiac list all kinds of positions. Individual associations and companies may also post job listings and descriptions, often as part of their World Wide Web pages. For example, IBM includes job openings on its Web page. Refer to the Appendix (Researching Information and Student Resources on the Internet) at the end of this book for more information on how to find the information you need on the Internet.

### Employment Agencies

Employment agencies are organizations that help people find work. Most employment agencies will put you through a screening process that consists of an interview and one or more tests in your area of expertise. For example, someone looking for secretarial work may take a word-processing test and a spelling test, while someone looking for accounting work may take accounting and math tests. If you pass the tests and interview well, they will try to place you in a job.

Most employment agencies specialize in particular career or skill areas, such as accounting, medicine, legal, computer operation, graphic arts, child care, and food services. Agencies may place job seekers in either part-time or full-time employment. Many agencies also place people in temporary jobs, which can work well for students who are available from time to time. Such agencies may have you call in whenever you are free and will see if anything is available that day or week.

Employment agencies are a great way to hook into job networks. However, they usually require a fee that either you or the employer has to pay. Investigate any agency before signing on. See if your school's career counselors know anything about the agency, or if any fellow students have used it successfully. Ask questions so that you know as much as possible about how the agency operates.

## Making a Strategic Job Search Plan

When you have gathered information on the jobs you want, formulate a plan for pursuing them. Organize your approach according to what you need to do and how much time you have to devote to your search. Do you plan to make three phone calls per day? Will you fill out three job applications a week for a month? Keep a record—on 3-by-5-inch cards, a computer file, or in a notebook—of the following:

➤ People you contact
➤ Companies to which you apply

➤ Jobs you rule out (for example, jobs that become unavailable or which you find out don't suit your needs)

➤ Response from your communications (phone calls to you, interviews, written communications) and the information on whoever contacted you (names, titles, times, and dates)

Keeping accurate records will enable you to both chart your progress and maintain a clear picture of the process. You never know when information might come in handy again. If you don't get a job now, another one could open up at the same company in a couple of months. In that case, well-kept records would enable you to contact key personnel quickly and efficiently. See Figure 9-3 for a sample file card.

## Your Résumé and Interview

Information on résumés and interviews fills many books. Therefore, your best bet is to consult some that will go into more detail, such as *The Resume Kit*, by Richard Beatty, or *Job Interviews for Dummies* by Joyce Lain Kennedy (don't be insulted by the title; it has lots of terrific information).

The following basic tips can get you started on giving yourself the best possible chance at a job.

FIGURE 9-3    SAMPLE FILE CARD

Job/company: Child-care worker at Morningside Day Care
Contact: Sally Wheeler, Morningside Day Care, 17 Parkside Road, Silver Spring, MD 20910
Phone/fax/e-mail: (301) 555-3353 phone, (301) 555-3354 fax, no e-mail
Communication: Saw ad in paper, sent résumé and cover letter on October 7
Response: Call from Sally to set up interview

—Interview on Oct. 15 at 2 p.m., seemed to get a positive response, she said she would contact me again by the end of the week

Follow-up: Sent thank-you note on October 16

Résumé.    Your résumé should always be typed or printed on a computer. Design your résumé neatly, using an acceptable format (books or your career office can show you some standard formats). Proofread it for errors, and have someone else proofread it as well. Type or print it on a heavier bond paper than is used for ordinary copies. Use white or off-white paper and black ink.

Interview.    Pay attention to your appearance. Be clean, neat, and appropriately dressed. Don't forget to choose a nice pair of shoes—people notice. Bring an extra copy of your résumé with you, and any other materials that you want to show the interviewer, even if you have already sent a copy ahead of time. Avoid chewing gum or smoking. Offer a confident handshake. Make eye contact. Show your integrity by speaking honestly about yourself. After the interview is over, no matter what the outcome, send a formal but pleasant thank-you note right away as a follow-up.

Earning the money you need is hard, especially if you work part-time in order to have time for school. Financial aid can take some of the burden off your shoulders. If you can gather one or more loans, grants, or scholarships, they may help make up for what you don't have time to earn.

*"And all that rubbish about placing the interviewee on a lower chair to make him feel inferior ... quite the opposite is true..."*

Source: Cartoon on page 11 by Bill Stott, from *The Crazy World of the Office*, reprinted with permission of Exley Publications Ltd, Watford, UK.

## WHAT SHOULD YOU KNOW ABOUT FINANCIAL AID?

Seeking help from various sources of financial aid has become a way of life for much of the student population. Education is an important but often expensive investment. The cost for a year's full-time tuition only (not including room and board) in 1995–96 ranged from $900 to $15,000, with the national average hovering around $2100 for public institutions and over $11,000 for private ones.[2] Not many people can pay for tuition in full without aid. In fact, according to data compiled in the academic year 1992–93, over 41 percent of students enrolled received some kind of aid,[3] and that number almost certainly continues to increase along with rising tuition costs.

Most sources of financial aid don't seek out recipients. Take the initiative to learn how you (or you and your parents, if they currently help to support you) can finance your education. Find the people on campus who can help you with your finances. Do some research to find out what's available, weigh the pros and cons of each option, and decide what would work best for you. Try to apply as early as you can. The types of financial aid available to you are loans, grants, and scholarships.

# Student Loans

A loan is given to you by a person, bank, or other lending agency, usually to put toward a specific purchase. You, as the recipient of the loan, then must pay back the amount of the loan, plus interest, in regular payments that stretch over a particular period of time. Interest is the fee that you pay for the privilege of using money that belongs to someone else.

## Making a Loan Application

What happens when you apply for a loan?

1. *The loaning agency must approve you.* You may be asked about what you and any other family members earn, how much savings you have, your credit history, anything you own that is of substantial value (a home or business), and your history of payment on any previous loans.

2. *An interest charge will be set.* Interest can range from 5 percent to over 20 percent, depending on the loan and the economy. Variable-interest loans shift charges as the economy strengthens or weakens. Fixed-rate loans have one interest rate that remains constant.

3. *The loaning agency will establish a payment plan.* Most loan payments are made monthly or quarterly (four times per year). The payment amount depends on the total amount of the loan, how much you can comfortably pay per month, and the length of the repayment period.

## Types of Student Loans

The federal government administers or oversees most student loans. To receive aid from any federal program, you must be a citizen or eligible noncitizen and be enrolled in a program of study that the government has determined is eligible. Individual states may differ in their aid programs. Check with your campus financial aid office to find out details about your state and your school in particular.

Following are the main student loan programs to which you can apply if you are eligible. Amounts vary according to individual circumstances. Contact your school or federal student aid office for further information. In most cases, the amount is limited to the cost of your education minus any other financial aid you are receiving. All the information on federal loans and grants comes from the *1997–1998 Student Guide to Financial Aid*, published by the U. S. Department of Education.[4]

Perkins Loans.    Carrying a low, fixed rate of interest, these loans are available to those with exceptional financial need (need is determined by a government-determined formula that indicates how large a contribution toward your education your family should be able to make). Schools issue these loans from their own allotment of federal education funds. After you graduate, you have a "grace period" (up to nine months, depending on whether you were a part-time or full-time student) before you have to begin repaying your loan in monthly installments.

Stafford Loans.   Students enrolled in school at least half-time may apply for a Stafford Loan. Exceptional need is not required. However, students who can prove exceptional need may qualify for a "subsidized" Stafford Loan, for which the government pays your interest until you begin repayment. There are two types of Stafford Loans. A Direct Stafford Loan comes from government funds, and an FFEL Stafford Loan comes from a bank or credit union participating in the FFEL (Federal Family Education Loan) program. The type available to you depends on your school's financial aid program. You begin to repay a Stafford Loan six months after you graduate, leave school, or drop below half-time enrollment.

Plus Loans.   Your parents can apply for a Plus Loan if they currently claim you as a dependent and if you are enrolled at least half-time. They must also undergo a credit check in order to be eligible, although the loans are not based on income. If they do not pass the credit check, they may be able to sponsor the loan through a relative or friend who does pass. Interest is variable; the loans are available from either the government or banks and credit unions. Your parents will have to begin repayment sixty days after they receive the last loan payment; there is no grace period.

For a few students, a loan from a relative is possible. If you have a close relationship with a relative who has some money put away, you might be able to talk to that person about helping you with your education. Discuss the terms of the loan as you would with any financial institution, detailing how and when you will receive the loan as well as how and when you will repay it. It may help to put the loan in writing. You may want to show your gratitude by offering to pay interest.

## Grants and Scholarships

Both grants and scholarships require no repayment, and therefore give your finances a terrific boost. Grants, funded by the government, are awarded to students who show financial need. Scholarships are awarded to students who show talent or ability in the area specified by the scholarship. They may be financed by government or private organizations, schools, or individuals.

### Federal Grant Programs

Pell Grants.   These grants are need-based. The Department of Education uses a standard formula to evaluate the financial information you report on your application, and determines your eligibility from that "score" (called an EFC, or Expected Family Contribution, number). You must also be an undergraduate student who has earned no other degrees to be eligible. The Pell Grant serves as a foundation of aid to which you may add other aid sources, and the amount of the grant varies according to the cost of your education and your EFC. Pell Grants require no repayment.

FSEOG (Federal Supplemental Educational Opportunity Grants). Administered by the financial aid administrator at participating schools, SEOG eligibility depends on need. Whereas the government guarantees that every student eligible for a Pell Grant will receive one, each school receives a limited amount of federal funds for SEOGs, and once it's gone, it's gone. Schools set their own application deadlines. Apply early. No repayment is required.

**Work-Study.** Although you work in exchange for the aid, work-study is considered a grant because a limited number of positions are available. This program is need-based and encourages community-service work or work related in some way to your course of study. You will earn at least the federal minimum wage and will be paid hourly. Jobs can be on-campus (usually for your school) or off-campus (often with a nonprofit organization or a local, state, or federal public agency). Find out who is in charge of the work-study program on your campus.

There is much more to say about these financial aid opportunities than can be touched on here. Many other important details about federal grants and loans are available in The *1997–98 Student Guide to Financial Aid.* You might find this information at your school's financial aid office, or you can request it by mail, phone, or on-line service:

| | |
|---|---|
| <u>Address:</u> | Federal Student Aid Information Center<br>P.O. Box 84<br>Washington, D.C. 20044 |
| <u>Phone:</u> | 1-800-4-FED-AID (1-800-433-3243)<br>*TDD for the hearing-impaired:* 1-800-730-8913 |
| <u>Internet address:</u> | www.ed.gov/prog_info/SFA/StudentGuide |

## Scholarships

Scholarships are given for different kinds of abilities and talents. Some reward academic achievement. Some reward exceptional abilities in sports or the arts. Some reward citizenship or leadership. Certain scholarships are sponsored by federal agencies. If you display exceptional ability and are disabled, female, of an ethnic background classified as a minority (such as African-American or Native American), or a child of someone who draws benefits from a state agency (such as a POW or MIA), you might find scholarship opportunities geared toward you.

All kinds of organizations offer scholarships. You may receive scholarships from individual departments at your school or your school's independent scholarship funds, local organizations such as the Rotary Club, or privately operated aid foundations. Labor unions and companies may offer scholarship opportunities for children of their employees. Membership groups such as scouting organizations or the Y might offer scholarships, and religious organizations such as the Knights of Columbus or the Council of Jewish Federations might be another source.

### Researching Grants and Scholarships

It can take work to locate scholarships and work-study programs because many of them aren't widely advertised. Ask at your school's financial aid office. Visit your library or bookstore and look in the section on College or Financial Aid. Guides to funding sources, such as Richard Black's *The Complete Family Guide to College Financial Aid,* catalogue thousands of organizations and help you find what fits you. Check out on-line scholarship search services. Use common sense and time management when applying for aid—fill out the application as neatly as possible and send it in on time or even early. In addition, be wary of scholarship scam artists who ask you to pay a fee up front for them to find aid for you.

No matter where your money comes from—financial aid or paychecks from one or more jobs—you can take steps to help it stretch as far as it can go. The next sections concentrate on developing a philosophy about your money and budgeting effectively. Using those skills, you can more efficiently cover your expenses, and still have some left over for savings and fun.

# HOW CAN STRATEGIC PLANNING HELP YOU MANAGE MONEY?

So you work hard to earn your wages and study hard to hold on to your grants and loans. What do you do with that money? Popular culture tells you to buy. You are surrounded by commercials, magazine ads, and notices in the mail that tell you how wonderful you'll feel if you indulge in some serious spending. On the other hand, there are some definite advantages to not taking that advice. Making some short-term sacrifices in order to save money can help you a great deal in the long run.

## Short-Term Sacrifices Can Create Long-Term Gain

When you think about your money, take your values and your ability to plan strategically into account. Ask yourself what goals you value most and what steps you will have to take over time to achieve those goals. You are already planning ahead by being in school and committing to paying for tuition. You may be scrimping now, but you are planning for a career that may reward you with job security and financial stability. Sometimes the most important goals are also the ones that require a long-term commitment. If you can make that commitment, the reward will be worth the short-term sacrifices.

Table 9-3 shows some potential effects of spending. Some effects are negative, some positive, and some more positive than others. Evaluate which you would prefer in the long run. You may find that the pleasure luxuries provide isn't worth the stress created by debt.

Critical thinking is the key to smart money planning. Impulsive spending usually happens when you don't take time to think through your deci-

## TABLE 9-3 POTENTIAL EFFECTS OF SPENDING

| OPTION | POTENTIAL SHORT-TERM EFFECTS | POTENTIAL LONG-TERM EFFECTS |
|---|---|---|
| Purchase new sound system | High-quality sound | If paid on credit, a credit card debt, with finance charges, that requires monthly payment; if paid in cash, a loss of benefits that could have come from saving that money |
| Reduce or pay off credit card debt | Less money for day-to-day expenses; reduction of monthly bills | Improved credit rating and credit history; increased ability to be approved for loans and mortgages; less money charged in interest and fees |
| Take a week's vacation | Fun and relaxation; stress reduction | Credit card debt or less money saved for future needs |
| Invest in mutual fund | Less money on hand; more money earning interest | More money earned, due to an interest rate higher than banks can offer |
| Buy a car | Transportation and independence; gas, maintenance, parking charges | Debt in the form of a car loan; monthly payments for a few years; gradual decrease in car value |
| Pay health-insurance bills | Health insurance coverage; a tighter monthly budget | The safety and security of knowing that your health and that of your family is protected |
| Invest in your family business | Commitment to family; less money to spend on extras | Involvement in a family business that can earn you money and provide solid employment for you and other family members |
| Put money toward tuition | Having to scrimp while in school due to less money on hand; fewer loans and debts | Less money to pay off later in student loans, which means less money charged in interest; more freedom to spend your money on getting settled after you graduate; shorter period of debt |

sion before you buy. To use your hard-earned money to your greatest benefit, take time to think critically about your finances. First, establish your needs, and be honest about what you truly need and what you just want. Second, brainstorm available options of what to do with your money; evaluate the positive and negative effects of each. Third, choose an option and carry it out. Finally, evaluate the result.

This section doesn't imply that you should never spend money on things that won't bring you any long-term satisfaction. The goal is to make choices that give short-term satisfaction while still providing for long-term money growth. If you need a vacation, drive to another state to visit friends instead of buying an expensive package deal at a resort. Buy a less expensive sound system instead of a state-of-the-art one that will test the limits of your credit card. Buy clothes at an outlet and choose pieces that you can mix and match. When you spend wisely, you will appreciate it later.

> "It is thrifty to prepare today for the wants of tomorrow."
>
> Aesop

## Develop a Financial Philosophy

You can develop your own personal philosophy about spending, saving, and planning. Following are a couple of strategies that you might want to incorporate into that philosophy.

**Live beneath your means.**    Spend less than you make. This strategy helps you create savings, no matter how much or how little. Any amount of savings will give you a buffer zone that can help with emergencies or bigger expenditures. Sometimes your basic needs will cost more than you make, in which case living beneath your means becomes very difficult. If you find, however, that extras are putting your spending over your earnings, cut back.

**Pay yourself.**    After you pay your monthly bills, put whatever you can save from your monthly earnings in a savings account. Paying yourself helps you store money in your savings where it can grow. That savings could become security when you grow older, financing for your children's college education, help with a financial crisis, or a down payment on a large purchase. Don't think of the money left after paying bills as automatically available for spending. Make your payment to yourself a high priority so that you honor it as you do your other bills.

# HOW CAN YOU CREATE A BUDGET THAT WORKS?

**Budgeting,**
Making a plan for the coordination of resources and expenditures; setting goals with regards to money.

Every time you have some money in your pocket and have to figure out whether it will pay for what you want at that moment, you are budgeting your money. It takes some thought and energy to budget efficiently. The more money you can save each month, the more you will thank yourself later when you need it. Consider your resources (money coming in) and expenditures (money flowing out). A smart budget adjusts the money flow for the best possible chance that what comes in will be more than what goes out. Smart budgeting is a worthwhile investment in your future.

## The Art of Budgeting

Budgeting involves following a few basic steps in order. These steps are: determining how much money you make, determining how much money you spend, subtracting the second number (what you spend) from the first number (what you make), evaluating the result, and making decisions about how to adjust your spending or earning based on that result. Budgeting regularly is easiest. Use a specified time frame, such as a week or month. Most people budget on a month-by-month basis.

### Determine How Much You Will Make

Do this by adding up all your money receipts from the month. If you currently have a regular full-time or part-time job, add your pay stubs. If you have received any financial aid, loan funding, or scholarship money, determine how much of that you can allow for each month's income and add it to your total. For example, if you received a $1200 grant for the year, each month would have an income of $100. Be sure, when you are figuring your income, to use the amounts that remain *after* taxes have been taken out.

## Figure Out How Much You Spend

You may or may not have a handle on your spending. Many people don't take the time to keep track. If you have never before paid much attention to how you spend money, examine your spending patterns. Over a month's time, record expenditures in a small notebook or on a piece of paper on a home bulletin board. You don't have to list everything down to the penny. Just indicate expenditures over five dollars, making sure to count smaller expenditures if they are frequent (a bus pass for a month, soda or newspaper purchases per week). In your list, include an estimate of the following:

- ➤ Rent/mortgage/school room fees
- ➤ Tuition or educational loan payments (divide your annual total by 12 to arrive at a monthly figure)
- ➤ Books, lab fees, and other educational expenses
- ➤ Regular bills (heat, gas, electric, phone, car payment, water)
- ➤ Credit card or other payments on credit
- ➤ Food, clothing, toiletries, and household supplies
- ➤ Child care
- ➤ Entertainment and related items (eating out, books and publications, movies)
- ➤ Health, auto, and home/renters' insurance
- ➤ Transportation and auto expenses

Subtract what you spend from what you make. Ideally, you will have a positive number. You may end up with a negative number, however, especially if you haven't made a habit of keeping track of your spending. This indicates that you are spending more than you make, which over a long period of time can create a nasty debt.

## Evaluate the Result

After you arrive at your number, determine what it tells you. If you have a positive number, decide how to save it if you can. If you end up with a negative number, ask yourself questions about what is causing the deficit—where you are spending too much or earning too little. Of course, surprise expenses during some months may cause you to spend more than usual, such as if you have to replace your refrigerator, pay equipment fees for a particular course, or have an emergency medical procedure. However, when a negative number comes up for what seems to be a typical month, you may need to adjust your budget over the long term.

### Make Decisions About How to Adjust Spending or Earning

Looking at what may cause you to overspend, brainstorm possible solutions that address those causes. Solutions can involve either increasing resources or decreasing spending. To deal with spending, prioritize your expenditures and trim the ones you really don't need to make. Do you eat out too much? Can you live without cable, a beeper, a cellular phone? Be smart. Cut out unaffordable extras. As for resources, investigate ways to take in more money. Taking a part-time job, hunting down scholarships or grants, or increasing hours at a current job may help.

## A Sample Budget

Table 9-4 shows a sample budget of an unmarried student living with two other students. It will give you an idea of how to budget (all expenditures are general estimates, based on averages).

To make up the $190 that this student went over budget, he can adjust his spending. He could rent movies or check them out of the library instead of going to the theater. He could socialize with friends at someone's apartment instead of paying high prices and tips at a bar or restaurant. Instead of buying CDs and tapes, he could borrow them. He could also shop for specials and bargains in the grocery store or go to a warehouse supermarket to stock up on staples at discount prices. He could make his lunch instead of buying it and walk instead of taking public transportation.

Not everyone likes the work involved in keeping a budget. While linear, factual, reflective, and verbal learners may take to it more easily, active, holistic, theoretical, and visual learners may resist the structure and detail (see Chapter 2). Visual learners may want to create a budget chart like the one shown in the example or construct a think link that shows the connections between all the month's expenditures. Use images to clarify ideas, such as picturing a bathtub you are filling that is draining at the same time. Use strategies that make budgeting more tangible, such as dumping all of your receipts into a big jar and tallying them at the end of the month. Even if you have to force yourself to do it, you will discover that budgeting can reduce stress and help you take control of your finances and your life.

## Savings Strategies

You can save money and still enjoy life. Make your fun less-expensive fun—or save up for a while to splurge on a really special occasion. Here are some suggestions for saving a little bit of money here and there. Small amounts can add up to big savings after a while.

- ➤ Rent movies or attend bargain matinees.
- ➤ When safe for the fabric, hand-wash items you ordinarily dry-clean.
- ➤ Check movies, CDs, tapes, and books out of your library.
- ➤ Make popcorn instead of buying bags of chips.
- ➤ Walk instead of paying for public transportation.

## TABLE 9-4  A STUDENT'S SAMPLE BUDGET

Part-time salary: $10 an hour, 20 hours a week. 10 × 20 = $200 a week, × 4 1/3 weeks (one month) = $866. Student loan from school's financial aid office: $2000 divided by 12 months = $166. Total income per month: $1032.

| MONTHLY EXPENDITURES | AMOUNT |
|---|---|
| Tuition ($6500 per year) | $ 542 |
| Public transportation | $ 90 |
| Phone | $ 40 |
| Food | $ 130 |
| Medical insurance | $ 120 |
| Rent (including utilities) | $ 200 |
| Entertainment/miscellaneous | $ 100 |
| **Total spending** | **$1222** |

$1032 (income) – $1222 (spending) = $-190 ($190 over budget)

➤ If you have storage space, buy detergent, paper products, toiletries, and other staples in bulk.

➤ Shop in secondhand stores.

➤ Keep your possessions neat, clean, and properly maintained—they will last longer.

➤ Take advantage of weekly supermarket specials and bring coupons when you shop.

➤ Reuse grocery bags for food storage and garbage instead of buying bags.

➤ Return bottles and cans for deposits if you live in a state that accepts them.

➤ Trade clothing with friends and barter services (plumbing for baby-sitting, for example).

➤ Buy display models of appliances or electronics (stereo equipment, TVs, VCRs).

➤ Take your lunch instead of buying it.

➤ Find a low-rate long distance calling plan, use e-mail, or write letters.

➤ Save on heat by dressing warmly and using blankets; save on air conditioning by using fans.

➤ Have pot-luck parties; ask people to bring dinner foods or munchies.

Add your own suggestions here!

_____

_____

_____

_____

You can also maximize savings and minimize spending by using credit cards wisely.

## Managing Credit Cards

Most credit comes in the form of a powerful little plastic card. Credit card companies often solicit students on campus or through the mail. When choosing a card, pay attention to the *annual fee* and *interest rates*, the two ways in which a credit card company makes money from you. Some cards have no annual fee; others may charge a flat rate of $10 to $70 per year. Interest rates can be fixed or variable. A variable rate of 12 percent may shoot up to 18 percent when the economy slows down. You might be better off with a mid-range fixed rate that will always stay the same.

Following are some potential effects of using credit.

### Positive Effects

**Establishing a good credit history.** If you use your credit card moderately and pay your bills on time, you will make a positive impression on your creditors. Your *credit history* (the record of your credit use, including positive actions such as paying on time and negative actions such as going over your credit limit) and *credit rating* (the score you are given based on your history) can make or break your ability to take out a loan or mortgage. How promptly you make loan payments and pay mortgage and utility bills affects your credit rating as well. Certain companies track your credit history and give you a credit rating. Banks or potential employers will contact these companies to see if you are a good credit risk.

**Emergencies.** Few people carry enough cash to handle unexpected expenses. Your credit card can help you in emergency situations such as when you need towing.

**Record of purchases.** Credit card statements give you a monthly record of purchases made, where they were made, and exactly how much was paid. Using your credit card for purchases that you want to track, such as work expenses, can help you keep records for tax purposes.

### Negative Effects

**Credit can be addictive.** Credit can be like a drug, seeming fun because the pain of paying is put off until later. If you get hooked, though, you can wind up thousands of dollars in debt to creditors. The high interest will enlarge

**Creditors,**
People to whom debts are owed, usually money.

*"Put not your trust in money, but put your money in trust."*

Oliver Wendell Holmes

# REAL WORLD PERSPECTIVE

## What should I do about all these credit card offers?

### Brett Cross, University of Washington

I am a pre-engineering student at the University of Washington. Recently, I have been receiving a number of credit card applications offering a low interest rate. In fact, I get at least one offer a week. I've been thinking it would be nice to establish credit, but I'm not sure if getting a credit card right now is a good idea. Even though I have a part-time job hauling and have financial aid, it seems like there's never enough to make it to the end of the semester.
Should I apply for one of these credit cards? It would be really great to have some extra cash every now and then.

### Tim Short, Washington State University

Dealing with financial hardships while in college is a part of life for many people these days. Credit card offers are in abundance for college students, and for good reason. Credit companies know that most college students won't be able to pay off their cards until after they graduate, and that they tend to carry balances and pay interest and hefty fees until they are solvent. Believe me, I know. Throughout my past four years at college, I have acquired several credit cards.
On them I have charged things such as books, car repairs, auto insurance, and other personal items. I am still paying interest on these cards monthly and will not be able to pay them off until after I graduate.

My suggestion to you is this: Don't take out a credit card unless you absolutely have to. If you can take out student loans or borrow from your parents, do that instead. Most academic loans hold a 6–8 percent interest rate which is much lower than the 18–21 percent that most credit card companies charge. Don't be fooled by offers for a card with a low rate. These invariably expire after one year and then the rate jumps up. If you miss a payment during that year, some companies will raise your rates immediately. Rationalizing that you will pay the card off before that time frame is up is also not a good idea. Unless you are on the verge of graduation, you will probably not have any more cash in a year than you do now. Overall, my advice is this: If you can avoid borrowing from credit card companies, do so! You will be a lot happier in the long run.

your debt; your credit rating may fall, potentially hurting your eligibility for loans and mortgages; and you may lose your credit cards altogether.

**Credit spending can be hard to monitor.** Paying by credit can seem so easy that you don't realize how much you are spending. When the bill comes at the end of the month, the total can hit you hard.

**You are taking out a high-interest loan.** Buying on credit is similar to taking out a loan—you are using money with the promise to pay it back. Loan rates, however, especially on fixed-interest loans, are often much lower than the 11 to 23 percent on credit card debt. Fifteen percent interest per year on a credit card debt averaging $2000 is approximately $300; 5 percent interest per year on a loan in the same amount is $100.

**Bad credit ratings can haunt you.** Any time you are late with a payment, default on a payment, or in any way misuse your card, a record of that occurrence will be entered on your credit history, lowering your credit rating. If a prospective employer or loan officer discovers a low rating, you will seem less trustworthy and may lose the chance at a job or a loan.

## Managing Credit Card Debt

There are ways to manage credit card debt so that it doesn't get worse. Stay in control by having only one or two cards and paying bills regularly and on time. Try to pay in full each month. If you can't, at least pay the minimum. Make as much of a dent in the bill as you can.

If you get into trouble, three steps will help you deal with the situation. First, *admit* that you made a mistake, even though you may be embarrassed. Then, *address* the problem immediately and honestly in order to minimize the damages. Call the bank or credit card company to talk to someone about the problem. They may draw up a payment plan that allows you to pay your debt gradually, in amounts that your budget can manage. Creditors would rather accept small payments than nothing at all.

Finally, *prevent* this problem from happening again. Figure out what got you into trouble and take steps to avoid it in the future if you can. Some financial disasters, such as medical emergencies, may be beyond your control. Overspending on luxuries, however, is something you have the power to avoid. Make a habit of balancing your checkbook. Cut up a credit card or two if you have too many. Don't let a high credit limit tempt you to spend. Pay every month, even if you pay only the minimum. If you work to clean up your act, your credit history will gradually clean up as well.

## Sacrifici

In Italy, parents often use the term *sacrifici*, meaning "sacrifices," to refer to tough choices that they make in order to improve the lives of their children and family members. They may sacrifice a larger home so that they can afford to pay for their children's sports and after-school activities. They may sacrifice a higher-paying job so that they can live close to where they work. They give up something in exchange for something else that they have decided is more important to them.

Think of the concept of *sacrifici* as you analyze the sacrifices you can make in order to get out of debt, reach your savings goals, and prepare for a career that you find satisfying. Many of the short-term sacrifices you are making today will help you do and have what you want in the future. Keep that notion as a light to guide you through the ups and downs of student life.

# Chapter 9: Applications

Name _____ Date _____

## ? Key Into Your Life: Opportunities to Apply What You Learn

### Exercise 1: Career Possibilities

Establish career possibilities for yourself by investigating some career areas. Consider what you know about yourself, and consult others if you want additional opinions. Write here two career areas that you would like to investigate.

1. _____  2._____

    Investigate both areas. You may want to talk to people in those fields, do research at the library, meet with someone at your career planning and placement office, or talk to someone who teaches in those fields. Make notes in a separate notebook as you investigate. Then, summarize your impressions here. What do you like or dislike? What suits your needs and what would be difficult to handle? Do you plan to keep these areas as possibilities or discard them?

1. _____

_____

_____

2. _____

_____

_____

### Exercise 2: Mentors

First, consider the people you go to with problems and questions, people whom you trust and with whom you share a lot of yourself. Name up to three—don't fill the list unless you can really think of three people you trust.

1. _____

2. _____

3. _____

Evaluate your list according to the description of mentoring that you read in the chapter. With which of those people do you feel you could have a mentoring relationship? Name up to two; for each, name two steps you can take to invest even further in your relationship.

1. _____

_____

2. _____

_____

## Exercise 3: Your Job Priorities

What kind of a job could you manage while you're in school? How would you want a job to benefit you? Discuss your requirements in each of the following areas.

Salary/wage level _____

Time of day _____

Hours per week (part time vs. full time) _____

Duties _____

Location _____

Flexibility _____

Affiliation with school or financial aid program_____

What kind of job might fit all or most of your requirements? List two possibilities here.

1. _____

2. _____

## Exercise 4: Savings Brainstorm

As a class, brainstorm areas that require financial management (such as funding an education, running a household, or putting savings away for the future) and write them on the board. Divide into small groups. Each group should choose one area to discuss (make sure all areas are chosen). In your group, brainstorm strategies that can help with the area you have chosen. Think of savings ideas, ways to control spending, ways to earn more money, and any other methods of relieving financial stress. Agree on a list of possible ideas for your area and share it with the class.

## Key to Self-Expression: Discovery Through Journal Writing

*To record your thoughts, use a separate journal or the lined page at the end of the chapter.*

**Credit Cards**  Describe how you use credit cards. Are you conservative, overindulgent, or in between? Do you pay on time, and do you pay the full balance of the card, or not? How does using a credit card make you feel—powerful, excited, apprehensive, or nervous? For what sort of purchases do you use credit cards? If you would like to change how you use credit, discuss any changes you want to make and how they would help you.

Name _____ Date _____

## Journal Entry

Name _____ Date _____

Journal Entry

# MOVING AHEAD:
## Building A Flexible Future

The end of one path can be the beginning of another. For example, graduation is often referred to as commencement, because the end of your student career is the beginning or renewal of your life as a working citizen. As you come to the end of your work in this course, you have built up a wealth of knowledge. Now you have more power to make decisions about what directions you want your studies, your career, and your personal growth to take.

This chapter will explore how to manage the constant change you will encounter. Developing your flexibility will enable you to adjust goals, make the most of successes, and work through failures. You will consider what is important about giving back to your community and continuing to learn throughout your life. Finally, you will revisit your personal mission, exploring how to revise it as you encounter changes in the future.

In this chapter, you will explore answers to the following questions:

➤ How can you live with change?

➤ What will help you handle success and failure?

➤ Why give back to the community and the world?

➤ Why is college just the beginning of lifelong learning?

➤ How can you live your mission?

# HOW CAN YOU LIVE WITH CHANGE?

Even the most carefully constructed plans can be turned upside down by change. In this section, you will explore some ways to make change a manageable part of your life by accepting the reality of change, maintaining flexibility, and adjusting your goals.

## Accept the Reality of Change

As Russian-born author Isaac Asimov once said, "It is change, continuing change, inevitable change, that is the dominant factor in society today. No sensible decision can be made any longer without taking into account not only the world as it is, but the world as it will be."[1] Change is a sure thing. Two significant causes of change on a global level are technology and the economy.

### Technological Growth

Today's technology has spurred change. Tasks that people have performed for years are now taken care of by computer in a fraction of the time and for a fraction of the price. Advances in technology come into being daily: Computer companies update programs, new models of cars and machines appear, and scientists discover new possibilities in medicine and other areas. People make changes in the workplace, school, and home to keep up with the new systems and products that technology constantly offers. People and cultures are linked around the world through the Internet and World Wide Web.

The dominance of the media, brought on by technological growth, has increased the likelihood of change. A few hundred years ago, no television or magazines or Internet existed to show people what was happening elsewhere in the world. A village could operate in the same way for years with very little change, because there would be little to no contact with anyone from the outside who could introduce new ideas, methods, or plans. Now, the media constantly presents people with new ways of doing things. When people can see the possibilities around them, they are more likely to want to find out whether the grass is truly greener on the other side of the fence.

### Economic Instability

The unpredictable economy is the second factor in this age of constant change. Businesses have had to cut costs in order to survive, which has affected many people's jobs and careers. Some businesses discovered the speed and cost-effectiveness of computers and used them to replace workers. Some businesses have had to downsize and have laid off people to save money. Some businesses have merged with others, and people in duplicate jobs were let go. The difficult economy has also had an effect on personal finances. Many people face money problems at home that force them to make changes in how much they work, how they pursue an education, and how they live.

**Downsize,**
To reduce in size; streamline.

# Maintain Flexibility

The fear of change is as inevitable as change itself. When you become comfortable with something, you tend to want it to stay the way it is, whether it is a relationship, a place you live, a job, a schedule, or the racial/cultural mix of people with whom you interact. Change may seem to have only negative effects, and consistency only positive effects. Think about your life right now. What do you wish would always stay the same? What changes have upset you and thrown you off balance?

You may have encountered any number of changes in your life to date, many of them unexpected. You may have experienced ups and downs in relationships, perhaps marriage or divorce. You may have changed schools, changed jobs, or moved to a new home. You may have shifted your course of study. You may have added to your family or lost family members. Financial shifts may have caused you to change the way you live. All of these changes, whether you perceive them as good or bad, cause a certain level of stress. They also cause a shift in your personal needs, which may lead to changing priorities.

## Change Brings Different Needs

Your needs can change from day to day, year to year, and situation to situation. Although you may know about some changes ahead of time, such as when you plan to attend school or move in together with a partner, others may take you completely by surprise, such as losing a job, illness, or an unexpected pregnancy. Even the different times of year bring different needs, such as a need for extra cash around the holidays or a need for additional child care when your children are home for the summer.

Some changes that shift your needs will occur within a week or even a day. For example, an instructor may inform you that you have a quiz or extra assignment at the end of the week, or your supervisor at work may give you an additional goal for the week. During the course of a day, your daughter might tell you that she needs you to drive her somewhere that evening, or a friend may call and need your help with something that has come up suddenly. Table 10-1, on the following page, shows how the effects of certain changes can lead to new priorities.

## Flexibility vs. Inflexibility

When change affects your needs, *flexibility* will help you shift your priorities so that you address those needs. You can react to change with either inflexibility or flexibility, each with its resulting effects.

**Inflexibility.**   Not acknowledging a shift in needs can cause trouble. For example, if you lose your job and continue to spend as much money as you did before, ignoring your need to live more modestly, you can drive yourself into debt and make the situation worse. Or if you continue to spend little time with a partner who has expressed a need for more contact, you may lose your relationship.

**Flexibility.**   Being flexible means acknowledging the change, examining your different needs, and addressing them in any way you can. As frightening

## TABLE 10-1 CHANGE PRODUCES NEW PRIORITIES

| CHANGE | EFFECTS AND CHANGED NEEDS | NEW PRIORITIES |
|---|---|---|
| Lost job | Loss of income; need for others in your household to contribute more income | Job hunting; reduction in your spending; additional training or education in order to qualify for a different job |
| New job | Change in daily/weekly schedule; need for increased contribution of household help from others | Time and energy commitment to new job, maintaining confidence, learning new skills |
| Started school | Fewer hours for work, family, and personal time; responsibility for classwork; need to plan semesters ahead of time | Careful scheduling; making sure you have time to attend class and study adequately; strategic planning of classes and of career goals |
| Relationship/marriage | Responsibility toward your partner; merging of your schedules and perhaps your finances and belongings | Time and energy commitment to relationship |
| Breakup/divorce | Change in responsibility for any children; increased responsibility for your own finances; possibly a need to relocate; increased independence | Making time for yourself, gathering support from friends and family, securing your finances, making sure you have your own income |
| Bought car | Responsibility for monthly payment; responsibility for upkeep | Regular income so that you can make payments on time; time and money for upkeep |
| New baby | Increased parenting responsibility; need money to pay for baby's needs or if you had to stop working; need help with other children | Child care, flexible employment, increased commitment from a partner or other supporter |
| New cultural environment (from new home, job, or school) | Exposure to unfamiliar people and traditions; tendency to keep to yourself | Learning about the culture with which you are now interacting; openness to new relationships |

as it can be, being flexible can help you move ahead. Discovering what change brings may help you uncover positive effects that you had no idea were there. For example, a painful breakup or divorce can lead you to discover greater capability and independence. A loss of a job can give you a chance to reevaluate your abilities and look for another job in an area that suits you better. An illness can give you perspective on what you truly value in life. In other words, a crisis can spur opportunity; you may learn that you want to adjust your goals in order to pursue that opportunity.

Sometimes you may need to resist for a while, until you are ready to face an important change. When you do decide you are ready, being flexible will help you cope with the negative effects and benefit from the positive effects.

# Adjust Your Goals

Your changing life will often result in the need to adjust goals accordingly. Sometimes goals must change because they weren't appropriate in the first place. Some turn out to be unreachable; some may not pose enough of a challenge; others may be unhealthy for the goal-setter or harmful to others.

## Step One: Reevaluate

Before making adjustments in response to change, take time to *reevaluate* both the goals themselves and your progress toward them.

**The goals.** First, determine whether your goals still fit the person you have become in the past week, or month, or year. Circumstances can change quickly. For example, an unexpected pregnancy might cause a female student to rethink her educational goals.

**Your progress.** If you feel you haven't gotten far, determine whether the goal is out of your range or simply requires more stamina than you had anticipated. As you work toward any goal you will experience alternating periods of progress and stagnation. Sticking with a tough goal may be the hardest thing you'll ever do, but the payoff may be worth it. You may want to seek the support and perspective of a friend or counselor as you evaluate your progress.

## Step Two: Modify

If after your best efforts it becomes clear that a goal is out of reach, *modifying* your goal may bring success. Perhaps the goal doesn't suit you. For example, an active, interpersonal learner might become frustrated while pursuing a detail-oriented, sedentary career such as computer programming.

Based on your reevaluation, you can modify a goal in two ways:

1. Adjust the existing goal. To adjust a goal, change one or more aspects that define that goal—for example, the time frame, the due dates, or the specifics of the expectations. For example, a woman with an unexpected pregnancy could adjust her educational due date, taking an extra year or two to complete her course work. She could also adjust the time frame, taking classes at night if she had to care for her child during the day.

2. Replace it with a different, more compatible goal. If you find that you just can't handle a particular goal, try to find another that makes more sense for you at this time. For example, a couple who wants to buy a home but just can't afford it can choose to work toward the goal of making improvements to their current living space. Because you and your circumstances never stop changing, your goals should keep up with those changes.

Being open to adjusting your goals will help you manage both failure and success along the way.

"Risk! Risk anything! Care no more for the opinion of others, for those voices. Do the hardest thing on earth for you. Act for yourself. Face the truth."

Katherine Mansfield

# WHAT WILL HELP YOU HANDLE SUCCESS AND FAILURE?

The perfect, trouble-free life is only a myth. The most wonderful, challenging, fulfilling life is full of problems to be solved and difficult decisions to be made. If you want to handle the bumps and bruises without losing your self-esteem, you should prepare to encounter setbacks along with your successes.

## Dealing With Failure

Things don't always go the way you want them to go. Sometimes you may come up against obstacles that are difficult to overcome. Sometimes you will let yourself down or disappoint others. You may make mistakes or lose your motivation. All people do, no matter who they are or how smart or accomplished they may be. What is important is how you choose to deal with what goes wrong. If you can arrive at reasonable definitions of failure and success, accept failure as part of being human, and examine failure so that you can learn from it, you will have the confidence to pick yourself up and keep improving.

### Measuring Failure and Success

Most people measure failure by comparing where they are to where they believe they should be. Since individual circumstances vary widely, so do definitions of failure. What you consider a failure may seem like a positive step for someone else. Here are some examples:

➤ Imagine that your native language is Spanish. You have learned to speak English well, but you still have trouble writing it. Making writing mistakes may seem like failure to you, but to a recent immigrant from the Dominican Republic who knows limited English, your command of the language will seem like a success story.

➤ If two people apply for internships, one may see failure as receiving some offers but not the favorite one, while someone who was turned down may see any offer as a success.

➤ Having a job that doesn't pay you as much as you want may seem like a failure, but to someone who is having trouble finding any job, your job is a definite success.

## Accepting Failure

No one escapes failure, no matter how hard he or she may try (or how successful he or she may be at hiding mistakes). The most successful people and organizations have experienced failures and mistakes. For example, the producers of the film "Waterworld" spent over $140 million on a film that made only a fraction of that cost at the box office. America Online miscalculated customer use and offered a flat rate per month, resulting in thousands of customers having trouble logging onto the service. Many an otherwise successful individual has had a problematic relationship, a substance-abuse problem, or a failing grade in a course.

You have choices when deciding how to view a failure or mistake. You can pretend it never happened, blame it on someone or something else, blame yourself, or forgive yourself.

**Pretending it didn't happen.** Avoiding the pain of dealing with a failure can deny you valuable lessons and could even create more serious problems. HIV is one example of this idea. Imagine that a person has unprotected sex with a potentially HIV-infected partner and then denies it ever happened. If that person later discovers that he or she has contracted HIV from the first partner, the deadly virus may have been passed on to any subsequent partners.

> "The word impossible is not in my dictionary."
> Napoleon

**Blaming others.** Putting the responsibility on someone else stifles opportunities to learn and grow. For example, imagine that an unprepared and inappropriately dressed person interviews for a job and is not hired. If he or she decides that the interviewer is biased, the interviewee won't learn to improve preparation or interview strategies. Evaluate causes carefully and try not to assign blame.

**Blaming yourself.** Getting angry at yourself for failing, or believing that you should be perfect, can only result in your feeling incapable of success and perhaps becoming afraid to try. Negative self-talk can become self-fulfilling.

**Forgiving yourself.** This is by far the best way to cope. First, although you should always strive for your best, don't expect perfection of yourself or anyone else. Expect that you will do the best that you can within the circumstances of your life. Just getting through another day as a student, employee, and/or parent is an important success. Second, forgive yourself when you fail. Your value as a human being does not diminish when you make a mistake. Forgiving yourself will give you more strength to learn from the experience, move on, and try again.

Once you are able to approach failure and mistakes in a productive way, you can explore what you can learn from them.

## Learning From Failure

Learning from your failures and mistakes involves thinking critically through what happened. The first step is to evaluate what happened and decide if it was within your control. It could have had nothing to do with you at all. You could have failed to win a job because someone else with equal qualifi-

## How can I prepare to make a difference in the world when I finish college?

### Norma Espina, University of Texas—El Paso

Right after high school I tried college and was very unsuccessful at it. I didn't realize what I was getting into. When I was in high school, I was surrounded by my friends. If someone didn't know me personally, they at least knew who I was. College was so different; no one knew me. I wanted to appear grown up so I didn't risk very much. This was one of my downfalls. I was  afraid to ask for help or get involved because I wanted to be mature, and I was too afraid to make a mistake. This backfired on me because I started to fall behind in classes. When I didn't understand something, I just let it slide by. Before long, I was avoiding classes. I had excuse after excuse after excuse until finally I didn't want to go to college anymore. That's when I gave up.

Seven years later, after a divorce and two children, I decided to return and finish my education. I was very motivated to succeed. I believe the reason I am successful this time is because I am willing to get involved. I ask questions in class or talk to the professor right after. Through speaking up I began making friends and forming study groups.

My dream is to finish college so I can begin making a difference in the world. I believe I'm on the right track and have a positive attitude about the direction I'm headed. What specific steps do you recommend I take as I prepare for my future outside of college?

### Mike Jackson, Baltimore City Community College

Whether you are in school or beginning your career, one of the things that will contribute to your success is to feel positive about who you are and the dreams you have. Sometimes people who enter the job force allow the job or the group they're in to define them. I personally feel it's better to let the group or the job *enhance* who you  are, but not control your life. That's why it's also important to have balance between your work and your personal life. The more balanced you are, the greater the chance you'll have a healthier perspective on your job and on people in general.

I also believe that life is a series of opportunities, so when one comes along, you've got to grab onto it. It's important to not let life just happen to you. Otherwise you could find yourself in circumstances which are very unpleasant, to say the least. Growing up in an inner-city environment as I did opens your eyes to what can occur when you let life happen to you. Fortunately for me, I had parents with very strong values to help point me in the right direction. But even without supportive parents like mine, if you believe that your goals are worth having, you can make it out of the worst of circumstances.

Finally, have a plan. Decide what you want to do with your life and then formulate steps to achieve that goal. Have some alternatives, too, in case your original ideas don't pan out. But don't worry if you stray from your original plan. Some detours can actually be better than the goal you had in the first place.

cations was in line for it ahead of you. A family crisis that disrupted your sleep could have affected your studying, resulting in a failing grade on a test. These are unfortunate circumstances, but they are not failures. On the other hand, something you did or didn't do may have contributed to the failure.

If you decide that you have made a mistake, your next steps are to analyze the causes and effects of what happened, make any improvements that you can, and decide how to change your action or approach in the future.

For example, imagine that after a long night of studying you forgot your part-time work-study commitment the next day.

**Analyze causes and effects.** *Causes:* Your exhaustion and your concern about your test caused you to forget to check on your work schedule. *Effects:* Because you weren't there, a crucial curriculum project wasn't completed. An entire class and instructor who needed the project have been affected by your mistake.

**Make any possible improvements on the situation.** You could apologize to the instructor and see if there were still a chance to finish up part of the work that day.

**Make changes for the future.** You could set a goal to note your work schedule regularly in your date book—maybe in a bright color—and to check it more often. You could also arrange your future study schedule so that you will be less exhausted.

Think about the people you consider exceptionally successful. They didn't rise to the top without taking risks and making their share of mistakes. They have built much of their success upon their willingness to recognize and learn from their shortfalls. You too can benefit from staying open to this kind of active, demanding, hard-won education. Learning involves change and growth. Let what you learn from falling short of your goals inspire new and better ideas.

## Think Positively About Failure

When you feel you have failed, how can you boost your outlook?

**Stay aware of the fact that you are a capable, valuable person.** People often react to failure by becoming convinced that they are incapable and incompetent. Fight that tendency by reminding yourself of your successes, focusing your energy on your best abilities, and knowing that you have the strength to try again. Realize that your failure isn't a setback as long as you learn from it and rededicate yourself to excellence. Remember that the energy you might expend on talking down to yourself would be better spent on trying again and moving ahead.

**Share your thoughts and disappointment with others.** Everybody fails. Trading stories will help you realize you're not alone. People refrain from talking about failures out of embarrassment, often feeling as though no one else could have made as big a mistake as they did. When you open up, though, you may be surprised to hear others exchange stories that rival your own. Be careful not to get caught in a destructive cycle of complaining. Instead, focus on the kind of creative energy that can help you find ways to learn from your failures.

Look on the bright side.    At worst, you at least have learned a lesson that will help you avoid similar situations in the future. At best, there may be some positive results of what happened. If your romance flounders, the extra study time you suddenly have may help you boost your grades. If you fail a class, you may discover that you need to focus on a different subject that suits you better. What you learn from a failure may, in an unexpected way, bring you around to where you want to be.

## Dealing With Success

Success isn't reserved for the wealthy, famous people you see glamorized in magazines and newspapers. Success isn't money or fame, although it can bring such things. Success is being who you want to be and doing what you want to do. Success is within your reach.

Pay attention to the small things when measuring success. You may not feel successful until you reach an important goal you have set for yourself. However, along the way each step is a success. When you are trying to drop a harmful habit, each time you stay on course is a success. When you are juggling work, school, and personal life, just coping with what every new day brings equals success. If you received a C on a paper and then earned a B on the next one, your advancement is successful.

Remember that success is a process. If you deny yourself the label of "success" until you reach the top of where you want to be, you will have a much harder time getting there. Just moving ahead toward improvement and growth, however fast or slow the movement, equals success.

Here are some techniques to handle your successes.

First, appreciate yourself.    You deserve it. Take time to congratulate yourself for a job well done—whether it be a good grade, an important step in learning a new language, a job offer, a promotion or graduation, or a personal victory over substance abuse. Bask in the glow a bit. Everybody hears about his or her mistakes, but people don't praise themselves (or each other) enough when success happens. Praise can give you a terrific vote of confidence.

Take that confidence on the road.    This victory can lead to others. Based on this success, you may be expected to prove to yourself and others that you are capable of growth, of continuing your successes and building upon them. Show yourself and others that the confidence is well founded.

Stay sensitive to others.    There could be people around you who may not have been so successful. Remember that you have been in their place, and they in yours, and the positions may change many times over in the future. Enjoy what you have, work to build on it and not to take it for granted, and support others as they need it.

Staying sensitive to others is an important goal always, whether you are feeling successful or less than successful. Giving what you can of your time, energy, and resources to the community and the world is part of being aware of what others need. Your contributions can help to bring success to others.

# WHY GIVE BACK TO THE COMMUNITY AND THE WORLD?

Everyday life is demanding. You can become so caught up in the issues of your own life that you neglect to look outside your immediate needs. However, from time to time you may feel that your mission extends beyond your personal life. You have spent time in this course working to improve yourself. Now that you've come so far, why not extend some of that energy and effort to the world outside? With all that you have to offer, you have the power to make positive differences in the lives of others. Every effort you make, no matter how small, improves the world.

## Your Imprint on the World

As difficult as your life can sometimes seem, looking outside yourself and into the lives of others can help put everything in perspective. Sometimes you can evaluate your own hardships more reasonably when you look at them in light of what is happening elsewhere in the world. There are always many people in the world in great need. You have something to give to others. Making a lasting difference in the lives of others is something to be proud of.

Your perspective may change after a volunteering at a soup kitchen. Your appreciation of those close to you may increase after you spend time with cancer patients at the local hospice. Your perspective on your living situation may change after you help people improve their housing conditions.

If you could eavesdrop on someone *talking about you* to another person, what do you think you would hear? How would you like to hear yourself described? What you do for others makes an imprint that can have far more impact than you may imagine. Giving one person hope, comfort, or help can improve his or her ability to cope with life's changes. That person in turn may be able to offer help to someone else. As each person makes a contribution, a cycle of positive effects is generated. For example, Helen Keller, blind and deaf from the age of two, was educated through the help of her teacher

Annie Sullivan, and then spent much of her life lecturing to raise money for the teaching of the blind and deaf. Another example is Betty Ford, who was helped in her struggle with alcoholism and founded the Betty Ford Center to help others with addiction problems.

How can you make a difference? Many schools and companies are realizing the importance of community involvement and have appointed committees to find and organize volunteering opportunities. Make some kind of volunteering activity a priority on your schedule. Join a group from your company that tutors at a school. Organize a group of students to clean, repair, or entertain at a nursing home or shelter. Look for what's available to you or create opportunities on your own. Table 10-2 lists organizations that provide volunteer opportunities; you might also look into more local efforts or private clearinghouses that set up a number of different smaller projects.

Volunteerism is also getting a great deal of attention on the national level. The government has made an effort to stress the importance of community service as part of what it means to be a good citizen, and it provides support for that effort through AmeriCorps. AmeriCorps provides financial awards for education in return for community service work. If you work for AmeriCorps, you can use the funds you receive to pay current tuition expenses or repay student loans. You may work either before, during, or after your college education. You can find more information on AmeriCorps by contacting this organization:

The Corporation for National and Community Service
1201 New York Avenue, NW
Washington, DC 20525
1-800-942-2677

Sometimes it's hard to find time to volunteer when so many responsibilities compete for your attention. One solution is to combine other activities with volunteer work. Get exercise while cleaning a park or your yard or bring the whole family to sing at a nursing home on a weekend afternoon. Whatever you do, your actions will have a ripple effect, creating positive impact for those you help and those they encounter in turn. The strength often found in people surviving difficult circumstances can strengthen you as well.

## Valuing Your Environment

Your environment is your home. When you value it, you help to maintain a clean, safe, and healthy place to live. What you do every day has an impact on others around you and on the future. One famous slogan says that if you are not part of the solution, you are part of the problem. Every saved bottle, environmentally aware child, and reused bag is part of the solution. Take responsibility for what you can control—your own habits—and develop sound practices that contribute to the health of the environment.

## TABLE 10-2 ORGANIZATIONS THAT CAN USE YOUR HELP

| | | |
|---|---|---|
| AIDS-related organizations | American Red Cross | Amnesty International |
| Audubon Society | Battered women shelters | Big Brothers and Big Sisters |
| Churches, synagogues, temples, and affiliated organizations such as the YM/WCA or YM/WHA | Educational support organizations | Environmental awareness/ support organizations such as Greenpeace |
| Hospitals | Hotlines | Kiwanis/Knights of Columbus/ Lions Club/Rotary |
| Libraries | Meals on Wheels | Nursing homes |
| Planned Parenthood | School districts | Scouting organizations |
| Share Our Strength/other food donation organizations | Shelters and organizations supporting the homeless | Sierra Club/World Wildlife Fund |

**Recycle anything that you can.** What can be recycled varies with the system set up in your area. You may be able to recycle any combination of plastics, aluminum, glass, newspapers, and magazines. Products that make use of recycled materials are often more expensive, but if they are within your price range, try to reward the company's dedication by purchasing the products.

**Trade and reuse items.** When your children have grown too old for the crib, baby clothes, and toys, give away whatever is still usable. Give clothing you don't wear to others who can use it. Organizations like the Salvation Army may pick up used items in your neighborhood on certain days or if you make arrangements with them. Wrap presents in plain newspaper and decorate with markers. Use your imagination—there are many, many items that you can reuse, all around you.

**Respect the outdoors.** Participate in maintaining a healthy environment. Use products that reduce chemical waste. Pick up after yourself. Through volunteering, voicing your opinion, or making monetary donations, support the maintenance of parks and the preservation of natural, undeveloped land. Be creative. One young woman planned a cleanup of a local lakeside area as the main group activity for the guests at her birthday party (she joined them, of course). Everyone benefits when each person takes responsibility for maintaining the fragile earth.

Remember that valuing yourself is the base for valuing all other things. Improving the earth is difficult unless you value yourself and think you deserve the best living environment possible. Valuing yourself will also help you understand why you deserve to enjoy the benefits of learning throughout your life.

# WHY IS COLLEGE JUST THE BEGINNING OF LIFELONG LEARNING?

Although it may sometimes feel more like a burden, being a student is a golden opportunity. As a student, you are able to focus on learning for a period of time, and your school focuses on you in return, helping you gain access to knowledge, resources, and experiences. Take advantage of the academic atmosphere by developing a habit of seeking out new learning opportunities. That habit will encourage you to continue your learning long after you have graduated, even in the face of the pressures of everyday life.

Learning brings change, and change causes growth. As you change and the world changes, new knowledge and ideas continually emerge. Absorb them so that you can propel yourself into the future. Visualize yourself as a student of life who learns something new every single day.

Here are some lifelong learning strategies that can encourage you to continually ask questions and explore new ideas.

**Investigate new interests.**    When information and events catch your attention, take your interest one step further and find out more. If you are fascinated by politics on television, find out if your school has political clubs that you can explore. If a friend of yours starts to take yoga, try out a class with him. If you really like one portion of a particular class, see if there are other classes that focus on that specific topic. Turn the regretful, "I wish I had tried that," into the purposeful, "I'm going to do it."

**Read books, newspapers, magazines, and other writings.** Reading opens a world of new perspectives. Check out what's on the bestseller list at your bookstore. Ask your friends about books that have changed their lives. Stay on top of current change in your community, your state, your country, and the world by reading newspapers and magazines. A newspaper that has a broad scope, such as *The New York Times* or *Washington Post*, can be an education in itself. Explore religious literature, family letters, and Internet news groups and web pages. Keep something with you to read for those moments when you have nothing to do.

**Spend time with interesting people.**    When you meet someone new who inspires you and makes you think, keep in touch. Have a potluck dinner party and invite one person or couple from each corner of your life—your family, your work, your school, a club to which you belong, your neighborhood. Sometimes, meet for reasons beyond just being social. Start a book club, a home-repair group, a play-reading club, a hiking group, or an investing group. Get to know people of different cultures and perspectives. Learn something new from each other.

**Pursue improvement in your studies and in your career.**    When at school, take classes outside of your major if you have time. After graduation, continue your education both in your field and in the realm of general knowledge. Stay on top of ideas, developments, structural changes, and new technology in your field by seeking out continuing education courses. Sign up for career-related seminars. Take single courses at a local college or community learning center. Some companies offer additional on-the-job training or will pay for their employees to take courses that will improve their knowledge and skills. If your company doesn't, you may want to set a small part of your income aside as a "learning budget." When you apply for jobs, you may want to ask about what kind of training or education the company offers or supports.

> **Continuing education,** Courses that students can take without having to be part of a degree program.

**Nurture a spiritual life.** You can find spirituality in many places. You don't have to regularly attend a house of worship to be spiritual, although that may be an important part of your spiritual life. "A spiritual life of some kind is absolutely necessary for psychological 'health,'" says psychologist and author Thomas Moore in his book *The Care of the Soul.* "We live in a time of deep division, in which mind is separated from body and spirituality is at odds with materialism."[2] The words *soul* and *spirituality* hold different meaning for each individual. Decide what they mean to you. Whether you discover them in music, organized religion, friendship, nature, cooking, sports, or anything else, making them a priority in your life will help you find a greater sense of balance and meaning.

**Experience what others create.** Art is "an adventure of the mind" (Eugene Ionesco, playwright); "a means of knowing the world" (Angela Carter, author); something that "does not reproduce the visible; rather, it makes visible" (Paul Klee, painter); "a lie that makes us realize truth" (Pablo Picasso, painter); a revealer of "our most secret self" (Jean-Luc Godard, filmmaker). Through art you can discover new ideas and shed new light on old ones. Explore all kinds of art and focus on any forms that hold your interest. Seek out whatever moves you—music, visual arts, theater, photography, dance, domestic arts, performance art, film and television, poetry, prose, and more.

**Make your own creations.** Bring out the creative artist in you. Take a class in drawing, in pottery, or in quilting. Learn to play an instrument that you have always wanted to master. Write poems for your favorite people or stories to read to your kids. Invent a recipe. Design and build a set of shelves for your home. Create a memoir of your life. You are a creative being. Express yourself, and learn more about yourself, through art.

Lifelong learning is the master key that unlocks every door you will encounter on your journey. If you keep it firmly in your hand, you will discover worlds of knowledge—and a place for yourself within them.

# HOW CAN YOU LIVE YOUR MISSION?

As you learn and change, so may your life's mission. Whatever changes occur, your continued learning will give you a greater sense of security in your choices. Recall your mission statement from Chapter 3. Think about how it is changing as you learn and develop. It will continue to reflect your goals, values, and strength if you live with integrity, roll with the changes that come your way, continue to observe the role models in your life, and work to achieve your personal best in all that you do.

## Live With Integrity

**Integrity,**
Adherence to a code of moral values; incorruptibility, honesty.

You've spent a lot of time exploring who you are, how you learn, and what you value. Integrity is about being true to that picture you have drawn of yourself while also considering the needs of others. Living with integrity will bring you great personal and professional rewards.

Honesty and sincerity are at the heart of integrity. Many of the decisions you make and act upon in your life are based on your underlying sense of what is "the right thing to do." Having integrity puts that sense into day-to-day action.

### The Marks of Integrity

A person of integrity lives by the following principles:

1. *Honest representation of him or herself, and his or her thoughts.* For example, you tell your partner when you are hurt over something that he or she did or didn't do.
2. *Sincerity in word and action.* You do what you say you will do. For example, you tell a co-worker that you will finish a project when she has to leave early, and you follow through by completing the work.
3. *Consideration of the needs of others.* When making decisions, you take both your needs and the needs of others into account. You also avoid hurting others for the sake of your personal goals. For example, your sister cares for your elderly father in her home where he lives with her. You spend three nights a week with him so that she can take a course toward her degree.

### The Benefits of Integrity

When you act with integrity, you earn trust and respect from yourself and from others. If people can trust you to be honest, to be sincere in what you say and do, and to consider the needs of others, they will be more likely to encourage you, support your goals, and reward your hard work. Integrity is a must for workplace success. To earn promotions, it helps to show that you have integrity in a variety of situations.

Think of situations in which a decision made with integrity has had a positive effect. Have you ever confessed to an instructor that your paper is late without a good excuse, only to find that despite your mistake you have

*"And life is what we make it, always has been, always will be."*

Grandma Moses

earned the instructor's respect? Have extra efforts in the workplace ever helped you gain a promotion or a raise? Have your kindnesses toward a friend or spouse moved the relationship to a deeper level? When you decide to act with integrity, you can improve your life and the lives of others.

Most importantly, living with integrity helps you believe in yourself and in your ability to make good choices. A person of integrity isn't a perfect person, but one who makes the effort to live according to values and principles, continually striving to learn from mistakes and to improve. Take responsibility for making the right moves, and you will follow your mission with strength and conviction.

## Roll With the Changes

Think again about yourself. How has your idea of where you want to be changed since you first opened this book? How has your self-image changed? What have you learned about your values, your goals, and your styles of communication and learning? Consider how your educational, professional, and personal goals have changed. As you continue to grow and develop, keep adjusting your goals to your changes and discoveries.

Stephen Covey says in *The Seven Habits of Highly Effective People*, "Change—real change—comes from the inside out. It doesn't come from hacking at the leaves of attitude and behavior with quick fix personality ethic techniques. It comes from striking at the root—the fabric of our thought, the fundamental essential paradigms which give definition to our character and create the lens through which we see the world."[3]

Examining yourself deeply in that way is a real risk. Most of all, it demands courage and strength of will. Questioning your established beliefs and facing the unknown are much more difficult than staying with how things are. When you have the courage to face the consequences of trying something unfamiliar, admitting failure, or challenging what you thought you knew, you open yourself to growth and learning opportunities. You can make your way through changes you never anticipated if you make the effort to live your mission—in whatever forms it takes as it changes—each day, each week, each month, and for years to come.

**Paradigm,**
An especially clear pattern or typical example.

## Learn From Role Models

People often derive the highest level of motivation and inspiration from learning how others have struggled through the ups and downs of life and achieved their goals. Somehow, seeing how someone else went through difficult situations can give you hope for your own struggles. The positive effects of being true to one's self become more real when an actual person has earned them.

Learning about the lives of people who have achieved their own version of success can teach you what you can do in your own life. Bessie and Sadie Delany, sisters and accomplished African-American women born in the late 1800's, are two valuable role models. They took risks, becoming professionals in dentistry and teaching at a time when women and minorities were often denied both respect and opportunity. They worked hard to fight racial division

**Role model,**
A person whose behavior in a particular role is imitated by others.

and prejudice and taught others what they learned. They believed in their intelligence, beauty, and ability to give, and lived without regrets. Says Sadie in their *Book of Everyday Wisdom*, "If there's anything I've learned in all these years, it's that life is too good to waste a day. It's up to you to make it sweet."[4]

## Aim for Your Personal Best

Your personal best is simply the best that you can do, in any situation. It may not be the best you have ever done. It may include mistakes, for nothing significant is ever accomplished without making mistakes and taking risks. It may shift from situation to situation. As long as you aim to do your best, though, you are inviting growth and success.

Aim for your personal best in everything you do. As a lifelong learner, you will always have a new direction in which to grow and a new challenge to face. Seek constant improvement in your personal, educational, and professional life, knowing that you are capable of that improvement. Enjoy the richness of life by living each day to the fullest, developing your talents and potential into the achievement of your most valued goals.

*Kaizen* is the Japanese word for "continual improvement." Striving for excellence, always finding ways to improve on what already exists, and believing that you can impact change, is at the heart of the industrious Japanese spirit. The drive to improve who you are and what you do will help to provide the foundation of a successful future.

Think of this concept as you reflect on yourself, your goals, your lifelong education, your career, and your personal pursuits. Create excellence and quality by continually asking yourself, "How can I improve?" Living by *kaizen* will help you to be a respected friend and family member, a productive and valued employee, and a truly contributing member of society. You can change the world.

# Chapter 10: Applications

Name _____    Date _____

**? Key Into Your Life: Opportunities to Apply What You Learn**

### Exercise 1: Changes in Goals

Have you experienced any shifts in your goals? Think about what may have changed since you began this course. List three major goals for each of the five goal areas. In each area, highlight or circle the goal that has changed the most and discuss why the change occurred.

**Personal**

1. _____

2. _____

3. _____

Discuss changes:

_____

_____

**Family**

1. _____

2. _____

3. _____

Discuss changes:

_____

_____

**Lifestyle**

1. _____

2. _____

3. _____

Discuss changes:

_____

_____

**Career**

1. _____

2. _____

3. _____

Discuss changes:

_____

_____

**Financial**

1. _____

2. _____

3. _____

Discuss changes:

_____

_____

## Exercise 2: Looking at Change, Failure, and Success

Life can go by so fast that you don't take time to evaluate what changes have taken place, what failures you could learn from, and what successes you have experienced. Take a moment now and answer the following questions for yourself.

What are the three biggest changes that have occurred in your life this year?

1. _____

2. _____

3. _____

Choose one that you feel you handled well. What shifts in priorities or goals did you make?

_____

_____

_____

Choose one that you could have handled better. What happened? What do you think you should have done?

_____

_____

_____

Now name a personal experience, occurring this year., that you would consider a failure. What happened?

_____

_____

How did you handle it—did you ignore it, blame it on someone else, or admit and explore it?

_____

_____

_____

What did you learn from experiencing this failure?

_____

_____

Finally, describe a recent success of which you are the most proud.

_____

_____

How did this success give you confidence in other areas of your life?

_____

_____

## Exercise 3: Volunteering

Research volunteering opportunities in your community. What are the organizations? What are their needs? Do any volunteer positions require an application, letters of reference, or background checks? List three possibilities for which you have an interest or a passion.

1. _____

2. _____

3. _____

    Of these three, choose one that you feel you will have the time and ability to try next semester. Suggestions that don't take up too much time include spending an evening serving in a soup kitchen, or driving for Meals on Wheels during a lunch or dinner shift. Name your choice here and tell why you selected it.

_____

_____

    Research the suggestion you have chosen. Describe the activity. What is the time commitment? Is there any special training involved? Are there any problematic or difficult elements to this experience?

_____

_____

_____

_____

_____

_____

_____

## Exercise 4: Lifelong Learning

Review the strategies for lifelong learning in this chapter. Which ones mean something to you? Which do you think you can do, or plan to do, in your life now and when you are out of school? Name them and briefly discuss the role they play in your life.

_____

_____

_____

_____

## Key to Self-Expression: Discovery Through Journal Writing

*To record your thoughts, use a separate journal or the lined page at the end of the chapter.*

**One Hundred Positive Thoughts**  Make a list for yourself. The first fifty items in the list should be things you like about yourself. You can name anything—things you can do, things you think, things you've accomplished, things you like about your physical self, and so on. The second fifty items should be things you'd like to do in your life. These can be of any magnitude—anything from trying a Vietnamese food to traveling to the Grand Canyon to keeping your room neat to getting to know someone. They can be things you'd like to do tomorrow or things that you plan to do in twenty years. Be creative. Let everything be possible.

Name _____ Date _____

## Journal Entry

# APPENDIX

## Researching Information and Student Resources on the Internet by Cynthia Leshin

Searching for information is like a treasure hunt. Unless a researcher has knowledge of all the resources and tools available, then the search for useful information may be a time-consuming and frustrating process.

## INTERNET RESEARCH TOOLS

The Internet contains many tools that speed the search for information and resources. Research tools called "search directories" and "search engines" are extremely helpful.

### Search Directories

Search directories are essentially descriptive subject indexes of Web sites. They also have searching options. When you connect to their page, you will find a query box for entering keywords. The search engine at these sites searches only for keyword matches in the directories' databases. Directories are excellent places to begin your research.

### Search Engines

Search engines are different from search directories in that they search World Wide Web sites, Usenet newsgroups, and other Internet resources to find matches to your descriptor keywords. Many search engines also rank the results according to a degree of relevancy. Most search engines provide options for advanced searching to refine your search.

## Basic Guidelines for Internet Research

Search directories and search engines are marvelous tools to help you find information on the Internet. Search directories are often the best places to begin a search, as they frequently yield more relevant returns on a topic than does a search engine, which may produce a high proportion of irrelevant information.

Search engines can be frustrating to use and may not prove to be the best Internet resources to begin with, often providing thousands of links on your keyword search. Although these search tools have advanced options for refining and limiting a search, researchers may find that locating the desired information is not easy and that search results frequently provide a high percentage of irrelevant and useless information. For example, using a search engine for a search with the keywords *business management* returned 500,000 occurrences (*hits*) of the words *business* and *management*. Many of the occurrences of these words were in job listings or companies that were advertising their services. This is why search directories are frequently an excellent resource to begin with when starting your research. The search directory may lead you to the goldmine collection of electronic resources you are searching for.

When researching information on the Internet it is essential that you use several search tools. The basic approach to finding information involves the following steps:

1. Use search directories such as Yahoo (**http://www.yahoo.com**), Excite (**http://www.excite.com**), Galaxy (**http://galaxy.einet.net/galaxy.html**), Magellan (**http://magellan.mckinley.com**) or Infoseek (**http://guide.info-seek.com**) to search for the information under a related topic or category. Explore the links that seem relevant to your topic, and make bookmarks of the ones you would like to investigate further. Look for one site that has a large collection of links on your topic. This is the resource goldmine you are looking for.

2. Use search engines to further research your topic by determining one or more descriptive words (keywords) for the subject. Enter your keywords into the search dialog box.

3. Determine how specific you want your search to be. Do you want it to be broad or narrow? Use available options to refine or limit your search. Some search engines permit the use of *Boolean operators* (phrases or words such as "and," "or," and "not" that restrict a search). Others provide HELP for refining searches, and some have pull-down menus or selections to be checked for options.

4. Submit your query.

5. Review your list of hits (a search return based on a keyword).

6. Adjust your search based on the information returned. Did you receive too much information and need to narrow your search? Did you receive too little or no information and need to broaden your keywords?

7. Use several search directories and search engines for your research. No one search tool will provide a complete resource list.

# SEARCH DIRECTORIES

## Yahoo

Yahoo is one of the most popular search tools on the Internet and is an excellent place to begin your search. Although Yahoo is more accurately described as a search directory, this Web site has an excellent database with search options available. There are two ways to find information using Yahoo: Search through the subject directory, or use the built-in search engine. Yahoo can be accessed from your browser's **Search** button, or by entering this URL: **http://www.yahoo.com**.

Using Yahoo to Search for Information    Follow these steps to use Yahoo to search for information:

1. Begin by browsing the subject directory. For example, if you were searching for information on environmental on-line resources you would first select the *Society and Culture* directory, then follow the

**FIGURE 1** Yahoo's *Environment and Nature* subject index search form in which the keyword *recycling* has been entered:

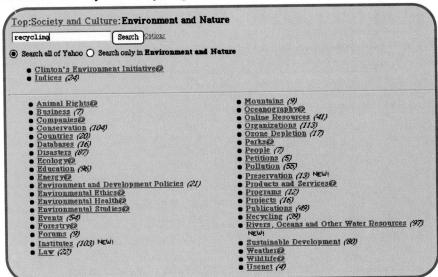

*Environment and Nature* category. Explore categories and see if the information you are searching for can be found under the categories (see Fig. 1).

2. Yahoo's search engine can also be used to find information. Enter a descriptive keyword for your subject, one that uniquely identifies or describes what you are looking for. It is often helpful to do a broad search first, though results may often provide information on the need to change descriptive keywords or to refine your query.

   Perhaps you are looking for information on recycling and were not able to find it easily under one of the Environment categories. Enter the keyword, in this case *recycling*, in Yahoo's query box (See Fig. 1).

3. Click on the **Search** button and review your query results (See Fig. 2).

4. You may now want to refine your search. Most search engines have options for advanced searching using Boolean logic or more carefully constructed database queries. Review the search page for **Options** or **Advanced Options**. When using Yahoo, click on the **Options** button.

**FIGURE 2** Yahoo search results from the keyword *recycling*:

Found **6** Category and **332** Site Matches for **recycling**.

**Yahoo! Category Matches**    **(1 - 6 of 6)**

Business and Economy: Companies: Environment: **Recycling**

Society and Culture: Environment and Nature: **Recycling**

Business and Economy: Companies: Industrial Supplies: Machinery and Tools: **Recycling**

Regional: Countries: Canada: Business: Companies: Environment: **Recycling**

Regional: Countries: United States: Dependent Areas: Puerto Rico: Business: **Recycling**

Regional: Countries: United Kingdom: Business: Companies: Environment: **Recycling**

**FIGURE 3** Yahoo **Options** for refining a search:

If you are using two or more keywords, do you want Yahoo to look for either word (Boolean **or**), both keywords (Boolean **and**), or all words as a single string? For example, to refine your recycling search for only information on commercial recycling, select Boolean **and** because you want to find resources that contain the words "commercial" **and** "recycling" in their titles (See Fig. 3). Otherwise the search would be too broad and would find all resources that contained any of the keywords "commercial" **or** "recycling."

**TIP**

Yahoo suggests putting a phrase in double quotes such as "commercial recycling."

5. Further limit or expand your search by selecting a search method, search area (Yahoo categories, Web sites, Today's News, or Net Events), a period of time for the listing to have occurred, and the number of results returned per page.

6. Submit your query.

7. Review your return list of hits and adjust your search again if necessary.

8. Review your return list for other descriptive words that have been used when summarizing search results. For example, when using the keyword "recycling," search result summaries produced other important descriptive words such as "recycling consumer," "pollution," or "waste management in the home."

9. Conduct a search using other descriptive words.

## Other Search Directories

Explore the search directories listed below Figure 4. You will find that their subject categories vary; most have advanced search options for refining your search; and several (Infoseek and Excite) have powerful search engines built in.

**FIGURE 4** Home page for Infoseek showing search directory: (Reprinted by permission. Infoseek, Ultrasmart, Ultraseek, iSeek, Quickseek, Imageseek, Ultrashop, "proof of intelligent life on the net" and the Infoseek logos are trademarks of Infoseek Corporation which may be registered in certain jurisdictions. Other trademarks shown are trademarks of their respective owners. Copyright © 1995–1997 Infoseek Corporation. All rights reserved.)

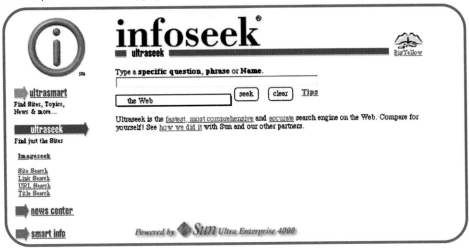

> ➤ Magellan     **http://magellan.mckinley.com**
> ➤ Galaxy     **http://galaxy.einet.net/galaxy.html**
> ➤ Excite     **http://www.excite.com**
> ➤ Infoseek     **http://guide.infoseek.com**

Notice the option for connecting to its powerful search engine—Infoseek Ultra (See Fig. 4).

# SEARCH ENGINES

Search engines require a keyword(s) or phrase that is descriptive of the information you are looking for. Begin by listing keywords or phrases on your topic. When you connect to a search engine, look for its own Search Tips or Advanced Search Options to help you conduct a more efficient and effective search. Taking this step will save time and help to prevent information overload frustration.

## Excite

Excite is one of the most widely used search engines providing a full range of services. Excite searches scanned Web pages and Usenet newsgroups for keyword matches and creates summaries of each match. Excite also has a Web directory organized by category (See Fig. 5).

### Searching With Excite

1. Type in a word or phrase that fits your information need. Be as specific as you can, using words that uniquely relate to the information you are looking for, not simply general descriptive words. For example, if you

**FIGURE 5** Excite Web page displaying services:

are looking for information on health and healing outside of tradition-al medicine you might begin by using keywords such as *holistic health* (See Fig. 6). Since we are using more than one word, read any **Help** information to find the best way to enter in multiple words or a phrase.

2.  If the search result does not contain the information you are looking for, or if the returns provide too much irrelevant information, use the Advanced Search options.

3.  Advanced features include the use of a plus sign (**+**) in front of a search word to ensure that all the returns contain that word. Use a minus sign (**−**) in front of a search word and Excite will make sure that **no** documents contain the word. Excite also supports the use of Boolean operators (**AND, OR, NOT**). Search engines also may suggest the use of double quotation marks around the words or phrase.

4.  Excite lists ten search results at a time in decreasing order of confidence. Each result lists a title, a URL, and a brief summary of the document. The percentage to the left of the return is the confidence rating

**FIGURE 6** Search query for holistic health:

**FIGURE 7**   Search results with a percentage of confidence rating for finding relevant information:

**Excite Search** found **16138** document(s) about : **holistic AND health**.
Documents **1-10** sorted by **Relevance**. Sort by Site.

**84% About the American Holistic Medical Asso...** [More Like This]
*URL:* http://www.doubleclickd.com:80/about_ahma.html
*Summary:* Later, associate membership was expanded to include all state-licensed holistically oriented practitioners, such as chiropractors, naturopaths, nurses, psychologists, dentists, etc. The mission of the AHMA is to support physicians in their evolving personal and professional development and to promote an art and science of health care which acknowledges all aspects of the individual, the.

**82% Holistic Healing Web Page** [More Like This]
*URL:* http://www.tiac.net:80/users/mgold/health.html
*Summary:* The holistic health-related information presented on this WWW page is not meant as medical advice. Environmental Issues Relating to Human & Planetary Health.

**81% HOLISTIC CONCEPTS OF HEALTH AND DISEASE ...** [More Like This]
*URL:* http://www.med.auth.gr:80/~karanik/english/vet/holist6.htm
*Summary:* HOLISTIC CONCEPTS OF HEALTH AND DISEASE #6. HOLISTIC CONCEPTS OF HEALTH AND DISEASE Answers.

**81% Holistic Health Link** [More Like This]
*URL:* http://www.kdcol.com:80/~daniel/prolink.htm
*Summary:* ....Holistic Health Services Holistic Health Care Practitioners Holistic Health Care Manufacturers, Distributors, and Suppliers. [Natural Connection] [Holistic Health Care] [Health Food Store] [Books] [E-Mail].

**81% The Fosters: Holistic Health and Native ...** [More Like This]
*URL:* http://www.blvl.igs.net:80/~bfoster/
*Summary:* The Fosters: Holistic Health and Native Herbs. A Homepage for Kristina and Bob Foster.

(Figure 7), with 100% being the highest confidence rating attainable. To see the next listing of documents related to your phrase or keywords, click the "next documents" button. Click the "sort by site" button to view the Web sites that have the most pages relevant to your search.

## Other Search Engines

There are many search engines to help you find information. You will need to use each of them at least several times before you can select the ones that best meet your needs. Listed below are additional search engines to explore.

Alta Vista  by Digital (http://altavista.digital.com) is an excellent search engine, with one of the largest Web-search databases.

Image Surfer  (http://isurf.interpix.com) differs from most search tools in that it focuses on finding images on the Web.

Infoseek Ultra  (http://ultra.infoseek.com), under development for two years at Infoseek and introduced in the fall of 1996, utilizes the next generation of search technology. Ultra promises to provide new levels of speed, accuracy, and currency unmatched by other search technologies.

Lycos,  one of the older search tools, has recently expanded their services with new search capabilities for images and sounds, information on cities, road maps, companies on line, stock quotes, and an excellent link to the top 5 percent Web sites. Lycos at http://www.lycos.com moves to the top of the bookmark list (See Fig. 8).

**FIGURE 8**    Lycos home page:    (The Lycos "Catalog of the Internet" Copyright © 1994–1997 Carnegie Mellon University. All rights reserved. Lycos is a trademark of Carnegie Mellon University. Used by permission.)

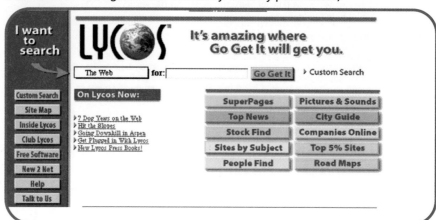

HotBot  (http://www.hotbot.com) is a new and very hot search tool.

Inktomi  (http://inktomi.berkeley.com) is a search engine from Berkeley.

Open Text  (http://www.opentext.com) has one of the most comprehensive collections of search tools and is one of the best designed search engines on the Internet.

Wired Source  at http://www.wiredsource.com/wiredsource has a collection of search engines to use for your research.

# USING INTERNET SOURCES FOR RESEARCH

Internet resources provide a valuable source for finding information that you can use for class presentations, papers, research, dissertations, and theses. However, the Internet should never be your sole source of information but rather another resource that you use to find information on a topic. The Internet can be a valuable resource for accessing

➤ information collections and databases,

➤ government documents,

➤ exhibitions,

➤ research papers,

➤ publications,

➤ news,

➤ on-line educational events,

➤ the latest and most current information on a topic, and for

➤ communicating with experts on your topic.

In this section you will learn

➤ how to evaluate Internet information sources, and

➤ how to reference Internet sources.

# Evaluating Internet Information

Unlike scholarly publications, there is no editorial board for most Internet information. With an estimate of between 20 to 50 million pages of data created from a variety of sources—individuals, business, corporations, nonprofit organizations, schools, special interest causes, or illicit (if not illegal) sources—it is not surprising that not all the information is accurate, unbiased, reputable, scientifically valid, or up-to-date. It is therefore essential that you understand how to evaluate information you research on the Net.

How strict you are with your evaluation will depend on what you are using the information for. For example, if you are writing a factual report, dissertation, thesis, or paper that others will rely on for accurate content, it will be essential that you are judicious in choosing what information will be reported from the Net.

The first thing you must do when using Internet sources for your studies is to determine which resources to use. The following guidelines will assist you with evaluating which sources to use.

> **Information Source.**  Where does the information come from—an individual, organization, educational institution, or other source? One way to quickly determine the source of the information is to look at the URL—Net site address. The first address protocol often will provide you with information on the source of the information, name of institution, and domain. For example, an address such as **http://gort.ucsd.edu** provides the name of the institution—University of California, San Diego—and the edu ending indicates an educational institution. An educational institution has a good chance of being a reputable source. Other address endings that are highly likely to be reputable are *gov* for government or *mil* for military. Naturally, you will want to evaluate the information further. Just because the information is from an educational institution, government, or military source does not ensure that the content is factual and reliable.

Check to see if the document resides in an individual's personal Internet account or is part of the organization's official Internet site. This information can often be determined by looking at the URL address pathway.

Is the organization that publishes this document recognized in the field you are studying? Is the organization qualified to be an expert in this topic?

> **Authorship.**  Closely related to the information source is the reputation of the data and the reliability of its source. Although the information may be from an educational institution, who wrote and compiled the data—a professor, student, or other source? Information on an educational institution Web site may be compiled by a student or graduate student who is not as yet an authority on the subject and may enter written errors or present incorrect data without realizing it. The content may not have been reviewed for accuracy and reliability.

Who is the author? Does the author have credentials to be an expert on the topic? Consider educational background, experience, and other published writings. Have you encountered the author's name in your reading or bibliographies?

Does the Internet document provide information on the author such as institutional affiliation, position, and experience and credentials? If none of this is provided, is there an e-mail address or a mailing address where you can request biographical information? Correspond with the author to obtain more information about the source of the content.

➤ **Accuracy.**    Is the data accurate? Check to see if there is a reference for the information. Where does the information come from—a published research paper or report, historical document, news publication, or is it a personal viewpoint? Does the document include a bibliography? Does the author acknowledge related knowledge sources?

Although information may be written from a personal point of view, don't necessarily invalidate it. Bias is to be expected especially if one is a participant in an event. If the writing seems biased, look for inconsistencies or incorrect thinking. Does the author acknowledge that his treatment of the subject is controversial? Are there political or ideological biases? Can you separate fact from opinion? Do any statements seem exaggerated or overly simplified? Has the author omitted any important details? Is the writer qualified to be authoritative?

One example of inaccuracy in Web writing is the use of the words *endangered species* when referring to animals that may in fact be only threatened or vulnerable. Many authors loosely use the words *endangered species*. To cross-check this information, a reliable source such as the Convention on International Trade and Endangered Species (CITES) and the International Union for the Conservation of Nature (IUCN) must be used. These international organizations keep the working lists of which species are categorized as either extinct, endangered, threatened, vulnerable, indeterminate, or out of danger.

➤ **Verifiable.**    Can the data be verified? Does it appear to be well researched? Does the author make generalizations without proof or validation? Always be thinking, "Show me why or how." In some instances you may need to ask if the data has statistical validity (is supported by statistical testing). Watch for errors or omissions.

When numbers or statistical information are reported, it is critical that the data be cross-checked with a reliable publication source. For example, some Web factual data contain errors due to carelessness in copying and transposing numbers from a print version to a Web site. Reporting that 17,000 acres of rain forest are destroyed daily when the correct number is 700 acres is an inexcusable error in sloppy copy.

➤ **Consistency of data.**    Is the data consistent or does it reflect contradictions with other information on the topic? Are definitions used consistently throughout?

For example, in our rain forest research a search for reputable Web sites such as the Public Broadcasting System (PBS) or the Rain Forest Action Network are excellent on-line references to cross-check the consistency of data.

➤ **Quality.**    Is the text error free; is it well organized and grammatically correct? Check for the misspelling of names or carelessness and lack of attention to details in other areas. Information that contains these types of careless errors probably should not be relied on.

Is the tone scholarly, technical, factual, authoritative, or personal?

➤ Currency.    Is the information current and up-to-date? Does the document include a publication date or a date of copyright? Does it appear to be appropriate and relevant for today? Information that was reported in 1985 is probably not valid today. Look for the most current information unless currency is not an issue.

Bonus guidelines—other important suggestions:

➤ Whenever possible, check on-line information against other sources. Never use information that you cannot verify.

➤ Question everything you read. Learn to be critical and skeptical.

➤ Information found on the Internet should complement information from traditional research resources. Never use Internet information as your sole source of knowledge.

➤ "When in doubt, leave it out."

### Tip

If you don't know where to find a reliable source to cross-check your information, go talk with a resource librarian, teacher, or professor. These individuals can be excellent resources for finding publications to verify your data. You can also call a reputable organization.

## Referencing Electronic Media

As with any published reference, the goal of an electronic reference is to credit the author and to enable the reader to find the material. The International Standards Organization (ISO) continues to modify a uniform system of citing electronic documents. The following guidelines and examples have been compiled from *The American Psychological Association (APA) Publication Manual*, *MLA-Style*, and *The Chicago Manual of Style*.

➤ Be consistent in your references to on-line documentation or information.

➤ Capitalization follows the "accepted practice for the language or script in which the information is given."

➤ Use your discretion for the choice of punctuation used to separate elements and in the use of variations in typeface or underscoring to distinguish or highlight elements.

➤ If a print form is available and the same as the electronic form, referencing of the print form is preferred.

Include the following in your reference:

➤ The author's name if it is available or important for identification.

➤ The most recent date of publication or a modification date if document undergoes revision.

➤ The date you accessed the document on the Internet.

➤ Title of the document, file, or World Wide Web site.

➤ Specify the protocol: Telnet, Gopher, FTP, World Wide Web.

> ➤ Provide the Internet address or retrieval path for accessing the information, including the file name, directory, and pathway.

> ➤ Do not end a path statement with a period, because it is not part of the Internet address and may hinder retrieval if used.

> ➤ If the information is available via a listserv mailing list, provide subscription information.

### Format for Referencing On-Line Information—APA Style

Author, I. (date of work). <u>Title of full work</u> [online] . Available: Specify protocol and path (date document was accessed).

Author, I., & Author, I. (date). <u>Title of full work</u> [online]. Specify protocol and path (date document was accessed).

**NOTE**

The examples provided in this section use APA style. Although the type of information required for referencing is similar, the format for the references varies between the APA, MLA, and the Chicago styles. Check with your professor to see which style to use. Refer to the style manual for the reference format.

## Examples of APA Style

### World Wide Web

The World Wide Web provides many types of information you may want to reference: text, images, video, or sound. To reference these information sources, provide the following:

> ➤ Author's name (if known)

> ➤ Date of Web site information (if known or different from date you accessed)

> ➤ Title of the page or article

> ➤ Any additional information such as version or edition

> ➤ The URL for the page you are referencing

> ➤ Date you accessed this page

### EXAMPLE 1: Referencing World Wide Web site

The first example is from CNET (See Fig. 9). CNET is a computer network that integrates television programming with a network. CNET's Web site takes advantage of the Web's interactive capabilities to deliver valuable information on computer technology, the Internet, and the future of technology in a well-designed, creative, and rich multimedia environment.

### World Wide Web Reference #1

Farell, C. (1997, February). Get animated: How to make your GIFs dance [Online]. Available: http://www.cnet.com/Content/Features/Howto/Webanim/index.html (March 1997).

**FIGURE 9**   World Wide Web page from CNET.COM to be referenced:
(Reprinted with permission from CNET, Inc. Copyright 1995-7. www.cnet.com)

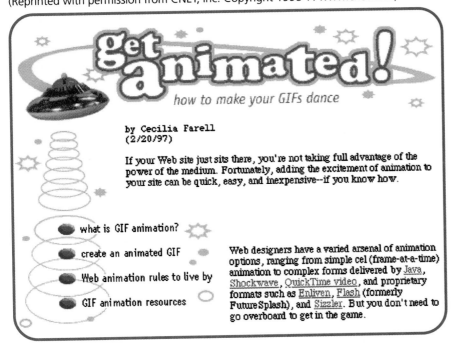

EXAMPLE 2: World Wide Web

This example references an article on Netscape World's site (See Fig. 10).

**FIGURE 10**   Article From Netscape World:   (Copyright 1996 Netscape
Communications Corp. Used with permission. All rights reserved. This electronic file or
page may not be reprinted or copied without the express written permission of Netscape)

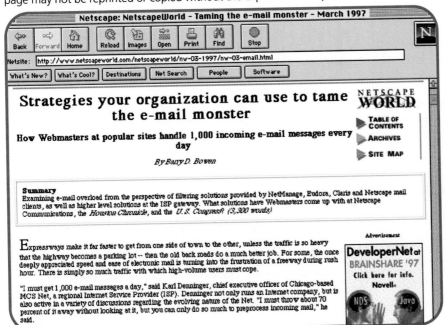

World Wide Web Reference #2

Bowen, B. D. (1997). Strategies your organization can use to tame the e-mail monster [Online]. Available : http://www.netscapeworld.com (March 1997).

## Gopher

When referencing Gopher sites, include the following information.

- ➤ Author's name (if known)
- ➤ Date of publication
- ➤ Title of the page, article, or file
- ➤ Any additional information such as version or edition
- ➤ The URL for the page you are referencing and the pathway to this information
- ➤ Date you accessed this page

### EXAMPLE 1: Gopher Reference

The Library of Congress has information on copyright basics that should be referenced when used in a document (See Fig.11).

Gopher Reference #1

Library of Congress (updated 9/95). Copyright basics [Online]. Available: gopher://marvel.loc.gov:70/00/.ftppub/copyright/circs/circ01 (March 1997).

### EXAMPLE 2: Gopher Reference

The second example is a NASA Gopher site (See Fig. 12). The figure below shows the first page for this site (**gopher://naic.nasa.gov**). For this page numerous pathways must be taken (links) to find the information on the M.U.S.E report. It is essential that this information be provided for others to find this article.

Gopher Reference #2

Part I - M.U.S.E. Report (1993, December). [Online]. Available Gopher: gopher://naic.nasa.gov/ Pathway: /Guide to NASA Online Resources/ NASA Scientific, Educational, and Governmental Resources/ Government

**FIGURE 11**   Library of Congress document at their Gopher site:

```
Circular 1

                       COPYRIGHT BASICS


WHAT COPYRIGHT IS

Copyright is a form of protection provided by the laws of the
United States (title 17, U.S. Code) to the authors of "original
works of authorship" including literary, dramatic, musical,
artistic, and certain other intellectual works.  This protection
is available to both published and unpublished works.  Section 106
of the Copyright Act generally gives the owner of copyright the
exclusive right to do and to authorize others to do the following:

  --  To reproduce the copyrighted work in copies or phonorecords;

  --  To prepare derivative works  based upon the copyrighted work;
```

**FIGURE 12**   The opening menu for NASA's Gopher server:

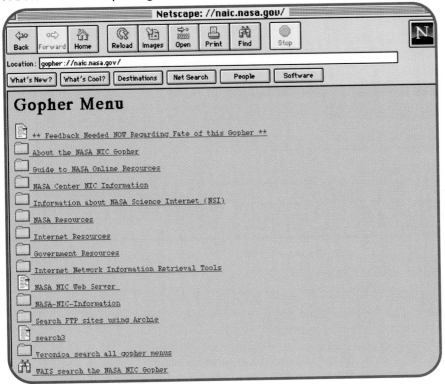

Resources/Americans Communicating Electronically/ Electronic Mail Issues for
the Federal Government/ Unified Federal Government Electronic Mail Users
Support Environment Report

## File Transfer Protocol

When referencing documents that you have accessed using FTP, include the
following:

- ➤ Author's name (if known)
- ➤ Date of publication (if available)
- ➤ Title of the document, article, or file
- ➤ The address for the FTP site you used along with the pathway to this
  information
- ➤ Date you accessed this site

### EXAMPLE 1: FTP Reference

This example is an article with information on how to use e-mail to access
Internet resources (See Fig. 13).

FTP Reference #1

Rankin, B. (1994, August). Accessing the Internet by e-mail, 2nd edition [Online].
Available: ftp://dftnic.gsfc.nasa.gov/general_info/internet.by-email (March
1997).

**FIGURE 13**    Internet by e-mail document at NASA's FTP site:

```
          Accessing The Internet By E-Mail
             2nd Edition - August 1994


        Copyright (c) 1994,  "Doctor Bob" Rankin

    All rights reserved.  Permission is granted to make and distribute
    verbatim copies of this document provided the copyright notice and
         this permission notice are preserved on all copies.


How to Access Internet Services by E-mail
-----------------------------------------


If your only access to the Internet is via e-mail, you don't have to
miss out on all the fun!  Maybe you've heard of FTP, Gopher, Archie,
Veronica, Finger, Whois, WAIS, World-Wide Web, and Usenet but thought
they were out of your reach because your online service does not provide
those tools.  Not so!  And even if you do have full Internet access,
using e-mail servers can save you time and money.
```

## EXAMPLE 2: FTP Reference

This example is from Project Gutenberg's FTP site (See Fig. 14). The article to be referenced is on the history and philosophy of Project Gutenberg.

**FIGURE 14**    Article on an FTP site to be referenced:

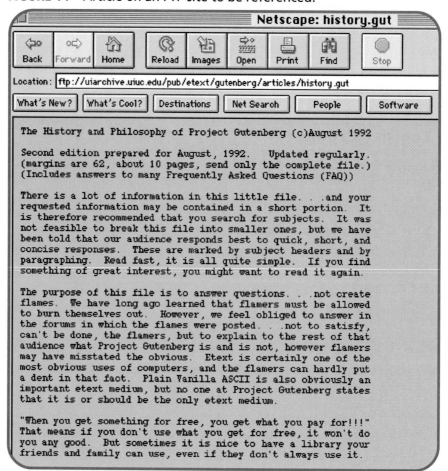

FTP Reference #2

History and philosophy of Project Gutenberg (1992, August). In Gutenberg
    Archives [Online]. Available FTP: ftp://uiarchive.uiuc.edu
    Directory: /pub/etext/gutenberg/articles/history.gut (April 1997).

# Telnet

When referencing telnet sites, include the following:

- ➤ Author's name (if known)
- ➤ Date of publication (if available)
- ➤ Title of the work or the name of the telnet site
- ➤ The address for the telnet site
- ➤ Directions for accessing the publication when connected
- ➤ Date you accessed this site

## EXAMPLE 1: Telnet Reference

The first example is from the Smithsonian Institution's telnet site (See Fig. 15).

Telnet Reference #1

S1 Chronology (Record 28). Rush leaves England with Smithson gold [Online].
    Available: telnet://siris.si.edu (March 1997).

## EXAMPLE 2: Telnet Reference

This example is from the MOO, Diversity University (See Fig. 16).

Telnet Reference #2

Diversity University_Guest. Welcome to Diversity University MOO [Online].
    Available: telnet://moo.du.org:8888 (March 1997).

**FIGURE 15**   Abstract on the history of the Smithsonian founder, James
Smithson:

**FIGURE 16**  Information on navigating within Diversity University's text-based virtual environment:

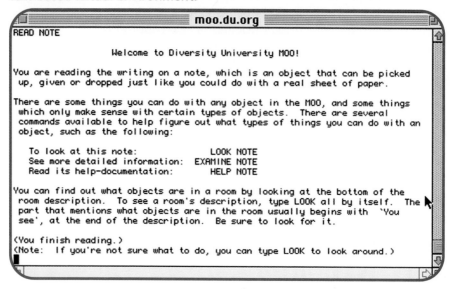

# E-mail, Listserv Mailing Lists, and Usenet Newsgroups

Information from e-mail, listservs, and newsgroups is both timely and personal, often representing an individual's point of view. This information must also be referenced. Do not reference personal e-mail. E-mail references will mainly come from listservs and newsgroups. To reference these information sources, provide the following:

➤ Author's name (if known)

➤ Date of the e-mail message, listserv message, or Usenet posting

➤ Subject

➤ Name of the listserv or newsgroup

➤ Address of the listserv or newsgroup

➤ Include information on how to find the group's archives if available

➤ Date accessed

### EXAMPLE 1: E-mail Reference

The latest document on how to use e-mail to access Internet resources is available by using e-mail (see FTP example #1).

E-mail Reference

Rankin, B. (1994, August). Accessing the Internet by e-mail [Online]. Available E-mail: LISTSERV @ubvm.cc.buffalo.edu: GET INTERNET BY-EMAIL NET-TRAIN F=MAIL

### EXAMPLE 2: Listserv Mailing List Reference

This example has been taken from a listserv for NASA's Galileo expedition (See Fig. 17).

Listserv Reference

Orton, G. (1997, February). Back from the original OFJ with some unexpected surprises [Online]. Available Email: listmanager@quest.arc.nasa.gov: subscribe updates-jup

**FIGURE 17**   NASA's listserv with updates on the Galileo mission:

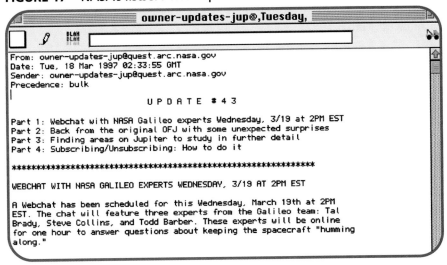

Also available: http://quest.arc.nasa.gov/galileo/people.html

## EXAMPLE 3: Usenet Newsgroup Reference

This example was taken from an environmental newsgroup (See Fig. 18).

**FIGURE 18**   Newsgroup discussion on solar energy viewed from Netscape's news reader:   (Copyright 1996 Netscape Communications Corp. Used with permission. All rights reserved. This electronic file or page may not be reprinted or copied without the express written permission of Netscape)

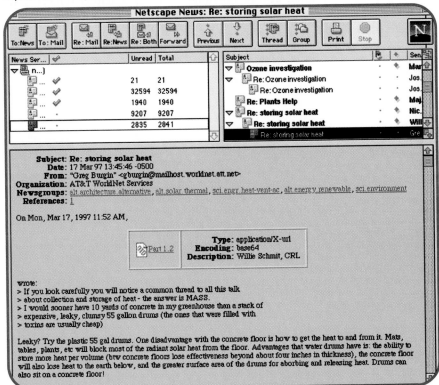

Newsgroup Reference

Burgin, G. (1997, March). Storing solar energy [Online]. Available Newsgroup: sci.environment (March 1997).

### NOTE

For more information on referencing Internet resources visit the following Web site: MLA Reference at

**http://www.cas.usf.edu/english/walker/mla.html**

An excellent online resource, "Beyond the MLA Handbook: Documenting Electronic Sources on the Internet" can be found at

**http://english.ttu.edu/kairos/1.2/inbox/mla_archive.html**

Visit their Home Page for discussions on problems researchers encounter in cyberspace:

**http://www.smpcollege.com/online-4styles~help**

For more information on utilizing the internet for research and services, please refer to *Student Resource Guide to the Internet: Student Success Online* by Cynthia Leshin (© 1998 by Prentice Hall, Inc. ISBN: 0-13-621079-1).

### Appendix Notes

"Netscape Communications Corporation has not authorized, sponsored, or endorsed, or approved this publication and is not responsible for its content. Netscape and the Netscape Communications Corporate Logos are trademarks and trade names of Netscape Communications Corporation. All other product names and/or logos are trademarks of their respective owners."

NASA has not authorized, sponsored, or endorsed, or approved this publication and is not responsible for its content.

Figures 5, 6, and 7 reprinted with permission by Excite. "Excite, Excite Search, Excite City.Net, City.Net, and the Excite logo are trademarks of Excite, Inc. and may be registered in various jurisdictions. Excite screen display copyright 1995–1997 Excite, Inc."

# ENDNOTES

## CHAPTER 1

[1] U. S. Department of Education, National Center for Education Statistics, *Nontraditional Undergraduates: Trends in Enrollment from 1986 to 1992 and Persistence and Attainment Among 1989–90 Beginning Postsecondary Students*, NCES 97–578, by Laura J. Horn. Dennis Carroll, project officer (Washington, D. C.: U. S. Government Printing Office, 1996), 16–17.

[2] U. S. Department of Education, National Center for Education Statistics, *Digest of Education Statistics 1996*, NCES 96–133, by Thomas D. Snyder. Production Manager, Charlene M. Hoffman. Program Analyst, Claire M. Geddes (Washington, D. C.: U. S. Government Printing Office, 1996), 167.

[3] Ibid.

[4] Ibid., 180.

[5] U. S. Department of Education, *Nontraditional Undergraduates*, 26.

[6] U. S. Department of Education, *Digest of Education Statistics 1996*, 168.

[7] Ibid., 177.

[8] Ibid., 176.

[9] U. S. Department of Education, National Center for Education Statistics, *Profile of Undergraduates in U. S. Postsecondary Education Institutions*, NCES 96–237, by Laura J. Horn, Mark D. Premo, and MPR Associates, Inc. Project Officer, Andrew G. Malizio (Washington, D. C.: U. S. Government Printing Office, 1996), 15.

[10] U. S. Department of Education, National Center for Education Statistics, *The Condition of Education 1996*, NCES 96-304, by Thomas M. Smith (Washington, D. C.: U. S. Government Printing Office, 1996), 60–61.

[11] *Baltimore City Community College 1996–1998 Catalog*. (Baltimore City Community College, Division of Planning and Advancement, 1996), 158.

## CHAPTER 2

[1] Barbara Soloman, North Carolina State University.

[2] Howard Gardner, *Multiple Intelligences: The Theory in Practice* (New York: HarperCollins, 1993), 5–49.

[3] Joyce Bishop, Ph.D., Psychology faculty, Golden West College, Huntington Beach, CA.

## CHAPTER 3

[1] Paul R. Timm, Ph.D., *Successful Self-Management: A Psychologically Sound Approach to Personal Effectiveness* (Los Altos, CA.: Crisp Publications, Inc., 1987), 22–41.

[2] Stephen Covey, *The Seven Habits of Highly Effective People* (New York: Simon & Schuster, 1989), 70–144, 309–318.

## CHAPTER 4

[1] Frank T. Lyman, Jr., Ph.D., "Think-Pair-Share, Thinktrix, Thinklinks, and Weird Facts: An Interactive System for Cooperative Thinking." In *Enhancing Thinking*

*Through Cooperative Learning*, ed. Neil Davidson and Toni Worsham (New York: Teachers College Press, 1992), 169–181.

[2] Roger von Oech, *A Kick in the Seat of the Pants* (New York: Harper & Row Publishers, 1986) 5–21.

[3] Dennis Coon, *Introduction to Psychology: Exploration and Application*, 6th ed. (St. Paul: West Publishing Company, 1992), 295.

## CHAPTER 5

[1] U. S. Department of Education, National Center for Education Statistics, *The Condition of Education 1996*, NCES 96–304, by Thomas M. Smith (Washington, D. C.: U. S. Government Printing Office, 1996), 84.

[2] Sherwood Harris, *The New York Public Library Book of How and Where to Look It Up* (Englewood Cliffs, NJ: Prentice Hall, 1991), 13.

[3] George M. Usova, *Efficient Study Strategies: Skills for Successful Learning* (Pacific Grove, CA: Brooks/Cole Publishing Company, 1989), 45.

[4] Francis P. Robinson, *Effective Behavior* (New York: Harper & Row, 1941).

[5] Sylvan Barnet and Hugo Bedau, *Critical Thinking, Reading, and Writing: A Brief Guide to Argument*, 2nd ed. (Boston: Bedford Books of St. Martin's Press, 1996), 15–21.

[6] John J. Macionis, *Sociology*, 6th ed. (Upper Saddle River, NJ: Prentice Hall, 1997), 174.

[7] Teresa Audesirk and Gerald Audesirk, *Life on Earth* (Upper Saddle River, NJ: Prentice Hall, 1997), 55–56.

## CHAPTER 6

[1] Walter Pauk, *How to Study in College*, 5th ed. (Boston: Houghton Mifflin Company, 1993), 110–114.

[2] Analysis based on Lynn Quitman Troyka, *Simon & Schuster Handbook for Writers* (Upper Saddle River, NJ: Prentice Hall, 1996) 22-23.

## CHAPTER 7

[1] Ralph G. Nichols, "Do We Know How to Listen? Practical Helps in a Modern Age," *Speech Teacher* (March 1961): 118–124.

[2] Ibid.

[3] Herman Ebbinghaus, *Memory: A Contribution to Experimental Psychology*, trans. H. A. Ruger and C. E. Bussenius (New York: New York Teacher's College, Columbia University, 1885).

[4] Many of the examples of objective questions used in this chapter are from Gary W. Piggrem, Test Item File for Charles G. Morris, *Understanding Psychology*, 3rd ed. (Upper Saddle River, NJ: Prentice Hall, 1996).

## CHAPTER 8

[1] Edith Wharton. "False Dawn," In *Old New York* (New York: Simon & Schuster, 1951), 18–19.

[2] Sheryl McCarthy, *Why Are the Heroes Always White?* (Kansas City: Andrews and McMeel, 1995), 188.

[3] John Hockenberry, *Moving Violations* (New York: Hyperion, 1995), 78.

[4] Claude Steele, Ph.D., Professor of Psychology, Stanford University.

[5] Tamera Trotter and Joycelyn Allen, *Talking Justice: 602 Ways to Build and Promote Racial Harmony* (Saratoga, CA: R & E Publishers, 1993), 51.

[6] Sheryl McCarthy, *Why Are the Heroes . . . ?*, 137.

[7] Louis E. Boone, David L. Kurtz, and Judy R. Block, *Contemporary Business Communication* (Englewood Cliffs, NJ: Prentice Hall, 1994), 49–54.

[8] Adapted by Richard Bucher, Professor of Sociology, Baltimore City Community College, from Paula Rothenberg, William Paterson College of New Jersey.


## CHAPTER 9

[1] U. S. Department of Education, National Center for Education Statistics, *Profile of Undergraduates in U. S. Postsecondary Education Institutions: 1992–93*, NCES 96-237, by Laura J. Horn, Mark D. Premo, Andrew G. Malizio, Project Officer, and MPR Associates, Inc. (Washington, D. C.: U. S. Government Printing Office, 1996), 15.

[2] U. S. Department of Education, National Center for Education Statistics, *Digest of Education Statistics 1996*, NCES 96-133, by Thomas D. Snyder. Production Manager, Charlene M. Hoffman. Program Analyst, Claire M. Geddes (Washington, D. C: U. S. Government Printing Office, 1996), 320–321.

[3] Ibid., 324–325.

[4] U. S. Department of Education, *The 1997–98 Student Guide to Financial Aid*.


## CHAPTER 10

[1] Isaac Asimov, "My Own View," in *The Encyclopedia of Science Fiction*, ed. Robert Holdstock (1978).

[2] Thomas Moore, *The Care of the Soul* (New York: Harper Perennial, 1992), xi–xx.

[3] Stephen Covey, *The Seven Habits of Highly Effective People* (New York: Simon & Schuster, 1989), 70–144, 309–318.

[4] Sarah Delany and Elizabeth Delany with Amy Hill Hearth, *Book of Everyday Wisdom* (New York: Kodansha International, 1994), 123.

# INDEX

**Y**

**Z**

THINKTRIX MIND ACTIONS

Comparing notes with another student to see what facts and ideas you have both considered important

Contrasting a weekday when you work half-day and go to school with a weekday when you attend class and then have the rest of the day to study

When you pay phone and utility bills on time, the effects are a better credit rating, uninterrupted service, and a better relationship with your service providers.

Naming the steps of a geometry proof in order, or remembering your friends' phone numbers

You have trouble finding a baby-sitter. A classmate has had to bring her child to class. Your brother leaves his daughter at your mom's. From these examples, you derive the idea that your school needs a daycare on campus.

Your idea of changing major leads to supporting examples, such as you have already taken classes in the major you want to choose, you have worked in that field, and you don't like your current course of study.

You have a chance to cheat on a test. After considering the potential effects of not knowing the material after the test and of getting caught, you evaluate that cheating isn't worth it to you.

SIMILARITY

DIFFERENCE

CAUSE & EFFECT

RECALL

EXAMPLE to IDEA

IDEA to EXAMPLE

EVALUATION

EX →

→ EX